M3

THE LANDSCAPE OF MAN

GEOFFREY AND SUSAN JELLICOE

The Landscape of Man

SHAPING THE ENVIRONMENT
FROM PREHISTORY TO THE PRESENT DAY

with 702 illustrations and six maps

THAMES AND HUDSON · LONDON

© 1975 THAMES AND HUDSON LTD, LONDON

Printed and bound in England
by Jarrold and Sons Ltd, Norwich

CONTENTS

Part Two   # The Evolution of Modern Landscape

The Eighteenth Century

The Nineteenth Century

The Twentieth Century: 1900–1945

The Twentieth Century: 1945–1975

Introduction Landscape and Civilization

THE WORLD is moving into a phase when landscape design may well be recognized as the most comprehensive of the arts. The reasons for this are threefold: (*a*) the existing delicately balanced order of nature within the biosphere, or protective envelope of the planet, is being disturbed by the activities of man, and it seems that only his own exertions can restore a balance and ensure survival; (*b*) these exertions call first for ecosystems that are no more than a return to an efficient animal state of sustained existence; and (*c*) man's destiny being to rise above the animal state, he creates around him an environment that is a projection into nature of his abstract ideas. The first has aroused an intuitive urge in biological man and caused the 'green revolution', so described at the Stockholm Conference on Human Environment, 1972; the second has encouraged comprehensive ecological planning by experts; and the third is promoting a landscape art on a scale never conceived of in history.

The popular conception of landscape design has been that it is an art confined to private gardens and parks. This is understandable, because it is only in the present century that the collective landscape has emerged as a social necessity. If the universal demand for landscape is therefore so different from the past, what do we gain from a study of history?

Art is a continuous process. However new the circumstances may be, it is virtually impossible to create a work of art without antecedents. The challenge of history is not whether it should be studied, but rather the interpretation of what is constant and therefore alive today, and what is ephemeral and only academic. The mind of intellectual man, for instance, has always responded to the tranquillity and assurance of certain geometrical forms such as the square and the circle, although the manifestations of these in the landscape vary according to geography, society, economics, morals and philosophy, all of which are local and transitory. Similarly, the response of biological man to an artificial hill made today in England out of waste is probably identical with the response to such a hill made in ancient China, no matter how different the environment. But undoubtedly, the most constant factor has been the mechanism of the five senses themselves, with their peculiarities and distortions, which have scarcely changed since pre-history and through which all perceptions still pass to stimulate the emotions.

All design therefore derives from impressions of the past, conscious or subconscious, and in the modern collective landscape, from historic gardens and parks and silhouettes which were created for totally different social reasons. Fundamentally, these again derived from impressions of the world: the classical from the geometry of agriculture, the romantic from natural landscape. Only the small private garden remains true to its instinctive unchanged purpose of expressing, protecting and consoling the individual.

7

This study is a concise global view of the designed landscape past and present, inclusive of all environment, from gardens to urban and regional landscape. Town-planning is included only when it is also landscape-planning. It is written objectively, as though the planet were seen from outer space, in which both hemispheres were equated. Part I runs from prehistory to AD 1700, a convenient date to mark the change from the old world to the new, coinciding by chance with the death of the famous French landscape architect, André Le Nôtre; Part II runs from that date to the present day.

As with all subjects concerned with time and space, it is not possible, at one and the same time, to describe schools of landscape both concurrently as to date and according to their own historic process. For this reason, three major groups of civilizations have been recognized and their growth followed separately: Central (from Mesopotamia), Eastern (from India, China, Pre-Columbian America) and Western (from Egypt). Although these began independently one from another, they soon interlocked and by AD 1700 the cross-fertilization of ideas was world-wide. By the nineteenth century the Western civilization had far outstripped the others; but in modern times, and emanating from the Americas, East and West are beginning to amalgamate in the creation of ideas. Unlike architecture and the sister arts, landscape fortunately cannot be wholly internationalized and it is a purpose of this book to engender diversification within the framework of a world that is fast becoming stereotyped.

There are twenty-five sections. The text of each is divided into six paragraphs, continuously numbered. In Part I the paragraphs are titled *environment*, *social history* and *philosophy*, followed by the physical arts arising from these, namely, *expression*, *architecture* and *landscape*. In Part II the content of the paragraphs changes to suit the information, such as *economics*, which is now required. Until 1700 landscape design, with notable exceptions, was predominantly metaphysical; after that date intellectual man finally displaced intuitive man, and landscape – again with notable exceptions – became realistic and worldly. A postscript, *Towards the Landscape of Humanism*, is the authors' personal assessment of the way of things today.

G.A.J.   S.J.

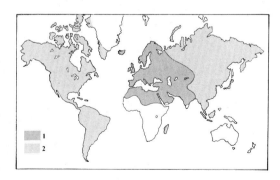

THE TWO PRINCIPAL RACES OF MANKIND
(BEFORE 1492)
1. Caucasoid   2. Mongoloid

THE CLIMATIC REGIONS OF THE WORLD
1. Tropical rainy   2. Dry
3. Temperate warm rainy
4. Cool   5. Polar

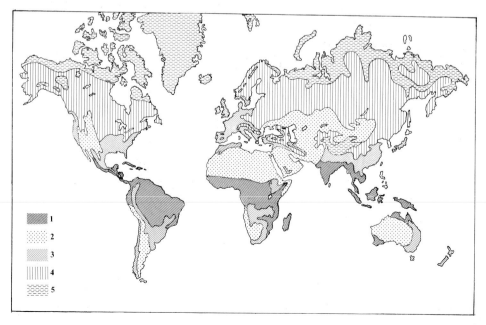

Part One

FROM PREHISTORY TO THE END OF THE SEVENTEENTH CENTURY

Since creation, the earth's surface continually worked its way, by trial and error, towards the condition of climate and racial groupings that existed at the beginning of recorded history. The length of time it took to do so is beyond comprehension: if the evolution of the world since creation corresponded in time to one year, then civilized man would have been upon it for only one minute.

1 Origins

Genesis *1.* The sun is the centre of a system of solid bodies – part of a galaxy that floats in an infinite void. It is a million and a quarter times the size of the earth which revolves round it at a mean distance of 98·82 million miles. The solar system is one of gravity balances and the orbits of the planets are ellipses slightly modified by the counter-attraction of each other. The earth appears to have been created out of gases about 4,700 million years ago, an imperfect sphere spinning upon its axis faster than today. The axis itself, originally parallel to the orbit, came imperceptibly to tilt and thus to present a differing surface to the sun. The surface was chaotic. Cloud masses hung over a barren volcanic landscape so hot that the constant rain instantly turned into steam. This weird scenery was illuminated by a sun that rose and set in much less time than today. There were no oceans, no atmosphere and no life.

Life *2.* The surface cooled, the water vapours condensed, atmosphere was created and life began. With life also began individuality, for evolution dictates that no two forms can be exactly alike. Life depends upon light and water, and in straining upwards towards light the plant evolved its own water reservoir and supply system. This enabled it to invade land. The first landscape of vegetation was one of shallow lagoons with mosses, ferns and swamp conifer forests that are the coal-measures of today. Animal life began and in this age became amphibious. After an interlude of barrenness came the reptiles, themselves extinguished by a further cooling of the climate. There followed the still-continuing movements of continents on their plates, either separating to form new oceans or colliding to form mountains, and the present landscape took general shape. Vegetation was now adapted to dry conditions. Grasses and flowers were abundant. The forests were of hardwood, such as birch, beech, holly, tulip tree, breadfruit and palm, alive with animal life. The mammal appeared. Among the apes and monkeys fashioned by nature with a form and instinct to survive a forest life was a species more gifted than the others. By 500,000 BC this creature had invented the tool and thus, as man, began the stupendous task of adjusting the environment to itself, as well as itself to the environment.

Paleolithic Man
500,000 BC to 8000 BC *3.* Despite the cold of succeeding glacial ages, man multiplied. He developed hunting skills and elementary protection against weather. Fifty thousand years ago the fourth and last Ice Age reached its maximum and began to decline, the glaciers receding northwards. Between that date and 8000 BC man appears to have spread over a greater part of the globe, and was probably most populous in Africa and south-west Asia. Where he settled he became conditioned by geography and climate into the present races of mankind: negroid, caucasoid, mongoloid, bushman and Polynesian. The caucasoid gave rise to the Central and Western civilizations, the mongoloid to the Eastern, including the Pre-Columbian American. The concept of mysterious forces behind all life was now almost universal, expressed in the worship of a Mother Goddess of fertility. The climax of instinctive man, as he may be called, is experienced in the cave arts of France and Spain. Here is an internal landscape art inspired only by observable happenings and direct experience; the mathematics and rhythms of the heavens that later

meant so much to civilization, meant nothing; there was no geometry, right angle or vertical straight line. It is pure biological art that can never be truthfully repeated, the junction between *Homo erectus* and *Homo sapiens* himself.

Neolithic Man
8000 BC to 4000 BC

4. The Neolithic Revolution introduced a new and profoundly important aspect of man's relation to environment. Previously he had been a hunter; now he was to become an agriculturist. His flint axes had allowed him to clear forests, he domesticated goats, sheep and pigs, and began to cultivate the wild wheat and barley which he found around him. The first major concentrations took place in the broad fertile river valleys, for only silt brought by a river could revivify soils that now supported heavy populations. Manuring was unknown. From Mesopotamia particularly the Neolithic farm culture spread westwards along the shores of the Mediterranean and Atlantic Europe, often carrying with it a megalithic memorial landscape of great stones and mounds to establish man's identity in what was still a hostile world. With the change of ceiling from a canopy of trees to the sky itself, forest dweller and caveman's short rhythm of day and night expanded into the vaster scale of the rhythm of the year. It was then inevitable that the concept of celestial gods should gradually evolve.

Bronze Age
4000 BC to 2000 BC

5. Because of changes of climate, the forests moved in directions that in some areas brought them into serious conflict with the agriculturists. The Sahara had lost its fertility and become arid, but the Mediterranean shores became the agreeable nursery of Western civilization. The discovery and exploitation of metallurgy now enriched the arts of war and peace, but of far greater importance was its encouragement of the diffusion of ideas. Metals were not found in the more prosperous agricultural centres of civilization, but in remote and generally poor lands. A system of barter therefore arose, with gradually extending lines of communication. In due time the prospectors reached Brittany, invading Cornwall for its tin and Wales and Ireland for their gold, and superseding the aborigines. Although Egypt and Mesopotamia were well past the Stone Age the periphery of civilization still expressed itself in megaliths. The monuments of Carnac in Brittany and Stonehenge in England date respectively from *c.* 2500 BC and 2000 BC. Similarly, towards the east, trade appears to have developed tentative routes to India, Mongolia and perhaps to China, to crystallize later into the silk road.

From 2000 BC

6. An observer from without would now see a curious change come over the surface of the earth. The forests were being cleared and the scene was changing from the natural to the man-made. Previously, such transformations had taken place mainly in the river valleys and these had developed into the centres and monuments of high civilization: Greece, Persia and China had all reached a philosophic climax by the fifth century BC. The geometric patterns of cultivation were now creeping all over the northern hemisphere, representing two opposing attitudes of mind to the earth mother that persist to this day: the one exploiting the capital resources of humus probably laid down by the forests, and the other creating a recurring ecosystem of stock-farming and crops. Exploitation was generally a one-purpose culture, showed quick returns, was essentially peripatetic and led to the denudation of forests and ultimately to waste, erosion and scars; the other was slow to mature, self-enriching and self-perpetuating. Although these patterns have profoundly influenced the course of landscape design, they have done so at different times and places in totally different ways: for man, searching eternally for the expression of abstract ideas, has either idealized them into an art form; or has been repelled by them; or has recognized their existence only as utilitarian, and therefore ignored them.

1

THE PROTECTIVE ATMOSPHERE, upon which all life depends, and which, in the view of **the Earth from Apollo 15 (1)** can be seen clinging precariously to the surface, was self-creative. The primary planet, without shield from the lethal solar rays and therefore barren, appears to have manufactured conditions for life on its own initiative, as follows: *c.* 4000–3000 million BC, volcanic eruption (**2, White Island, New Zealand**) releases vapour and gases and fabricates an atmosphere similar to the present, but without life-giving oxygen; exposure of these elements to solar radiation, together with vapour condensation into water, creates a small oxygen content sufficient to promote fermentation in shallow pools. About 2700 million BC, the pools activate the atmosphere to increase the oxygen content to one-hundredth part of the present, and the respiration of organisms begins. Between 600 and 340 million BC, the action of the organisms increases the oxygen content to one-tenth of the present and deepens the protective shield; plants appear above water and the great forests begin (**3, Saimaa, Finland**); the present biosphere is created, exactly balanced to receive no more of the devastating solar radiations than is necessary to give life-energy. *Within this biosphere, and only dimly aware of its fragility, the historic civilizations grew and prospered. Until the present day there has been no challenge to its authority.*

2, 3

4

THE FIRST LANDSCAPES consciously conceived by man appear in the cave paintings of France and northern Spain between 30,000 and 10,000 B C. The painting from **Lascaux, France (4)**, is a section only, measuring about twenty-six by nine feet. The drawings are instinctive, made before geometry was known, and probably based on 'sympathetic magic'. Despite varied

scales, the animals are closely related one to another, to their rock wall and to the cavern as a whole. The design is complex in time as well as space, for one animal has later been drawn over another with a respect for the past. Considered as a whole, the cave paintings are the first and still the most pure of all the intuitive arts of landscape design.

5

PRIMITIVE MAN set his mark on the landscape by raising artificial hills or re-arranging stones. The simple heaped mound, emulating a hill and silhouetted against the sky, was the almost universal record of a burial throughout the prehistoric world, as at the **Seven Barrows, Wiltshire** (painting by John Piper) (**5**). At **Carnac, Brittany** (**6**), the Ménec alignment, made after 2500 BC with over a thousand stones, is set with two other alignments in a crowded landscape of dolmens (burial chambers), menhirs (single stones) and cromlechs (groups of stones). The stones are regimented, probably for ritual; but each stone is individual, with an overwhelming personality. At the culmination of the alignments are the presumed **stones of sacrifice** (**7**). **Stonehenge, Wiltshire** (**8**), was completed about 1500 BC and is the climax of symbolic British circular sanctuary. The sarsen stones (weighing up to fifty tons) come from the Marlborough Downs (twenty-four miles away) and the blue stones from South Wales. The design and structure is highly skilled (possibly under Mycenaean influence), the enormous stones being shaped to a purpose. Geometric man had arrived, together with his instruments.

6

7

BOTH GODS AND ANCESTORS inspired primitive art. **The White Horse of Uffington** (**9**), on the Berkshire Downs, was cut by the Celts in about AD 100, perhaps the first engraving on any landscape of a major work of art. The Celts were innovators in agriculture and created new land forms that persist today. Celtic art, based on metal engraving, has a flavour of classicism, but its fantastic elongated animals seem to be influenced by the east, by the nomad art of the steppes. The White Horse, difficult to see from the ground, was almost certainly made for the gods. On the other side of the world and isolated in the Pacific, the huge **stone statues of Easter Island** (**10**), dating from about the fifteenth century AD, are an original expression of ancestor worship. The proportion of monuments to inhabitants is remarkable. Besides single statues, there are 260 *ahu*, or platforms, many with similar sculpture, that extended continuously along the seashore. Some of the images weigh over twenty tons, and may have been adorned with lightly coloured feathers and red earth washes. The whole island would seem to have been dedicated to sculpture on a colossal scale, among which, in time and space, men moved like pygmies.

The area of the Central civilizations, showing latitude, mountain barriers and selected place names.

THE CENTRAL CIVILIZATIONS

These comprise that part of the caucasoid race whose civilization began with the Sumerians in Mesopotamia, developed with the Assyrians, Persians and Sassanids, and under Islam spread west to Spain and east to India roughly about 35° north. Originally separated from the Western civilizations that began simultaneously in the Nile Valley, the two parallel and antithetical civilizations came to be so interlocked that there was an inevitable and continuous interchange of ideas. In contrast, the Eastern civilizations seemed remote and the influence of one group of civilizations upon another was less pronounced; even when the Muslim Mughuls overwhelmed Hindu India, the two cultures in principle remained independent. By AD 1700 the central Muslim civilizations had ceased to be an originating force, and culturally the world was thereafter broadly divided into *east* and *west*.

2 Western Asia to the Muslim Conquest

Environment   7. The evolution of man from hunter to agriculturist throughout the world probably began in the eighth millennium BC on the Anatolian plateau and in the foothills to the east of the Mesopotamian plain. Later he descended to the delta of the Tigris and Euphrates and in the alluvial silt, infertile until drained and irrigated, began more profitable cultivation of wild wheat and barley and the domestication of wild dogs, goats, sheep, cattle and pigs. The original scene must have been bleak. While the middle mountain slopes of the cooler, rainier north sustained scrub oak and forests of such species as plane, box, cedar, cypress and poplar, only willows grew in the northern river plains and date palms in the delta. Rocky desert bordered the western fringes of the Tigris-Euphrates basin; to the east were the Zagros Mountains. Undulating gypsiferous plains in the north gave way in the south to flat, salty silt and marsh – a featureless landscape except for the two rivers, which changed their course unpredictably; a land subject to cloud-bursts and inundations, but little regular rainfall. From these beginnings there emerged some four thousand years later the world's first literate civilization, known as 'Sumerian'.

Social History   8. The social structure of Sumer arose from the need to regulate the unpredictable Euphrates by means of irrigation works on a scale that was beyond the family or clan unit. Thus evolved the city states, later welded into a single empire with the capital established at Babylon in 2250 BC. Simultaneously, cuneiform writing on clay was invented and the first code of laws published. The social structure was civil, orderly and based on class, with the king at the summit and a priesthood with moderate influence. In 1275 BC Babylon fell to the Assyrians, a military autocracy, the capital was moved to Nineveh and the empire extended through the domestication of the horse. Nineveh was destroyed in 606 BC and re-established at Babylon under Nebuchadnezzar II. Conquest by Persia followed in 538 BC. The Persian Empire became the greatest known to the Western world, reaching its climax almost contemporaneously with Greece and China, between which it lay geographically. Persepolis, the capital, was destroyed by Alexander in 333 BC and for over five centuries thereafter the country was affected by Hellenistic culture. In AD 226 the Sassanids re-established an effective native dynasty until the conquest by the Muslims in AD 637.

Philosophy   9. The primitive peoples of the forest conceived a god to be within all touchable objects, whether animate or inanimate. When they moved into the open from under the canopy of trees, the objects seen in the night sky, untouchable, sparkling, remote, ordered and timeless as they seemed to be, acquired a significance that soon surpassed that of earthly objects. From this contemplation of the heavens there arose two great concepts: a pantheon of gods, with one god supreme, that benevolently administered human affairs; and an invisible timeless world to which all men could aspire. Both concepts were based upon the limits of imagination; the one reflected an ideal in human nature, the other an ideal in physical environment. Each city state had its own god, whose abode on earth was as close to the heavens as possible and above that of the king, who ruled by divine right but was not himself a god. The precariousness of life led to a philosophy of inevitability that was expressed on the one hand by enjoyment of the passing moment and on the other by the contemplation of a serene future life, symbolized by the sky at night.

Expression *10.* The ziggurat was the early expression of man's determination to place his mark upon an endless flat surface. Made by labour in the agricultural off-season, it was both a holy mountain on whose summit lived a god, and an observatory for the deduction as well as empirical study of astronomy; events in the heavens that affected agriculture were predictable, whereas on earth they were not. The ziggurat, which included the legendary Tower of Babel, disappeared under the materialistic Assyrians and Persians, its place on the skyline being later taken by dome and minaret. More lasting as a metaphysical expression was the paradise garden. The origins are found in Old Testament history, which placed the first garden north of Babylon: 'and the Lord planted a garden eastward of Eden . . . and a river went out of Eden to water the garden; and thence it was parted and became into four heads . . . and the fourth river is Euphrates.' This description contained the idea of heaven, whose shape on earth was symbolized by the square, and which has remained to this day the basic inspiration of garden design of the Central civilizations.

Architecture *11.* Lacking the stone that accounts for the crispness of architecture and sculpture in the Nile Valley, buildings in Babylonia were of brick made from burnt clay and consequently subject more to modelling than to carving. Structures were usually low and horizontal, the more important being raised on a podium to avoid floods and insects. Roofs were normally flat, inviting roof gardens to which water was lifted from the Euphrates. Arch and vault appear at Babylon, and were probably the basis of the legendary hanging gardens, for soil could be packed into the haunches. The palaces were extensive, often with square internal courts, and contrasted with the ziggurat which might be over a hundred feet in height. The ceremonial approach to the summit of the ziggurat was the first grand landscape stairway. The architecture of the Assyrian and Persian conquerors culminated in Persepolis, reflecting the post-and-lintel structures of both Egypt and Greece, with wide spans made possible by cedar beams from Lebanon; and based on a plan that was still composed of squares. The original stream of Iranian thought in architecture remained submerged under Hellenism, but reappeared under the Sassanids, when the early vault began to evolve into the dome, set upon a square.

Landscape *12.* The first designed garden rose from the contemplation of the miraculous effect of irrigation on a dead world. A rich green oasis, patterned solely according to the science of agriculture, spread like a vast carpet between the Tigris and Euphrates. All gardens were an idealization of this scene. They were laid out geometrically within protecting walls and their primary contents were channels of irrigation and trees beneath which to recline. The tree was always an object of veneration. The paradise garden itself in its purity was a square enclosed against a hostile world, crossed by water channels symbolic of the four rivers of heaven, and containing theoretically all the fruits of the earth. With the domestication of the horse under the Assyrians came the first hunting-park, the first landscape expansion into the environment; the park was laid out geometrically with trees often imported from afar; wild animals were introduced, and the hunting-box evolved into the first landscape pleasure pavilion. Expansion in idea as well as in reality continued under the Persians, for Persepolis was on a huge podium thrusting majestically outwards from the mountains to dominate the plain below. The only visible signs of religion in the Persian landscape were the fire sanctuaries in high places, and these continued under the Sassanids.

THE FIRST DESIGNED LANDSCAPES of the central civilizations were in southern Mesopotamia, emerging from extreme severity and hardship. One hundred thousand years ago, towards the end of the last Ice Age, parkland flourished in the now desolate landscape of the **Persian Gulf (11)**, whose water channels show dark against the sand. Roamed by lions, deer, antelopes, gazelles and, in the north, a few Paleolithic men, it was an Eden from which men and animals appear to have been banished by the northward-advancing heat – a physical enactment of the legendary expulsion of Adam and Eve by the angel with the flaming sword. In post-glacial times, fertility in this arid area has depended largely upon the Euphrates, one of the four rivers mentioned in *Genesis*. The **vegetation map of Mesopotamia (13)** shows the Fertile Crescent that Abraham followed from Ur to Palestine and indicates the desert that prevented contact between the Nile and the Sumerian civilizations. Flood control was as important as irrigation, since the flood waters reached Mesopotamia after the crops were well advanced. The silt deposits which enriched the delta also raised the river-bed above the surrounding land, requiring a large labour force to raise the irrigation and drainage channels. Babylonia was threaded with canals, used equally for transport and for trade with the north. Agriculture developed from the cultivation of wild barley and wheat, first grown as a garden rather than a field crop and held in such esteem as to become a decorative motif, as on a **sculptured vase from Uruk (12)**. Uruk was the second city state to arise in the Tigris–Euphrates delta and is described in the Sumerian *Epic of Gilgamesh* (*c.* 2000 BC): 'One third of the whole is city, one third is garden, and one third is field, with the precinct of the goddess Ashtar.' The poem tells of the 'groves of the plain' of willow and boxwood, the hills with 'forests stretching ten thousand leagues in every direction'.

11

12

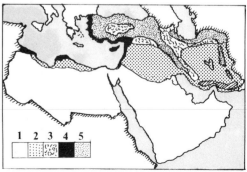

13 VEGETATION MAP OF MESOPOTAMIA
1 Desert 2 Semi-desert 3 Steppe 4 Maquis forest
5 Other forest

14

THE ZIGGURAT OF UR (**14**), Sumer's greatest surviving monument, is an artificial 'Hill of Heaven', dating from about 2250 BC, dedicated to Nanna the moon god and recalling the mountain home of the gods brought by the early settlers. According to the **reconstruction** (**15**) by Sir Leonard Woolley, the ziggurat was sixty-eight feet high on a ten-foot-high terrace above the city. The terraces appear to have been planted with trees, thus heightening the imagery of a rocky eminence. The outer walls were of baked brick round a core of mud brick. At least in the later period, it had painted walls: the lower stages black, the uppermost red; the shrine itself was covered with blue-glazed tiles, topped by a gilded dome. These colours stood, according to Woolley, for the dark underworld, the habitable earth, the heavens and the sun.

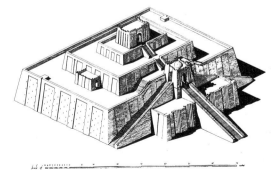

15

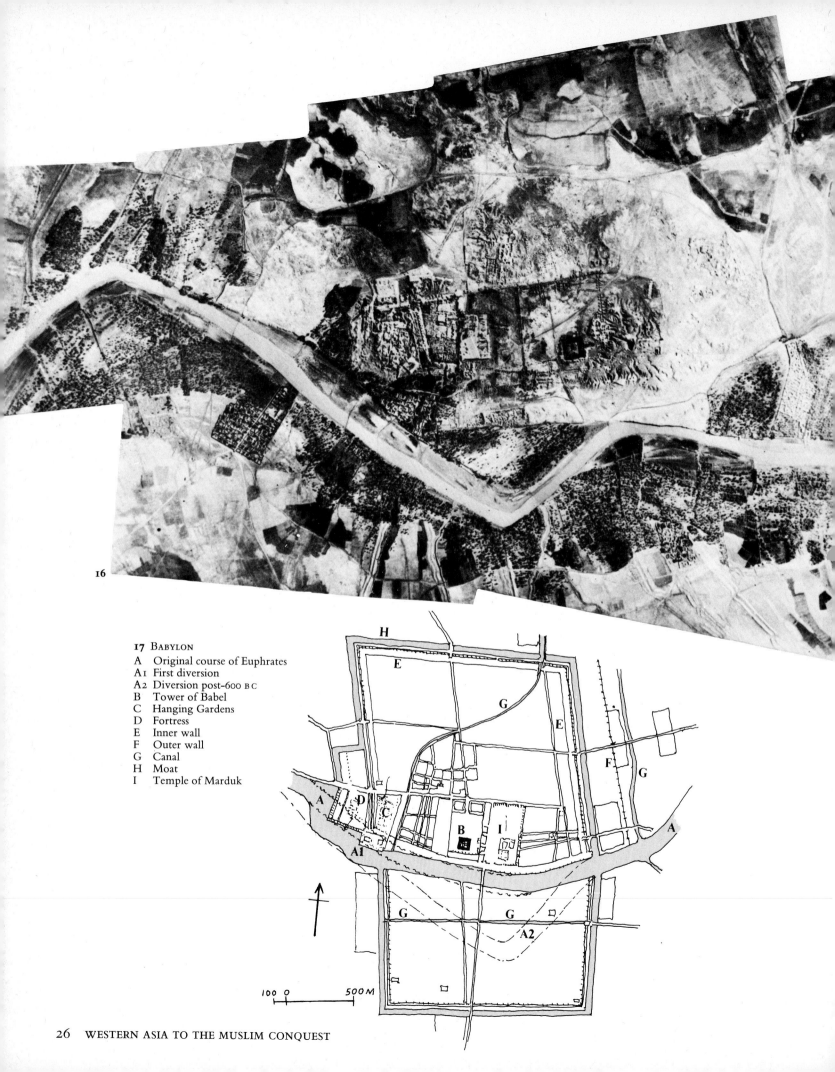

16

17 BABYLON
A   Original course of Euphrates
A1 First diversion
A2 Diversion post-600 BC
B   Tower of Babel
C   Hanging Gardens
D   Fortress
E   Inner wall
F   Outer wall
G   Canal
H   Moat
I   Temple of Marduk

100 0   500 M

BABYLON rose to power in the third millennium BC, following one of the Euphrates' many changes of course. The river acquired its present angularity soon after the seventh century BC, when, according to Herodotus, three artificial bends and a large lake upstream were excavated for military reasons; the old bed through the centre of the city can be traced in the **aerial photograph (16)** and in the **schematic plan** after E. Unger (**17**) of the late Babylonian city *c.* 600 BC. Thus Babylon might be described as the mother-city of the manufactured landscape as well as of gardens. Of the Tower of Babel only the remains of the base are still traceable. The terraces of the Hanging Gardens were built between 604 and 562 BC above two rows of seven vaulted chambers and may have risen in sequence up to seventy-five feet. The structure was waterproofed with bitumen, baked brick and lead, and covered with soil for trees, depth probably being obtained by use of the space between the haunches of the arches. Water seems to have been lifted from a well within the vaulted area. It had three shafts close to each other, which may have housed a chain pump worked by a wheel, similar to the *dolab* still in use locally.

The **Assyrians** were the dominant military power from 1350 BC onwards, and the cooler, more thickly wooded landscape of northern Mesopotamia encouraged the chase; this in turn encouraged the peaceful arts of landscape, from the vine trellis to the hunting-park, enriched by cedars, box trees and strange animals brought from the conquered lands. The carved panels which lined the walls of their sumptuous palaces, as at Nineveh, show scenes from the world of **hunting (18)**, **fishing (19)** – with a tree-topped palace as background – and the **king feasting in his garden (21)**. The temple and artificial hill at **Khorsabad (20)** was carved *c.* 715 BC and is therefore one of the earliest picturesque landscapes of the Western world.

18

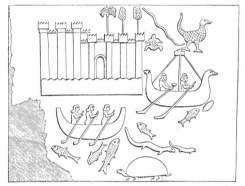
19

20

21

THE SITE OF PERSEPOLIS was chosen as the centre of the world *c.* 540 BC by Cyrus the Great in the tradition of the earlier Achaemenid fortresses. The **aerial view** (**22**) shows the built up geometrical plateau lying at the foot of the mountains. The buildings were begun by Darius I and continued by Xerxes I and Artaxerxes I, who needed not so much a stronghold as a demonstration of international power, forcibly expressed in the massive **sixty-foot podium** (**24**) projecting from the mountains. The **stairway** (**25**) and the **propylaea of Xerxes** (**26**) lead to the terraces, partly rock and partly huge blocks of stone, which are raised above the fortifications to create a new sense of expansion into the landscape, as seen particularly from the **Apadana** (**27**) or hall of audience. This sense of landscape was later to inspire the Mughul fortress palaces of India. The buildings themselves, covering thirty-three acres, are a complex of squares – reception palaces, official palaces of the kings, store rooms of the treasury and military head-quarters. Below the podium lay the royal town, protected by a double wall and moat; here, too, was Xerxes' private palace with gardens comprising an ornamental lake and the profusion of trees and flowers, especially the rose, so much venerated and loved by all Persians.

23 PERSEPOLIS   (The numbered arrows indicate the viewpoints of the photographs)

A   Entrance stairway
B   Propylaea of Xerxes
C   Hypostyle hall of Xerxes
D   Hall of 100 columns, Darius
E   Palace of Darius
F   Palace of Xerxes
G   Harem

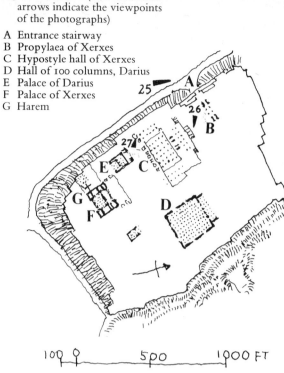

22

24

25, 26

27

CTESIPHON marks a return to ancient Iranian traditions after their interruption by Alexander and his Hellenizing successors. The Sassanians (third to sixth centuries A D) established control over much of the old Persian Empire, consciously linking themselves with the dynasty of Darius and Xerxes. Still surviving is the great hall and half the façade of the **palace of Chosroes I** (**28**), reputedly the widest single-span vault of unreinforced brickwork in the world, dominating the landscape as the ziggurat had done. The sky at night obsessed the Sassanians. Chosroes II's throne at Gandjak, surmounted by a gold and lapis-lazuli baldachin with symbols of the sky, the stars and the signs of the zodiac, bears witness, with the palace planetarium, to the age-long Persian awareness of the heavens – a word which they used for the round awnings of the royal tents.

On audience days, the floor beneath the vault was covered with carpets, one of which, the Spring Carpet of Chosroes, was one of the glories of Ctesiphon. This is recorded as being about a hundred feet square, depicting a garden with canals, flowers and trees worked in silk, gold and precious jewels. **Garden carpets of later ages** (**29**), such as this of the seventeenth century (from the collection of Daniel Wildenstein), are a continuation of the patterns of Chosroes' Spring Carpet, which are based on the traditional Persian paradise garden. The broad bands of wavy lines represent the canals – the 'four rivers of life' – that divide the garden into four smaller ones, whence the name *char-bagh* (four gardens) derives. The cartouche at the junction may indicate a pavilion or a large water tank. Round each circular intersection of the smaller canals are *chenars* (oriental plane trees). The cypresses that line the main canals symbolize death and eternity, the fruit trees represent life and fertility.

28

29

3 Islam: Western Asia

Environment   *13.* At the time of the Muslim conquest the settlements extending from the Mediterranean roughly along 34° north were culturally well advanced. They were set far apart in a desert landscape subject to extreme ranges of temperature; in Baghdad it can vary from 19 degrees F in winter to 123 degrees F in summer. Strong dust-laden winds blow from the north. Rainfall is less than ten inches per annum and limited to winter and spring. The settlements owed their prosperity to their position astride the main east–west trade route and their subsistence to an elaborate system of irrigation. Apart from the green surroundings of the cities lying beside rivers, small patches of cultivation extended wherever an underground stream had been tapped by underground water canals called *qanats*. To the north lay the wooded highlands of Kurdistan and Anatolia and beyond these the highly populated and fertile coastal fringe that extended along the Black Sea and culminated in Constantinople.

Social History   *14.* The Arab was a nomad from the south Arabian deserts. He was a shepherd, who moved with his flocks, dependent upon the stars at night. His worldly goods must be transportable, hence his love for jewels, fabrics and perfumes. Apart from weaving, his only art was that of eloquence and poetry. His religion was polytheistic, with Mecca as its centre. With awful suddenness the Prophet Mohammed welded this race into a single fanatical body of adventurers, conquering Persia in AD 637. The Caliphate capital was first established at Damascus but after a change of dynasty in AD 750 was removed to Baghdad. Here the Arabs set up the first educational systems, translated and distributed the Greek classics throughout the Empire, developed sciences of all kinds, including horticulture and the export of plants, and in every way made the city virtually the metropolis of the world. The capital fell in 1258 to the Mongols, who laid waste Mesopotamia, destroying the ancient irrigation systems. In 1326 the Ottoman Turks, heirs to the Seljuk Turks and converts to Islam, established their capital at Bursa; in 1453 they took Constantinople. Persia itself, after eclipse under both Arabs and Mongols, emerged in 1501 as an independent Islamic state under the Safavid dynasty, reaching the height of empire under the enlightened Abbas I (1587–1629), builder of the new capital of Isfahan.

Philosophy   *15.* The declaration and symbol of Muslim faith was the Koran, an inspired code of behaviour said to have been given to the Prophet Mohammed by the One God Allah, and incorporating much of the Hebrew Old Testament. The idea of the One God was simple and easily understood. The philosophy that 'the proof of God is in the perishable nature of that which is not Him' influenced all the works of Islam. Life was ephemeral: enjoy it while you may, but abide by the comparatively simple rules, mainly those of abstemiousness, cleanliness and regular tranquillizing prayer. This idea, applied with tolerance, appealed even to the conquered, who were easily converted to the new religion and language, and thereafter continued much as before. Parallel to this, and under the protection of a free-thinking Caliphate against a suspicious community, rose a school of logical philosophy based on that of the Greeks. Muslim philosophers were encyclopaedic, interested in such practical affairs as medicine, agriculture, alchemy, astronomy and zoology. Nor was the breadth of learning and experience confined to the philosophers: Persia's great poet, Omar Khayyám, was also a mathematician, reforming the calendar in AD 1079.

Expression *16.* Persian culture was absorbed by Islam and continued without apparent interruption. The garden proved itself able to comprehend and absorb the two opposing ways of thought of religious extremist and logical philosopher. To the one it remained the paradise of the Koran: 'For them [the good] the Gardens of Eden, under whose shade shall rivers flow'; to the other a place for contemplation and conversation, where body and spirit were in repose and the mind liberated from preconceptions. In the city with its dwellings and gardens, the new form and silhouette introduced into the scene was the mosque, the place of assembly for prayer. To this came to be added the *medresseh*, a place of learning attached to the mosque. The conception of architecture as the union of heaven and earth remained, enriched with the new symbolism of the relation of square to circle in the shape of the dome. In accordance with religious beliefs, little importance was attached to durability in buildings. Cities and buildings continued to be sited for strategic or other practical reasons, and it was not until the Ottoman Empire that a less restrictive conception of landscape emerged.

Architecture *17.* The dome, the minaret and the formal court dominated architecture. The Romans had created the dome on a circle or octagon, but the pure symbolism of circle on square was first achieved by the Sassanids at Sarvistan. Both Byzantine and Muslim were contemporaneously to exploit the full potentialities of shape: the Byzantine primarily preoccupied with the interior where a low dome was supported on plain pendentives, the Muslim externally with a freed and prominent dome that appeared to float upon internal stalactite pendentives. The illusion of weightlessness was created by an expanding silhouette, later enhanced by the turquoise tile that dissolved in the sky. The minaret developed from the ancient ziggurat, a curious return to tradition being found in the magnificent ensemble at Samarra. All true Muslim buildings were insubstantial, often seeming to be no more than stage scenery. Wall decoration was two-dimensional rather than sculptural, excluding human imagery on religious grounds. The patterns were either those of the geometry of brick or of highly coloured ceramics with flowing lettering from the Koran, interlaced plants and intricate stalactite forms.

Landscape *18.* Of the Baghdad of Harun al-Raschid, fabled for its palaces and gardens, nothing now remains but descriptions. Houses and gardens continued on traditional lines, but with interior and exterior more closely interwoven; there were terraces to catch the winds and from which to see the views; there were silver trees, mechanical birds of silver and gold and other marvels. After the invasion of the Mongols the initiative in landscape passed to the Ottoman Turks. Using Byzantine craftsmen, the Turks evolved the idea of the groupings of small low domes, which appear like liberated mushrooms in the landscape. This free conception may have arisen from the nomadic tent landscape which was their inheritance; it would seem that at Bursa and later at Constantinople the Turks evolved an art in which buildings were sited in the grand landscape primarily for aesthetic reasons. Two and a half centuries after the foundation of Bursa, Isfahan was laid out as a contained city, but with a sense of urban green landscape hitherto unknown. Monumental bridges extended like tentacles into the countryside. Based in principle upon a sequence of Persian gardens, the plan is characteristically Islamic inasmuch as it is composed of squares and rectangles that can be added to indefinitely; symmetry and finality in town-planning were avoided as a challenge to that perfection which only Allah could attain.

THE ROUND CITY OF BAGHDAD was founded by the Caliph al-Mansur as the new capital of the Abbasid dynasty in AD 762, in fertile country beside the Tigris. The Euphrates irrigated the land between the two rivers, while the Tigris watered the land beyond its eastern bank; the decisive urban circle is in contrast to the irregularity of the canals. Flowers were abundant and the city became the centre of a perfume industry.

Baghdad was not the first circular city, but it is the only one of which contemporary historians left detailed descriptions and measurements. The **plan (30)** is diagrammatic. A moat surrounded the outer wall; between a second, much thicker wall and the third, inner wall, were the houses, leaving a wide central area (to be crossed on foot by all but the Caliph) for public buildings, etc., with the mosque and the green dome of al-Mansur's palace at its heart. Outside the walls, on both river banks, were the fabulous gardens of the palaces, one of which is described below.

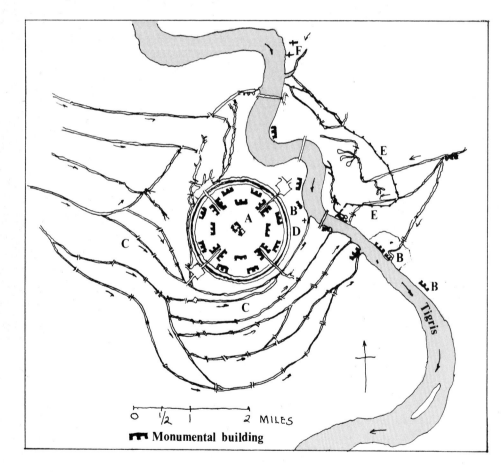

30 BAGHDAD
A Government centre
B Palaces
C Canals in domestic city
D Fortifications
E Wall
F Monasteries

Caliph Mktadir (acc. 908) added to the Palace of the Taj [on the east bank] and erected the Palace of the Tree, from the tree of silver which stood in the middle of the palace, surrounded by a great circular tank filled with clear water. The tree had eighteen branches, every branch having numerous twigs, on which sat various kinds of mechanical birds in gold and silver, both large and small. Most of the branches of the tree were of silver but some were of gold, and they spread in the air carrying leaves of divers colours, the leaves moving as the wind blew, while the birds, through a concealed mechanism, piped and sang. On either side of this palace, to right and left of the tank, stood life-sized figures in two rows, each row consisting of fifteen horsemen, mounted upon their mares, both men and steeds being clothed and caparisoned in brocade.

From *Baghdad during the Abbasid Caliphate* by Guy le Strange, quoting from contemporary Baghdad historians.

31

SAMARRA (**31**) was founded a century later, in AD 850, and its Great Mosque and the Manaret al-Malwiya (Spiral Minaret) are comparatively well preserved. Both owe their inspiration to other civilizations, for the Islamic Arabs had no architectural traditions of their own. The minaret derives from ziggurats such as the one at Babylon, with its winding outer staircase, still extant in the twelfth century. Early Arab mosques were usually adaptations from the aisled Christian churches in the cities they conquered, but the forest of columns at Samarra (whose foundations can be seen) is derived from Persian antecedents, such as Persepolis. The minaret, of baked brick like the ziggurats, stands on a 10-foot-high base, 108 feet square, from which it rises 164 feet by a spiral ramp 7½ feet wide, making five complete anti-clockwise turns and becoming steeper as it rises in order to keep a constant height for each successive stage. On top are the remains of a small pavilion, from which the call to prayer floated out above the one-storeyed houses of the town.

32, 33

34, 35

BURSA was founded by the Ottoman Turks in A D 1326 at the foot of Ulu Dağ (Mount Olympus), overlooking the fertile plain upon which it subsisted. In contrast to the neighbouring Christian Constantinople, whose power was now challenged and which could survive only within inhibiting fortifications, Ottoman Bursa points to a new way of thought on cities in relation to nature and landscape. Instead of a decisive break between town and country, caused by fortifications, the two are intermingled. The domes of the **royal Muradye cemetery** (**32**) are like free-growing mushrooms and are expressive of Ottoman personal philosophy. The dome of the **mausoleum of Murad II** (**33**) is open to the sky above the tomb of plain marble surrounding bare earth, since he wished to lie where rain could fall on his grave. Humility in death, often accompanied by awareness of the heavens, was a tradition handed down from Seljuk Turkish sultans. The royal *turbes* are surrounded by the tombstones of favourites, servants and friends, standing in rows on raised plinths.

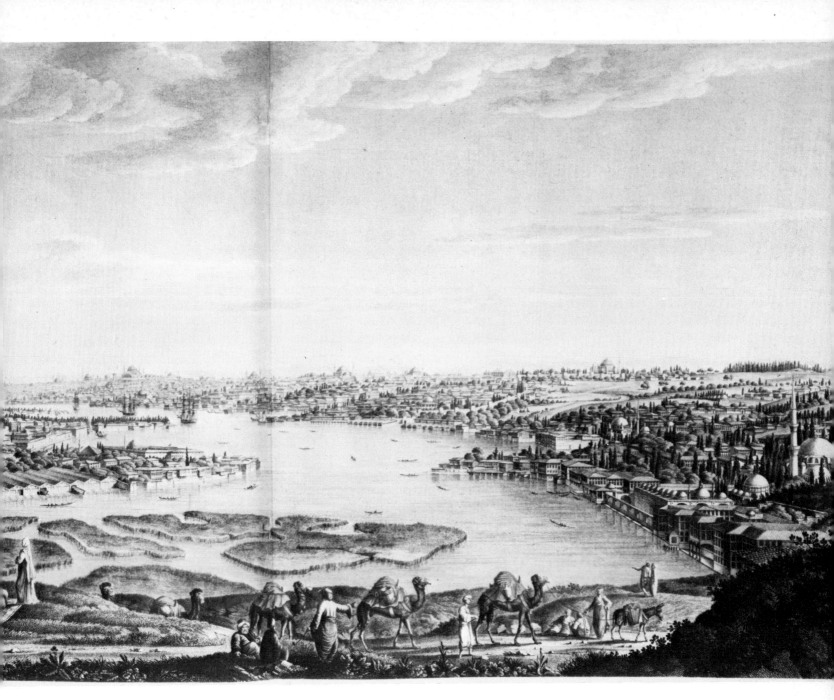

CONSTANTINOPLE (Istanbul) fell to the Ottomans in 1453, the capital being transferred here from Bursa. The Byzantine city had been tightly contained within walls, the skyline broken by low domes, the most prominent being that of St Sophia. With a feeling of jubilation and power after the conquest, and an expanding sense of landscape that had been exploited at Bursa, the sultans proceeded to develop the landscape spectacle of the Golden Horn. The Ottoman dome was almost a replica of the Christian Byzantine, but to it was now added the minaret, with its startling outline. Within two centuries, the **scene along the Golden Horn (34)** had been transformed from a fortress into a free and prosperous city, the silhouette enlivened by mosques and minarets designed to be seen from afar. The **Seraglio of the sultans (35)**, a city in itself, of courts and gardens, was sited on the dramatic promontory between St Sophia and the Bosphorus.

36

37, 38

ISFAHAN, CITY OF GARDENS and capital of the Safavid dynasty from 1598, flowering in an arid desert, was laid out by Shah Abbas I. The inspiration of the complete city plan can be found in the traditional Persian garden, whose elements are seen in miniatures such as that from the sixteenth-century **Nizami Khamsah** (36). The single *chenar* symbolizes a whole grove whose shade brought relief from the burning sun. According to Sir Thomas Herbert, in 1626 the royal parks abounded 'in lofty pyramidical cypresses, broad-spreading chenars, tough elm, straight ash, knotty pines, fragrant mastics, kingly oaks, sweet myrtles, useful maples; and of fruit trees are grapes, pomegranates, pomecitrons, oranges, lemons, pistachios, apples, pears, peaches, chestnuts, cherries, quinces, walnuts, apricots, plums, almonds, figs, dates and melons . . . also flowers rare to the eye, sweet to the smell and useful in physic'.

The **plan** (41) was a vast complex of gardens, palaces and mosques, the spine of which was the Chahar Bagh, a double avenue of *chenars*, with a central canal and flower-beds, linking the palace gardens with the Shah's terraced country garden across the Zaiandeh River. The imperial square linked the royal complex to the town itself. **The view** (40) is taken across the modern town towards Mount Soffeh. In the middle distance is the Maidan (the imperial square); the Ali Qapu, with its high veranda, is seen to the right and the Masjid-i-Shah (Shah's mosque, 1611–66) to the left. The larger of the two nearer domes is that of the Masjid-i-Sheikh Lotfollah (1602–19). Turquoise domes, minarets and palaces rose from a low urban architecture whose character of stage scenery can be seen in the rear of the Maidan arcades, and in the entrance to the mosque on the extreme left. Within the city, the royal palaces were designed for shade, cool breezes and views of all kinds. The massive columns of the verandas were teak, as at the **Ali Qapu** (37) and Chehel Sutun with its reflecting pool. Ablution tanks became light-reflecting pools, as in the **medresseh Madri-i-shah** (38). **Allahvardi Khan's bridge** (39) allows walkers to enjoy the seasonal water scenery (the river-bed is shown dry), undisturbed by passing vehicles, which are concealed.

39

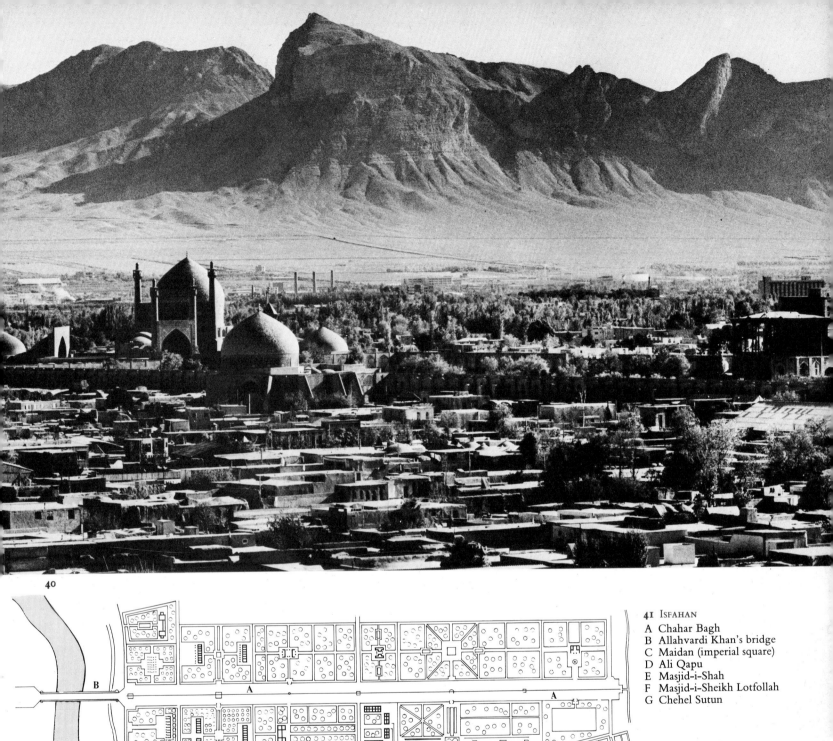

40

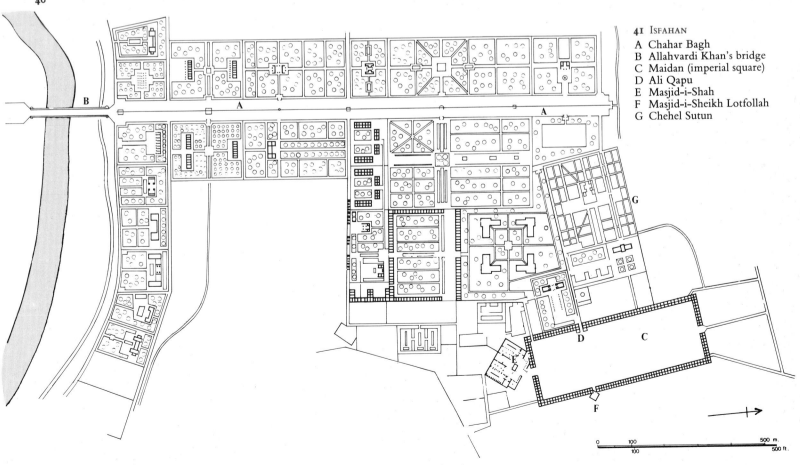

41 ISFAHAN

A Chahar Bagh
B Allahvardi Khan's bridge
C Maidan (imperial square)
D Ali Qapu
E Masjid-i-Shah
F Masjid-i-Sheikh Lotfollah
G Chehel Sutun

0 100   500 m.
100   500 ft.

4 The Western Expansion of Islam: Spain

Environment 19. Possibly as much for climatic as for strategic reasons, Islam was unable to retain a footing north of latitude 40°. Andalusia (Moorish Spain) lies mainly south of latitude 38° and has a Mediterranean climate and varied scenery more African than European. Much of the land is arid but along the coastal belt and the rivers the vegetation can be rich, the predominant evergreens being holm oak and olive. Under the irrigation introduced by the Moors the Valley of the Guadalquivir came to support a huge population. The valley is excessively hot in summer, Seville having a maximum temperature of 117 degrees F. Granada, on the other hand, is higher above the coastal plain on the edge of the Sierra Nevada and is well watered by melting snows. At the time of the Moorish conquest the remains of a rich Roman culture were everywhere, interspersed with those of a contemporary Visigoth civilization that had spread from France. Such structures as the ruins of the aqueducts were impressive to a conqueror little versed in massive architecture and engineering.

Social History 20. Having secured Syria, the Arabs advanced on Egypt in AD 640. Sixty years later they had overrun the south Mediterranean seaboard and reached the Atlantic. The continuous lure of plunder rather than religious fanaticism turned their eyes north to Spain rather than south to a more congenial environment. In AD 711 the first Muslims crossed the Strait of Gibraltar, overcame Visigoth opposition and consolidated positions in the south. Following the extinction of the Caliph dynasty of the Umayyads at Damascus, the one member who escaped was crowned independent Caliph of al-Andalusia in AD 750. Thereafter Muslim Spain was to stand on its own. The Moors welded the indigenous and new populations into a single whole, bringing in fresh methods of cultivation, including irrigation, and creating new wealth through commerce. In 1238 Cordova fell to the Christians and ten years later the fortress of the Alhambra in Granada was begun as a last Moorish stronghold. In 1492 Granada was taken by the Christians under Ferdinand and Isabella of Castile and the Moors were finally expelled from Spain.

Philosophy 21. The Muslim faith was carried without modification and with its accustomed tolerance across Egypt and North Africa. Although in direct religious opposition, Christians in Andalusia were allowed to live in their own way and follow their own customs, being subject only to extra taxation. Philosophy and learning flourished independently of religion. Cordova became the main link through which knowledge of the classics passed to medieval Europe, proving more reliable than transmission from the eastern Mediterranean by means of the Crusaders or by way of Sicily. The philosopher Averroes (1126–98), in opposition to both Muslim orthodoxy and Christian doctrines, held that the existence of God could be proved by reason independently of revelation, thus interpreting Aristotle and fore-shadowing the views of the most influential of Western scholastic philosophers, St Thomas Aquinas (1225–74). The orthodox, contented Muslim philosophy of day-to-day enjoyment of life, with its love of gardens, passed easily into the Early Italian Renaissance at a time when theocratic Europe north of the Alps still tended to forego the pleasures of this world in favour of their hopes of the next.

Expression 22. The metaphysical ideas that had arisen from the geography of the Middle East adapted themselves to the new circumstances in Andalusia. In the deserts the sky had predominated, eventually symbolized on earth by the dome. In Spain the sky was less significant because the more fertile and well-treed environment drew attention away from the force and majesty of the heavens. The dome gave way to the minaret and only appeared internally as the cool shadowed depths of a cavern. Attracted rather than repelled by the environment, internal courts now began to expand in imagination beyond the enclosing walls. An almost mystical weaving of interior and exterior can be experienced even today in the Great Mosque of Cordova. The final achievement was the dematerialization of wall and roof surfaces in the Court of the Lions at the Alhambra. Much of Moorish art passed into Western medievalism. The transfer of ideas can be seen in Tarragona, where a square Persian paradise garden was transmuted at the time of the Reconquest into the contemplative cloister garden of Christian monastery, cathedral and university quadrangle.

Architecture 23. The Valley of the Guadalquivir was rich in palaces, houses and gardens. In Cordova the prosperous dwelling would consist of one or more patio gardens, the complex enclosed in a high wall, with glimpses from without of water, fountains and greenery. The paved streets were narrow shady spaces between groups of buildings, without a determined or parallel building line. The urban silhouette was varied, broken by the minarets of four hundred mosques. The Great Mosque was almost totally enclosed within a box of bare walls and consisted of a mysterious forest of columns supporting horseshoe arches that may have derived from Roman remains but which, in their intricate perspective, are reminiscent of the palm groves of Morocco; the pattern, today interrupted by a wall, continues into the adjoining patio, where column is transmuted into tree. Similarly reminiscent of far-off origins is the fragile brick, timber and carved plaster architecture within the Alhambra, which recalls equally the desert nomad existence among tents and shady cases, and cool deep caverns with complex rock walls and ceilings.

Landscape 24. Contained within the shell of the Alhambra is a delicate composition of spaces whose relationship seems particular to Islam. The complex is not, in the Roman sense, a unified plan, for to the Muslim, symmetry on a commanding scale would appear arrogant and displeasing to Allah. The shapes accumulate in the mind rather than the eye, the whole apparently intricate composition being based very simply on the two contrasting forms of the Hall of the Ambassadors/Myrtle Court and the Court of the Lions. The spaces themselves are mathematically proportioned, human in scale, and in principle imaginatively unconfined. Where possible, the interior projects itself through the ramparts to admit views of the countryside, an idea later developed more splendidly by the Mughuls in the Delhi and Agra forts. The Generalife, built in the open country as a summer retreat under the protection of the walls, is in direct contrast to the introvert interior of the Alhambra. The gardens are an extension of the architecture of the house, lying openly along the falling landscape. The composition is based on a romantic view overlooking Granada and the extrovert nature of the design is a forerunner of the hillside villa of the Italian Renaissance.

SPANISH ISLAM represented a high civilization, of which the Reconquista left few remains. **The mosque of Abd er-Rahman I** at Cordova (AD 785–987), now a cathedral, is contained within a walled rectangle 570 feet by 425 feet, two-thirds of which is a dimly lit **internal forest of columns (43)**, and one-third the open-air **Patio de los Naranjos (44)** or Court of the Oranges. The **plan (42)** shows the mosque as it was in the tenth century, before conversion to Christianity and before the openings linking the two parts were walled up. The orange trees and their irrigation channels were a mathematical projection of the mystic interior into the open.

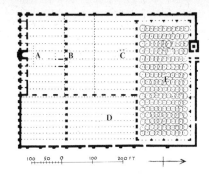

42 THE MOSQUE AT CORDOVA
A Additions by al-Hakim II B Additions by Abd er-Rahman II C Original building of Abd er-Rahman I D Additions by al-Mansur E Patio de los Naranjos

43

44

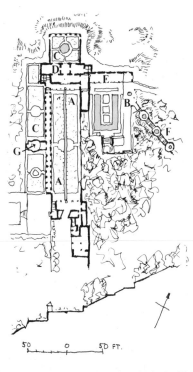

45 GENERALIFE
A Court of the Canal
B Patio de los Cipréses
C Terrace
D Casino
E Belvedere
F Water steps
G Mosque

The Generalife at Granada was built some three hundred years later (before AD 1319) as a summer residence of the Moorish kings. It lies high on the steep, well-watered slopes of the Cerro del Sol adjoining the Alhambra and is sited solely for the enjoyment of landscape in a way that foreshadows the Italian Renaissance. The **plan and section (45)** are based on a survey of 1812, since when there have been additions. Basically the design is a traditional patio garden sensitively placed along the contours, and without damage to enclosure the external world has been decisively drawn in on the north and west. The **high-level view of the Court of the Canal (49)** looks south towards the entrance. The **ground-level view (47)** shows the central rill and fountains, which served as an ablution tank for the small mosque on the outer wall but broke with tradition in not having a cross arm. The **Patio de los Cipréses (48)** was the secluded garden of the harem, defined by a U-canal and planted with oleanders that flower in June, the month when the Moorish Court arrived at the palace. The **water-staircase (46)** leads down from the treed hillside. The air is cooled and the senses delighted by the sight and sound of falling water, not only in the fountains but in the balustrades on each side.

46

47

48

49

50

THE FORTRESS PALACE OF THE ALHAMBRA, Granada, was begun by the founder of the Nasrid dynasty about AD 1250 as the final bastion of Spanish Islam, its construction being spread over 250 years. The **view from the Albaicin (50)** (the old Moorish town) shows the fortress set against the Sierra Nevada, its source of water supply; within its massive encompassing towers and walls is the supreme example of Moorish imagination and elegance in the design of enclosed landscape. The **Court of the Myrtles (52)** was used in conjunction with the Hall of the Ambassadors, as well as being the court of ablutions for the adjoining mosque. The myrtle hedges date from the Spanish Conquest in 1492, when the Muslim religion was suppressed and ablution rites forbidden. Part of the sense of interweaving space is given by windows such as that **looking outwards (53)** from the Hall of the Ambassadors and that **looking inwards (54)** towards the Garden of Daraxa. The climax lies in **the Court of the Lions (55–59** overleaf), originally enriched with orange trees. The columns are alabaster, the decorative surfaces are carved plaster and the fountain itself is bronze.

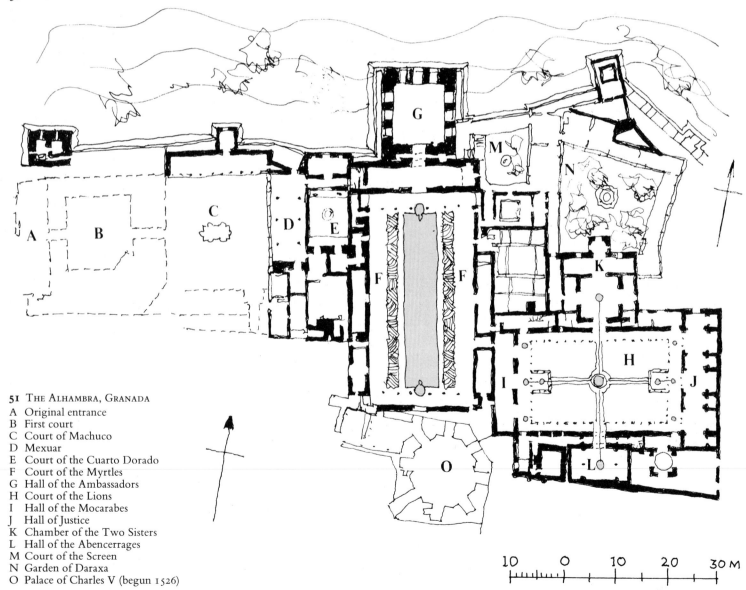

51 THE ALHAMBRA, GRANADA

A Original entrance
B First court
C Court of Machuco
D Mexuar
E Court of the Cuarto Dorado
F Court of the Myrtles
G Hall of the Ambassadors
H Court of the Lions
I Hall of the Mocarabes
J Hall of Justice
K Chamber of the Two Sisters
L Hall of the Abencerrages
M Court of the Screen
N Garden of Daraxa
O Palace of Charles V (begun 1526)

10 0 10 20 30 M

52

53

54

THE COURT OF THE LIONS AT THE ALHAMBRA, GRANADA

5 The Eastern Expansion of Islam: Mughul India

Environment   *25.* The Mughuls were mainly concerned with two areas: Agra/Delhi on latitude 28° and the Vale of Kashmir on latitude 35°. Agra lies on the Jumna, 110 miles south of Delhi. The climate is tropical, with monsoons from June to September and intense heat from March to June. The natural landscape is flat, jungle-treed and featureless except for the river. At the time of the Mughul invasion the existing civilization, both here and in Kashmir, was Hindu, interspersed with Muslims from a previous invasion. The Vale of Kashmir itself, approximately eighty miles by thirty, lies wholly within the Himalayas, some five hundred miles north of Delhi. There is an abrupt change of temperature. The climate of the Vale is equable and the land fertile, the surrounding snow-clad mountains giving abundance of water and protection from the monsoons. The characteristic trees are chenar, poplar, willow and orchard and the scene is enriched by contour-following water shapes of the rice-fields. Indigenous Hindu architecture has always been prominent in the towns and villages.

Social History   *26.* The social history is that of an autocracy dominated by conqueror and despot. The nomad race of the Mongols emerged in AD 1219 from east of the Altai Mountains to overrun Asia and under Genghis Khan create an empire that extended from the China Seas to the Dnieper. Having no civilization of their own, one group of Mongols adopted the Muslim faith. In the fourteenth century the first Mongol invader of India, Tamberlane, made his capital, Samarkand, a city of contemporary Persian architecture and gardens. From here his descendant Babur (1483–1530) again invaded India, making Agra his capital in 1526. Babur's grandson Akbar (1542–1605) expanded and consolidated the Mughul Empire in India, proving to be one of the world's greatest administrators. Akbar brought to India the vision of a society where reason would take precedence over mysticism and emotion, creating a civil service later to be taken over by the British. His son Jahangir (1569–1627) inherited fabulous power and wealth with which to indulge his passion for landscape design, as well as for cruelty; and his grandson Shah Jahan (1593–1666) his passion for architecture and building, which included the completion of the palaces at Delhi and Agra, and the Taj Mahal. The attraction of Kashmir to the six great emperors was irresistible, although the last, Aurangzib (1618–1707), paid only one visit.

Philosophy   *27.* Before their westward drive in the thirteenth century the Mongols were a nomadic race in a hard landscape, living in tents and subsisting on mare's milk products and meat. They drifted northwards for summer pasturage as the snows melted, and southwards for winter pasturage. Their religion was a primitive polytheism. These harsh conditions not only produced a unique fighting machine, the arts of which were learned from China, but a succession of ruthless leaders over the centuries, whose power of organization was matched by a remarkable capacity to move armies across the globe, traversing (and probably exhilarated by) some of the wildest and most varied landscape in Asia. When polytheism proved inadequate, the Muslim religion of the conquered was outwardly adopted, together with their culture. Akbar, three hundred years later and above all dogma and fanaticism, endeavoured unsuccessfully to create a form of world religion. The intuitive passion for wild and natural landscape that the Mughul emperors inherited from their ancestors was equalled by their intellectual preoccupation with the search for the tranquillity that lies in established and unchanging order. Unlike the true Muslim, they were pre-occupied with their own personal immortality in this world as well as the next, and never ceased to explore how best this could be assured.

Expression 28. The three main components of Mughul landscape were: the Agra/Delhi complex; the royal progress to Kashmir; and Kashmir itself. The first was the administrative centre of the emperors, comprising the huge red sandstone walls of the forts and the elegant white marble buildings upon them, and the splendid tombs that perpetuated their memory. The second was the gorgeous procession, some fifty thousand strong, that moved between alternating mile-long rectangular camps as far as the 'great Wall' of the Himalayas, there to shed its size but not its splendour to make the passage of the mountains to Kashmir. The third represented the realization of the objective of personal happiness on earth, symbolized by the inscription in the Shalamar Bagh in Kashmir: 'If there be a Paradise on earth, it is here, it is here.' The journey was no more than a gorgeous barbaric return to the nomadic way of life, but the monuments at Agra and in Kashmir were profound studies in the symbolism and the power of geometry to convey an idea to the human mind. Mughul symbolism was expressed basically in the relationship of circle, octagon and square.

Architecture 29. Like other elements of this civilization, architecture developed either directly under the influence of Persia or, secondarily, from earlier Muslim architecture in India. A Hindu character was encouraged by Akbar, giving a sense of strength, permanence and monumentality that the Muslim Persians had deliberately avoided. The main surviving works were the tombs of the emperors and the fortress palaces. The former were built in their lifetime and were festal. The silhouette of Akbar's tomb at Sikandra gives the effect of joyous viewing platforms high in the sky, the counterfeit of the tomb itself being aloft and in white marble, while the real is subterranean, immediately beneath. The fortress palaces consisted of a complex and exquisitely detailed architectural sequence of courts along the ramparts, designed to catch the breezes and interweave with the middle and distant view of countryside. The Taj Mahal is a final and intricate masterpiece of symbolism.

Landscape 30. While the geometry of the gardens themselves remained traditional to the point of monotony, the conception of the broader landscape was both original and on a grand scale. A single imaginative idea joined Agra to Kashmir, which in fact were linked by chenar avenues as far as Lahore. In Agra, the Taj lies poised between heaven and earth, the centre of a wide metaphysical landscape that comprehends the paradise garden on the one side and the Jumna on the other. Opposite, and connected by a bridge, Shah Jahan had planned his own tomb in black marble. In Kashmir the scene, in contrast, was worldly, transformed into a Mughul pleasure landscape of water. Gardens were set mainly on the lower slopes of the enclosing mountains, luscious with streams. Because of ground irregularities, gardens tended to break away from the standard plan, exploiting the spectacle of falling water and the view over the Vale. Shalamar Bagh was an exception, for it remained loyal to the traditional enclosed square, one following another in falling sequence. The association between tranquil pattern, ground modelling and mountainous environment, makes Shalamar Bagh a garden of contemplation as well as of delight.

60

61, 62

MUGHUL LOVE OF GARDENS AND SYMBOLISM was inherited from Persia. The miniature of the **Feast of the birth of Humayun** (**60**) (*c.* 1590) contains the classic features of design: the square tank with fountains, the watercourse and the stone *chabutra* or platform upon which the Emperor is seated, providing the setting for the life and growth and vitality in which the garden abounded. The rich carpet echoes the spring flowers; the *chenar*, the cypress and the canopy provide shade. The oldest Mughul garden now extant, **Ram Bagh**, was laid out by the Emperor Babur *c.* 1528 on the east bank of the Jumna opposite Agra, his capital. The first need was water. From **a huge well** (**61**) in the background of the picture, water for irrigation was fed into the garden by a raised canal. In the foreground is a stone *chadar*, scalloped to break the water surface and create sparkle. Water was carried along **raised causeways** (**62**), leading past the stone *chabutras* (one is visible in the distance) from which the Emperor contemplated the fruit blossom. Close to Agra, at Sikandra, is the **Tomb of Akbar** (**63**), grandson of Babur. From their Mongol forebears the Mughuls inherited the custom of building their tombs during their lifetime and using them for entertainment; after death the tombs were handed over to holy men. The tomb stands on a raised platform in the centre of a traditional *char-bagh*, or fourfold garden, linked by wide stone causeways to the gateways (three of them blind) set in the surrounding walls.

63

THE RED FORT AT DELHI was built by Shah Jahan between 1639 and 1648. The **plan** (**65**), drawn in 1850, is a vast complex of traditional paradise gardens. The siting, shown in a **painting from a Persian manuscript** (**64**), is reminiscent of Persepolis. The palace buildings were stretched along a two-thousand-foot terrace on high fortress walls, commanding a foreground where spectacles took place, a middle distance of cultivation beyond the River Jumna, and an imaginative far distance of snow-clad Himalayas.

64, 65

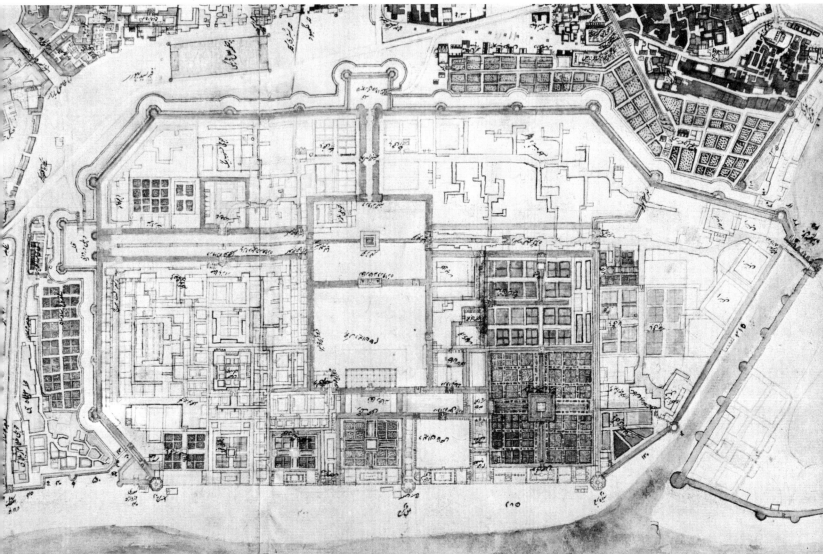

66

THE VALE OF KASHMIR is encircled by mountains that are rarely out of sight. The sketch shows the panorama of **Lake Dal** (**66**) adjoining the capital, Srinagar. On the left is Akbar's fort, in the centre is reclaimed land and on the lake itself are seen the artificial bunds (embankments) and islands which the Mughuls turned into a comprehensive waterscape. The gardens were sited between mountains and lake, to catch the water flow. Beyond the fourth spur lies **Shalamar Bagh**, the site chosen by Jahangir about 1620 and the gardens laid out by his son Shah Jahan. The **plan today** (**67**) has been curtailed, but originally consisted of three fourfold gardens (public audience, private garden and harem) threaded on a canal linked with Lake Dal. On both sides of the central *chenar* avenue were orchards. Each garden was levelled to fit the sloping site and each of the fourfold parts modelled for irrigation, together giving a sense of ground sculpture in low relief that was echoed in architecture. The **view from below the site of the Hall of Private Audience** (**70**) (which originally spanned the cascade) shows the Emperor's throne in the foreground and a smaller throne on the cascade behind, reached by stepping-stones. In the middle distance is the **Black Pavilion** (**68**), isolated in water. The fountains were fed by gravity. Within the cascade behind the Pavilion were **chini-kanas** (**69**), illuminated niches. While the Shalamar plan was strictly traditional, mathematical and symbolic, other gardens such as **Achabal** (**71**) varied the water proportions, but kept to the principle of a **central thread passing through buildings** (**72**).

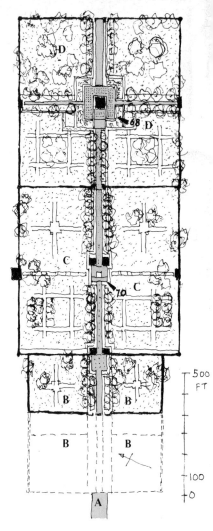

67 SHALAMAR BAGH, KASHMIR
A Canal approach from Lake Dal
B Curtailed court or public garden
C The Emperor's garden
D Ladies' garden

68   69

70

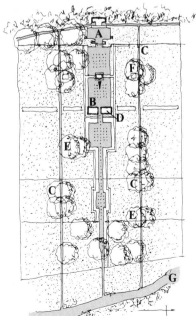

71 ACHABAL, KASHMIR

A Great cascade
B Water and fountains
C Water chutes
D Water pavilions
E Chenar trees
F Stone platforms
G River

72

THE TAJ MAHAL at Agra (77) was built 1632–54 by Shah Jahan in memory of his most cherished wife, Mumtaz Mahal. The **plan** (73) (made 1828 by the Surveyor General of India) breaks with precedent, since the tomb stands, not in the centre of the *char-bagh* but on a terrace to the north, overlooking the Jumna. It is, therefore, a link between two complementary landscapes: a universal paradise garden and a revered but particular riverscape. **From the river terrace (74)** the Fort is seen in the distance. The return **view from the Fort (75)** is that contemplated by Shah Jahan when a prisoner here in the last years of his life. The **final conception of the riverscape (76)** is said to have included his own black marble tomb opposite the Taj, which was never realized.

73

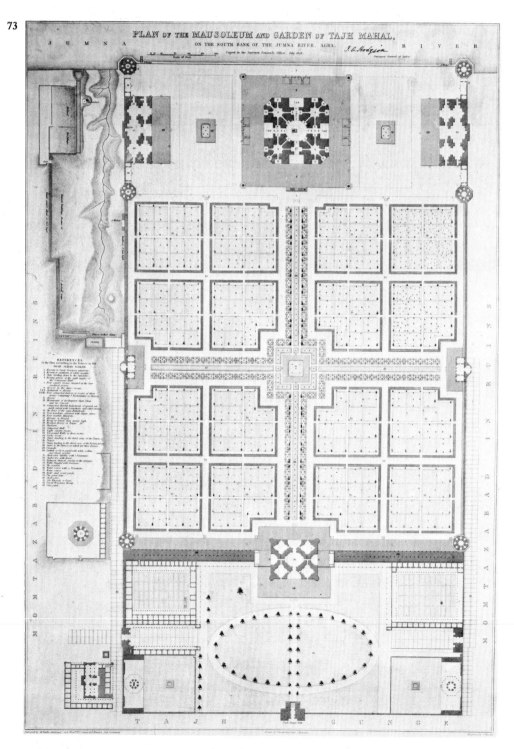

74, 75

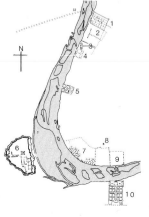

76 MUGHUL AGRA
1 Ram Bagh
2 Zahara Bagh
3 Chini ka Rauza
4 Wazir Khan ka Bagh
5 Tomb of 'Itimad-ud-Daula
6 Agra Fort
7 Chahar Bagh
8 Humayun's Mosque
9 Conjectured site of black marble tomb and bridge
10 Taj Mahal

77

MUMTAZ MAHAL came of a Persian family that for many years had brought to the Mughul Court an elegance and exquisite refinement which inspired all architecture and decoration. The Taj Mahal was to be a materialization of her spirit. The architecture is evocatively feminine and to many it is even the concept of Mumtaz Mahal herself, for ever seated by the banks of the Jumna.

The area of the Eastern civilizations, showing latitude, mountain barriers and selected place names.

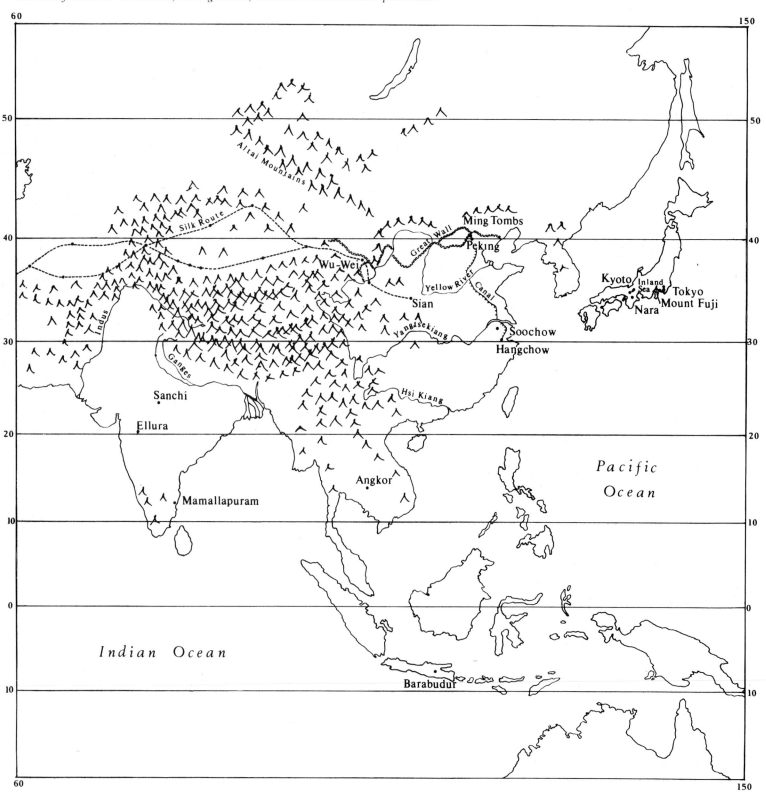

THE EASTERN CIVILIZATIONS

Composed of the mongoloid races of India, China, Japan and Pre-Columbian America. India and China were separated by physical barriers and the link came to be Buddhism filtering from India through the mountains. The civilization of India was based on *religion*; that of China on *ethics*. The mainspring of Chinese culture lay on the mainland, with Japan as an offshoot; the mongoloids of Pre-Columbian America appear to have been wholly independent. Although there had been for long some contact between China and the West, it was not until about AD 1700 that either began slowly to feel that the one might be complementary to the other, the West more so than the East.

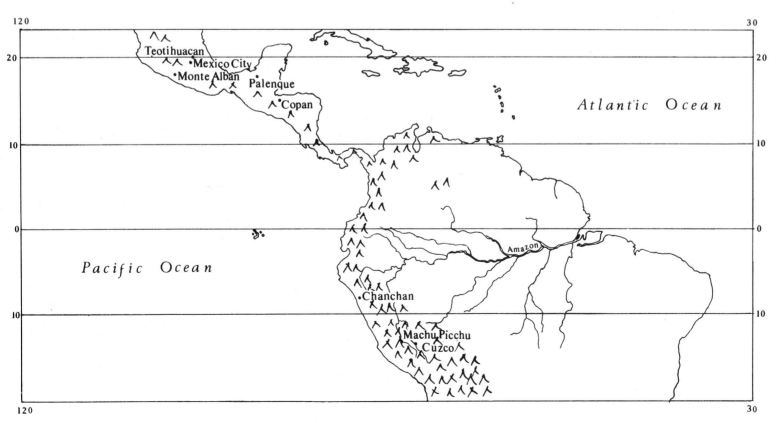

6 Ancient India

Environment *31.* In prehistory India was separated by sea from Asia. The movement northwards of the Indian continental 'plate' and subsequent collision that threw up the Himalayas made an even more formidable barrier to the mainland. Historic India was practically sealed from the Asiatic countries, becoming fundamentally introvert. The only passes were in the north-west, which link with the Iranian plateau, and it was from this corner that civilization, fertilized from outside, gradually spread from 32° north to the islands south of the Equator. The northern plains were watered by monsoons and by many rivers fed by the melting snows. The climate everywhere was tropical. The core of the peninsula was a granite plateau some two thousand feet high and the natural scene was one of peaks, mountains, rocks, rivers and a vast extent of jungle teeming with animal and vegetable life. In the plains there were few wild flowers because of the heat, but there were deep-rooted spring-blossoming trees. There was a second flowering in the autumn season of the rains: 'When the rank green growth chokes all but tall grasses and ferns, and the lotus flowers with their lovely curving leaves completely hide the surface of the ponds. Creepers flourish in the damp dripping forests, where the gnarled twisted limbs of the old mangoes are fringed with sweet-scented orchid sprays.' (C. Villiers Stuart, *Gardens of the Great Mughals*).

Social History *32.* Civilization began in the Indus Valley some time before the third millennium, probably through contact with Mesopotamia. In 1500 BC this indigenous Indus Valley civilization, or 'Harappan' culture, was overwhelmed by an Aryan race originating from the region of the Caspian Sea. The two cultures merged and it was this amalgamation that formed the basic character and philosophy of the future India. In 327 BC the Greeks under Alexander invaded India but retired almost immediately. The third emperor of the new Mauryan dynasty, Asoka (r. 272–232 BC), united most of India, becoming so abhorrent of bloodshed that he renounced war and dedicated himself to Buddhism. After Asoka, civilization in India was dominated by religion to the detriment of civil administration, experiencing many phases and disturbances. Indian influence penetrated into Ceylon, Cambodia, Siam, Burma and Java, through which there may have been contact with China. In AD 1175 came the first major Muslim invasion; the Mughul Empire was established in 1526; the East India Company in the seventeenth century; the British Empire in 1757; and independence in 1947.

Philosophy *33.* The fertility of nature all around him appears to have given the Indian the time, the inclination and the subsistence for metaphysical contemplation; he was wholly preoccupied in making visible the invisible world. The great religious systems that came to dominate Asia were all evolved during the period between the Aryan invasions and the establishment of the Mauryan dynasty. The pre-Aryan peoples worshipped place spirits, tutelary deities and the powers of nature conceived as personal beings (these included tree spirits, sap, water and the whole source of fertility of the vegetable and animal worlds). The Aryans, coming from a less fertile region, on the other hand cultivated the abstract idea of the heavens and of the gods of the sky. Hinduism was a formidable amalgamation of these two religions. It saw in nature the processes through which man has passed before becoming human and it taught reincarnation in animal form for the wicked; but for the good an absorption into a changeless and timeless state. The lotus became the symbol of the creation of the world, of beauty formed out of apparent waste. Buddha, born probably in the mid-sixth century BC, accepted Hindu principles of reincarnation. His teachings were primarily a moral code of conduct and urged that by self-control men, through meditation, could reach a state of Nirvana in which all consciousness of identity is transcended.

Expression   *34.* There were virtually no secular monuments. All were religious, symbolic, and not primarily intended to be aesthetic. They were created to be a materialization of the unseen world and were a unified expression of the indigenous and Aryan philosophies. The former was preoccupied with the forces behind biology, the latter with mathematics. In the south, the Dravidian influence was directed to the revelation through sculpture of the life force that lies unseen within all living things. Observation of nature was acute and accurate, but exact representation was a secondary consideration. The Aryan, on the other hand, was concerned with the order and mysteries of the universe. The symbol of this was the circle, and the materialization of it, the square. Aryan symbolism made the world mountain Meru a pillar between heaven and earth, relating it to the four quarters of the compass. The logical expression of these two philosophies was the rock temple mountain, interpenetrated with exuberant animal and vegetable life. This is the basis of Indian religious architecture, changing little throughout the centuries and reaching its climax in the Buddhist Temple of Barabudur in Java – a mandala in stone and an allegory of man's passage through the world to eternity.

Architecture   *35.* Secular architecture is of little consequence. The extensive palace and gardens of Pataliputra, built by Asoka's grandfather half a century after the destruction of Persepolis, showed decisive Persian influence. The indigenous architecture was solely religious. Although some of the forms were inherited from timber architecture, all structures were of stone, either built up to be as massive as mountains or carved direct from the rock, as in cave architecture, and were made for endurance. They appear to have been based on systems of mathematical proportions both in detail and as a whole. There was no personal expression by the architect. Although creative originality and fine craftsmanship is manifest everywhere, the general expression is that of the collective rather than individual subconscious. This is apparent in the realization of the allegory at Barabudur. The pilgrim proceeds spirally upwards from the worldly square to the ethereal circle and to the 'great emptiness of the upper terraces where sit the Buddhas of the world beyond form and thought'.

Landscape   *36.* Mountains and jungle were together an immense landscape from which the great monuments of spiritual man emerged to give significance and inner meaning. Like the lotus, these monuments were self-evolved out of apparent waste and like the lotus they needed no artifice to link them with their environment. Although conscious landscape design therefore formed no part of temple architecture, there is nevertheless, in the domestic sphere, evidence of early Hindu gardens that no longer exist. The epic poem *Mahabharata* describes gardens that, in the words of Constance Villiers Stuart, 'echoed to the cry of the peacock and the song of the cuckoo . . . there were numerous arbours covered by creepers, charming artificial hillocks, lakes filled to the brim with clear water, fish ponds carpeted with lotus and water lilies, covered by delicate aquatic plants, on which swam red geese, ducks and swans'. The approach to nature changed when the Mughul Emperor Babur laid out the first garden based on irrigation, imposing on the indigenous scene a foreign conception of practical landscape design and of a new relation to nature.

Man's relation to the universe is represented diagrammatically in Buddhist thought by the mandala, the basis of religious building. The **Tibetan Mandala** (**78**) is a late example of the eighteenth or nineteenth century, but the principle has remained unchanged. Benjamin Rowland, in *The Art and Architecture of India*, writes:

In the final development of Mahayana Buddhism in the eighth century we have the complete *mandala*, or magic diagram of the cosmos, with a universal Buddha of the zenith having his seat at the very centre of the cosmic machine, surrounded by four mythical Buddhas located at the four cardinal points of the compass. This concept of Five Buddhas may go back to earlier beliefs and numerologies, such as the Five Elements, the Five Senses, or as names to express the classic correlation of the human microcosm to the universe.

The Great Stupa at Sanchi (**79**, **80**) in central India, first built by Asoka and enlarged in the second century B C, is an example of the Indian concept of *pratibimba*, whereby architectural or sculptural form is given to the imagined structure of the cosmos and supernatural things or regions in order that men may have power over them through their symbols. The concept also includes the making of sacred mountains. Stupas originally were simple earthen burial mounds, but with the death of Buddha they acquired a deeper religious significance: his ashes were enshrined in eight stupas of earth and brick and re-distributed by the Emperor Asoka to stupas in the principal cities of India.

The solid hemisphere enclosing the central chamber symbolizes the dome of heaven enclosing the world-mountain, Meru, here indicated by the balcony at the summit, while the mast that rises above it represents the axis of the world. Round the base of the dome a fence encloses a path for clock-wise circumambulation, the worshipper performing a metaphysical journey, tracing with his footsteps a simple type of mandala.

Towards the end of the first century B C four gateways (*torana*) were added at the four cardinal points, reminiscent of the log or bamboo entrances to the Indo-Aryan villages of the Vedic period (*c.* 1500–800 B C). These were planned as rectangles whose sides faced the four quarters of the globe and were intersected by two avenues linking four gateways. Between the outer walls and the buildings ran a broad path round which the inhabitants might circulate while petitioning the gods – a custom later applied to the stupas. The carvings on the gateways of the stupa follow no preconceived scheme but were commissioned by private persons wishing to gain merit.

80

79

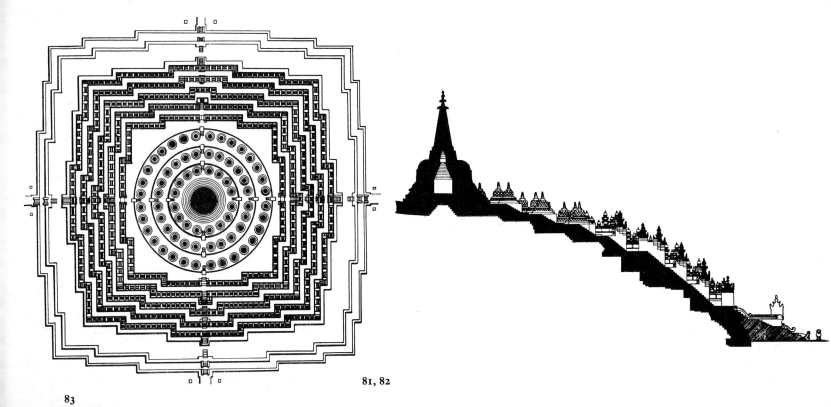

81, 82

83

84

MYSTIC BUDDHISM finds its supreme monument in the **Stupa of Barabudur** in Java, probably built in the mid-eighth century. It is a pure *mandala* created from a hill in the centre of the Kedu plain, a spiritual response to the surrounding volcanic peaks. As the pilgrim ascends, he passes through life from birth to death and thence to the realm of the Void or Absolute beyond form or thought. The sequences of this metaphysical journey are narrated in sculpture. The **plan (81), section (82)** and **terrestrial view (84)** show the five successive square terraces that are the earthly world. The square then changes to the circle of the cosmos: three terraces on which are seated seventy-two Buddhas in **latticed stupas (83)**. Above is the final terrace and stupa of the supreme Buddha. A hidden basement completed the symbolic nine storeys of an Indian Meru mountain, supposedly extending downwards to the foundations of the world.

85, 86

87, 88

DRAVIDIAN TEMPLES ranged from rock excavation to seashore. The mid-eighteenth-century panorama by Thomas Daniell shows the **Ellura hills (85)** near Aurangabad in the Deccan. In the right centre is the **Kailasanatha temple (86)**, one of the greatest Dravidian monuments, dedicated to Siva by Krishna I (AD 757–83) of the Rashtrakuta dynasty. Intended as an architectural replica of the sacred Mount Kailasa, its shrine originally painted white to link in idea with the sacred Himalayan peaks, the building is hewn direct from the rock face and carved like sculpture from the hillside. It is only one of a series of about thirty-four rock-cut temples and shrines of different religions carved out of the Ellura hills between the fifth and eighth centuries. **The shore temple at Mamallapuram (87)**, is on the sea coast below Madras, one of a complex of Dravidian monuments built by the rulers of the Pallava dynasty in the seventh century AD. There are some seventeen temples, five of which are carved from granitic outcrops. The shore temple, built after 674, is a structural building, planned so that the door of the sanctuary opens to the east in order to catch the first rays of the rising sun. Sculpture abounds throughout the complex. The **Descent of the Ganges from the Himalayas (88)** is carved on the face of a granite boulder over eighty feet long. A natural cleft in the rock, at one time a channel for water in reality, has been used to represent the river, in which elephants are wading.

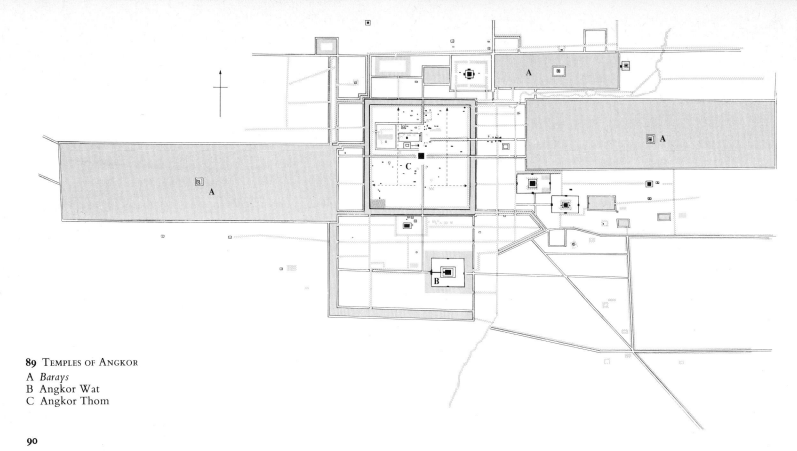

89 TEMPLES OF ANGKOR

A *Barays*
B Angkor Wat
C Angkor Thom

90

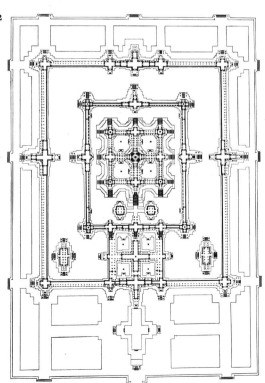

92

ANGKOR, jungle city of water and mountain-temples on the Cambodian Lake Tonle Sap, was founded as the capital of the Khmers about AD 900. By the fifteenth century its population may have been a million; thereafter it slowly returned to jungle. **The overall plan (89)**, shown here as it was in the fourteenth century, was shaped first by irrigation. The huge *barays*, or reservoirs were constructed by dikes rather than excavations, in order to catch flood waters and later release them over the land. The whole city was encompassed by a dike, appearing as an island during floods. Having ensured astonishing fertility and food supply, the King, God on Earth, then built his personal symbolic mountain-temple to house his kingly essence. Because of the ease with which life was sustained, spare labour was plentiful and its utilization to absorb energy clearly desirable. Stone was brought easily to the site by water, piled high according to a basic plan, and carved *in situ* as narrative. Plans of the separate temples, such as **Angkor Wat (92)**, were traditional, but the square was elongated on the east–west axis, and this directional tendency is seen throughout the whole complex. The last and greatest of the temple-mountains was Angkor Wat, seen here **from the air (90)** in its own vast water setting symbolic of the ocean. A view of one of the smaller complexes, **Angkor Thom (91)**, shows the huge pile-up of masses that broke into a jagged silhouette of symbolic towers, suitable to the misty light of the humid jungle.

ANCIENT INDIA 67

7 China

Environment   *37.* China proper lies between latitudes 40° and 20°, covering about one and a half million square miles. It is bounded on the west by the Himalayas and on the south and east by the Pacific Ocean; only on the north is there no natural boundary against historic invasion. Three great rivers cross it approximately from west to east: the Yellow River (Huang-Ho), the Yangtse-kiang and the Si-kiang. North China has extensive dry loess plains; central China has lakes, streams and flooded fields; south China, mountains and inaccessible valleys stretching into sub-tropical regions. The climate varies from Siberian to sub-tropical. The monsoon blows in from the sea from June to August, giving most of the rainfall and ensuring uniformity of temperature over much of the country. The winter is dry, short and sharp. The primeval forests were luxuriant and with a greater variety of species than anywhere in the world; wild flowers proliferated, and when cultivated for food the soil could produce two crops a year. From the geniality of environment there arose an understanding between man and landscape that was to be the basis of Chinese thought and philosophy.

Social History   *38.* Civilization crystallized along the Yellow River about 3000 BC, and evolved virtually uninterrupted for nearly five thousand years. The climax in philosophy and thought was reached in the sixth century BC contemporaneously with that of Greece, and in 221 BC the previous multiplicity of states was united in a single empire. The basis of stability was the family unit, with a society mainly of small proprietors and merchants. There was no hereditary aristocracy. The emperor rode supreme on this civilization, and all foreign conquerors were absorbed by it. Serious contact with the West began about the first century BC through the silk road north of the Himalayas. Under the Han (200 BC–AD 200) the population of China exceeded that of the entire Roman Empire, her technology was more advanced and her scale of Imperial building prodigious. The Sung (AD 960–1229) reorganized the state administratively, making their capital Hangchow, as Marco Polo described it, 'the greatest and most beautiful city in the world'. The accumulated knowledge, wisdom and intuitions of the long past were conserved and digested. Culture was intellectualized and standards set for the future. The foreign Mongol dynasty (AD 1288–1368) under Kubla Khan moved the capital to Peking, but preserved Hangchow from destruction. Peking remained the capital under the indigenous Ming dynasty (1368–1644) and the foreign Manchu dynasty (1644–1912).

Philosophy   *39.* The Chinese conceived that man emerged from the bowels of the earth like any mountain or plant, and therefore was one of them in spirit. Hence his love of antique tradition and the worship of ancestors, for the spirits in all nature were friendly. The philosopher Confucius (550–478 BC) systematized earlier rites and ideas into a moral code of behaviour rather than of religion, and this remained basic to future Chinese thought. Confucianism was paralleled with the more mystical Taoism, whose influence on painting and landscape was complete. Tao means 'the way': all men must live, work and die within the laws of nature ordained by the Lord of Heaven, who moves all things. It emphasized the individual rather than the community, and instinctual inner harmony rather than outward rule-keeping. Its cult of solitude led to a special sensitivity to landscape. About AD 58 the extreme mysticism of Buddhism filtered from India, having as its doctrine the emancipation of the soul from worldly desire and the negation of self. Buddhism reached its greatest influence in the seventh and ninth centuries A D, when with Zen Buddhism it passed to Japan. Thereafter China returned to its ethical rather than religious basis. Since nature appeared constant, rhythmic and unchanging, so man, having reached an ecological climax, remained constant also, like any other earthly species.

Expression 40. Art grew from calligraphy. The Chinese written character was a pictograph which conveyed to the mind, rather than the eye, the essence of the object. Similarly, landscape design later evolved through the painter. The basic conception was that of the lonely philosopher deep among the mountains or in communion with the mythical immortal islands that vanished and reappeared in the waters, wrapped in mist. The essence of these scenes was transmuted and brought to the home by the painter with arts similar to those of landscape design. 'In your fancy you enter a painting,' said Yuan Yen in the sixteenth century. Because he conceived himself in spirit akin to all physical objects, alive or inert, he could rely upon analogy and symbolism to convey his message. 'Never paint even a stone without spirit,' a Chinese master told his pupils. 'If a great mountain is the most important part of your picture, the mountain must seem like a host and the other hills and the trees like his guests; or the mountain must be like a prince and the other parts of your picture his vassals.'

Architecture 41. The first Chinese home was hollowed out of the earth and lightly roofed, and just as the family unit remained the basis of society so the domestic house remained the basis of all subsequent architecture. There was little external change of expression between classes of buildings, secular and sacred, and the Buddhists needed to introduce the pagoda to mark a sacred precinct. Once the architectural style had been evolved, there was little change. The buildings were timber framed, elegantly stabilized by massive tilted tile roofs that often seemed poised in flight above the ground. The buildings were brightly coloured. Cities, towns and emperor's urban palace were orientated and laid out according to cosmic calculation, heaven being considered a round and the earth counterpart to be a square. The huge urban complexes were axial, geometric and built to impress. Outside the massive stone walls the summer palaces, according to the records of the painters, were an idealization of the lonely philosopher's pavilion among the mountains. They were asymmetrical, modest in scale if vast in size and above all partook of the *genius loci*.

Landscape 42. The metaphysical science of geomancy, or land divination, was applied in choice of site and layout. It shared a cosmology with Taoism, stressing kinship, descent, relations between buildings and society; without harmony there could not later be peace for those who dwelt in them. The basic elements of a new landscape were that of rock, hill or mountain (the *yang*, the stimulating male force) and still water (the *yin*, the tranquillizing female force). All perceived forms were thought to be forms of cosmic forces with certain characters combining the *yin* and the *yang*. They were endowed with particular spirit, sometimes human and often animal, such as tortoise, serpent or dragon. Not until these were harmonized were the techniques of design applied. Gardens were then planned for every mood and occasion, daylight and moonlight, all the year round, and for mist, rain or clear skies. Boundaries were subdued or eliminated, for the imagination must roam in worldly space as well as that of spirit. Stillness was essential, for the gardens were for meditation, conversation and poetry-reading; and all were fragrant with trees, flowers and shrubs. The intuitive world of spirit appears to have reached its climax under the Sung. It was intellectualized, and in China gradually declined as an inner force as the physical and visible world increased in magnificence.

93

94

POETRY AND PAINTING were both originators and inspirers of early Chinese landscape design, revealing a deep and often mystical relationship between man and his environment. In painting, the viewpoint is always above ground level, as though the observer himself were some disembodied spirit, part of a scene already ethereal through atmosphere. Thus he himself (but not his body) seems to be actually inside Ma Yüan's **Landscape with Willows and Bridge** (**95**) (*c.* AD 1200). In scroll painting, the disembodied observer moved along as well as above the landscape. Both atmosphere and movement are contained in the section of Tung Yüan's **River Landscape** (**93**) (*c.* AD 1000), which also embodies the oldest of Chinese myths, the Mystical Islands of the Blest, on whose shores dwelt the immortals, and which were said to vanish and return. The translation of myths and scenes such as this into practical reality was the birth of landscape design.

The first recorded great artificial landscape, derived from the hunting- and fishing-park, was designed by the Han Emperor Wei (140–89 BC) as an interpretation of the mystic isles, with an artificial lake presumably large enough for the islands to disappear in mist. Thereafter, landscape design matured in all its aspects, but remained constant to its original principles. The magnitude of some of the works is almost beyond comprehension. In the year AD 607, for instance, the Sui Emperor Ti began his tremendous Western Park near his capital of Lo-Yang: 'The ground was broken over an area of about seventy-five square miles, and the labour of a million workers on the average was required. Earth and rock were brought to make hills, and the ground was excavated for the five lakes and four seas' (Loraine Kuck). Imaginary palaces in the landscape about this period were depicted by the T'ang painter Li Ssu-Hsun (*c.* AD 651–716) in such scenes as the **Palace by a River** (**94**). From these we can assess the modesty of architecture, however magnificent, that was an essence of Chinese landscape art.

北苑真筆

宣統辛亥□月□甲拔觀於
□□□越之□敬同□□

95

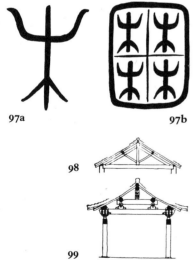

97a 97b

98

99

THE CREATION AND NATURE OF CHINESE ARCHITECTURE can be understood through the sixteenth-century painting **Dreaming of Immortality in a Thatched Cottage** (96). The artist has transmuted the earth-bound body of the sleeping sage into a floating weightless abstract form symbolic of his spiritual objectives and aspirations. This dream of immortality seems to inform all Chinese art, as though art itself were a middle distance between the visible and the invisible. Architecture itself, so peculiar to China and so constant in its spirit, seems to have evolved in a way which parallels the evolution of writing.

The character for **tree** (97a), for example, was originally used on bronze castings, and this in turn became the diagram for a **park** (97b). Parallel with the pictogram came the development of building technique. Timber was plentiful, needed painting for preservation (which called for colour) and its vulnerability as compared with stone was in harmony with the Chinese philosophy of the ephemeral. All structures were framed, not, as in Europe, with a **rigid triangular truss** (98) on load-bearing walls, but with a **complete frame system** (99) stabilized by a heavy roof of clay tiles. The tilted eave probably evolved from the practical need to throw off water, and only afterwards was translated into the aesthetic of flight already suggested in the pictogram and in the dream of the sage. The **Phoenix Hall at Byodo-in** (100) in Japan (eleventh century) is the only existing example of pure Chinese Tang/Sung architecture in which this sense of movement and flight reached its most complex form.

THE TOWN GARDEN had objectives which were laid down more than two thousand years ago and which in fact are applicable anywhere today. It must have privacy, quietness, protection from man and the elements; above all, the sense of an inner sanctuary and peacefulness that is obtained by association with nature in repose. The town dweller interpreted this last requirement as bringing into his home a symbol of his ideal life, such as the rural scene depicted in the **Landscape (101)** attributed to T'ung Ch'i-Ch'ang (d. 1636). The components were simple: water, rocks and, in this instance, pines and willows; but their arrangement was all-important. The urban dwelling grew from a single unit with a walled courtyard garden, in which the architecture was sufficiently low to allow views of the sky. A restrictive or hostile boundary would be eliminated, probably by planting. The symbolic principles were later fully developed by the Japanese.

The traditional plan of **a house in Soochow (102)**, bounded on three sides by canals, is a multiple family unit, an assembly of small dwellings and gardens ingeniously interlocked for seclusion and individuality; the **garden in Soochow (103)** was probably one of the more important. So powerful and constant has been the tradition of domestic individuality that it has been maintained in principle in the modern **Peace Hotel**, Peking (**104**).

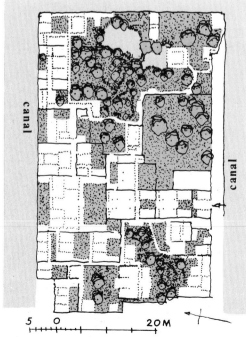

canal

canal

5 0 20M

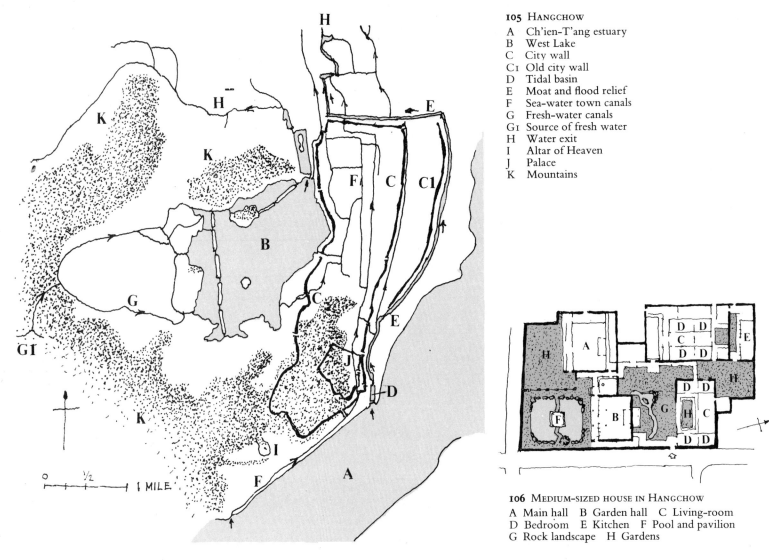

105 HANGCHOW
A Ch'ien-T'ang estuary
B West Lake
C City wall
C1 Old city wall
D Tidal basin
E Moat and flood relief
F Sea-water town canals
G Fresh-water canals
G1 Source of fresh water
H Water exit
I Altar of Heaven
J Palace
K Mountains

106 MEDIUM-SIZED HOUSE IN HANGCHOW
A Main hall B Garden hall C Living-room
D Bedroom E Kitchen F Pool and pavilion
G Rock landscape H Gardens

HANGCHOW was the capital of China under the Sung dynasty between 1127 and 1291 and it was here that landscape design, in common with all the arts, probably reached its zenith. **Beautifully sited (105)** in relation to an amphitheatre of hills and to the mile-wide tidal waters of the Ch'ien-T'ang estuary, the city was dependent on an elaborate water design that separated fresh water from sea. The sea-water town canals were flushed by the manipulation of tidal sluices. The shallow artificial **West Lake (107)**, made in the seventh century AD when the city was founded, was fresh-water-fed from the mountains; and the two systems had to be kept apart. This vast functional water project was the inspiration for a tranquil lake landscape active with artificial islands and bunds, and an urban scene of water streets that must have been clean and wholesome. The **plan of a medium-sized house (106)** shows a typical family complex with its individual units and gardens. The city was visited in 1280 by Marco Polo, who appears to have been inaccurate in stating that the canals were flushed into the lake, but otherwise gave a vivid if exaggerated description of the contemporary city. Part of it is given opposite.

107

On the borders of the lake are many handsome and spacious edifices belonging to men of rank and great magistrates. There are likewise many idol temples, with their monasteries, occupied by a number of monks, who perform the service of the idols. Near the central part are two islands, upon each of which stands a superb building, with an incredible number of apartments and separate pavilions. When the inhabitants of the city have occasion . . . to give a sumptuous entertainment, they resort to one of these islands, where they find ready for their purpose every article that can be required . . . which are provided and kept there at the common expense of the citizens, by whom also the buildings were erected. It may happen that at one time there are a hundred parties assembled there, all of whom, not withstanding, are accommodated with separate rooms or pavilions, so judiciously arranged that they do not interfere . . . with each other . . . there are upon the lake a great number of pleasure vessels or barges, calculated for holding ten, fifteen, to twenty persons, being from

fifteen to twenty paces in length, with a wide and flat flooring. . . . Such persons as take delight in the amusement, and mean to enjoy it, either in the company of their women or that of their male companions, engage one of these barges, which are always kept in the nicest order, with proper seats and tables, together with every other kind of furniture necessary for giving an entertainment. The cabins have a flat roof or upper deck, where the boatmen take their place, and by means of long poles, which they thrust to the bottom of the lake (not more than one or two fathoms in depth), they shove the barges along, until they reach the intended spot. These cabins are painted within-side of various colours and with a variety of figures; all parts of the vessel are likewise adorned with painting. There are windows on each side, which may either be kept shut, or opened, to give an opportunity to the company, as they sit at table, of looking out in every direction and feasting their eyes on the variety and beauty of the scenes as they pass them. And truly the gratification afforded in

this manner, upon the water, exceeds any that can be derived from the amusements on the land; for as the lake extends the whole length of the city, on one side, you have a view, as you stand in the boat, at a certain distance from the shore, of all its grandeur and beauty, its palaces, temples, convents, and gardens, with trees of the largest size growing down to the water's edge, whilst at the same time you enjoy the sight of other boats of the same description, continually passing you, filled in like manner with parties in pursuit of amusement. In fact, the inhabitants of this place, as soon as the labours of the day have ceased, or their mercantile transactions are closed, think of nothing else than of passing the remaining hours in parties of pleasure, with their wives or their mistresses, either in these barges, or about the city in carriages.

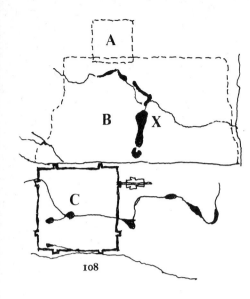

108

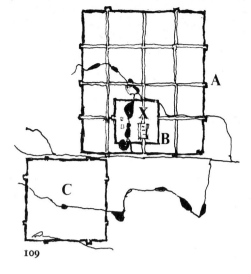

109

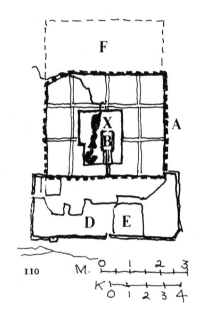

110

108 Peking. The Pre-Mongol city
A Site of the earliest city, twelfth century B C
B Park and Summer Palace, Chin Dynasty A D 1115–1234
C Liao Dynasty city A D 907–1114
X Coal Hill

109 Peking. The Mongol city
A Mongol city (1279–1367)
B Inner city
C Old Liao city
X Coal Hill

110 Peking. The Ming city
A Mongol city as reduced *c.* A D 1409
B Imperial Palace
D South extension
E Altar of Heaven
F Abandoned area
X Coal Hill

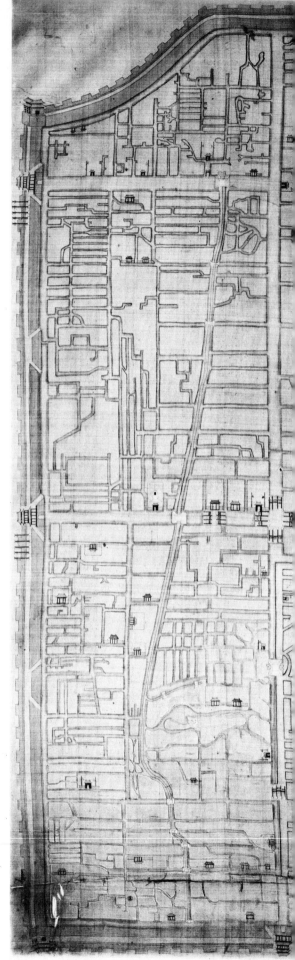

111

PEKING was sited on flat wet land and in evolution has been basically geometrical. The earliest **symbolic square town (108)** was followed by a second square, and under the Chin (1115–1234) the space between became a hunting-park. Fishing-lakes were formed and the excavations supposedly used to make Coal Hill. **The new city of Kubla Khan (109)** was built in the hunting-park, the lakes being retained and embellished and the axis of the Imperial Palace aligned with Coal Hill – 'an artificial mount, fully a hundred paces high, clothed with the most beautiful evergreen trees' (Marco Polo). **Under the Ming, the city (110)** was contracted in the north but extended in the south to include the Altar of Heaven. **The plan (111),** drawn in the eighteenth century, shows the system of boxes one within another: the inmost Imperial Palace, the inner city with the artificial landscape of the Sea Palaces, and the outer for the population. The philosophic history of China can be read from this exquisite drawing. The geometry is Confucian and the inconsequential penetration of natural form is Taoist; the two together are in harmony.

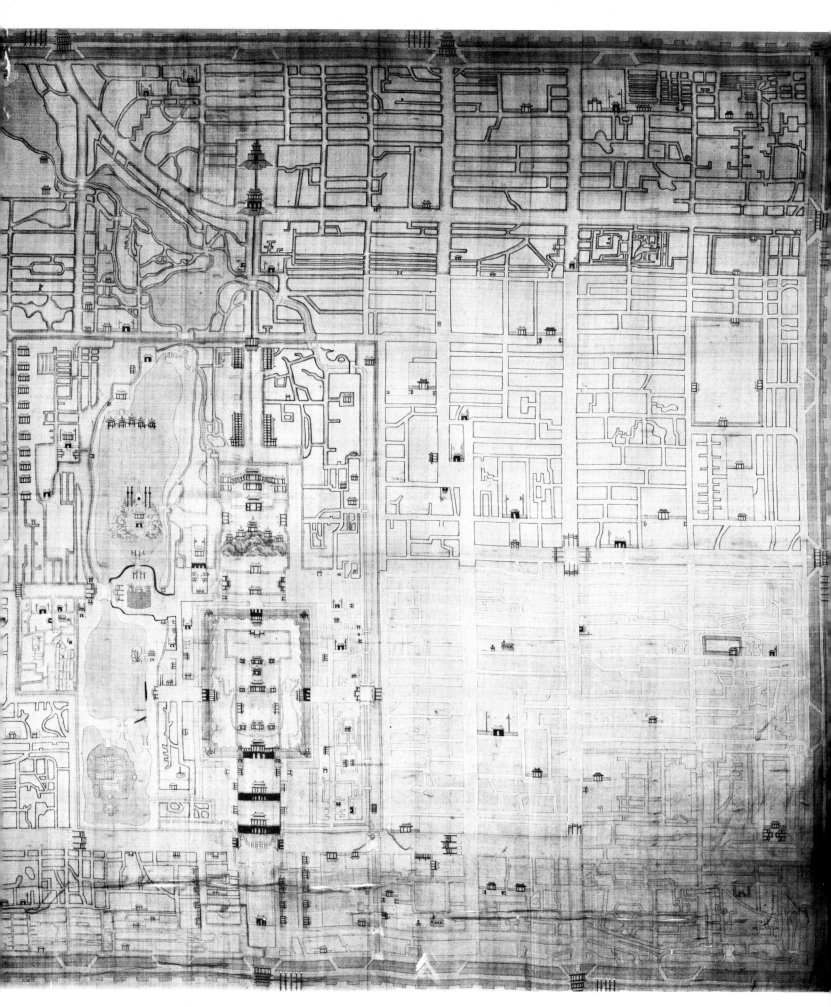

112

THE SUCCESSION OF SPACES which made up Peking was mainly the creation of Kubla Khan, followed by the Ming dynasty and the Manchus. The **view from Coal Hill** (112) over the Imperial Palace of Kubla Khan shows its symmetry without the emphatic central axis of Western planning. The modest axis passes under and through buildings and does not divide one side from the other. The otherwise excessive geometry is counter-balanced by the succession of lakes and Sea Palaces that now forms Pei-hai Park. As part of this romantic landscape, the **Jade Rainbow Bridge** (113) leads to the Emerald island of Kubla Khan, upon which stands the Buddhist White Dagoba (1652). South of the city and east of the central axis is the **Altar of Heaven** (114, 115), built by the Ming in 1420 (rebuilt 1889). Symbolic of the relationship between the heavenly circle and the earthly square, this magnificent conception of religion was placed insignificantly in the total plan and was used by the emperors only three or four times a year. The Chinese city was not theological in the Western medieval sense, and the overriding character always remained domestic.

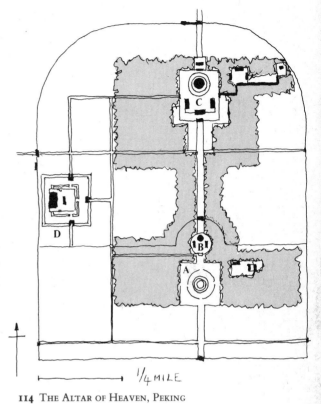

1/4 MILE

114 THE ALTAR OF HEAVEN, PEKING
A Altar of Heaven
B Imperial Lofty Throne
C Temple of Heaven
D Palace of Fasting

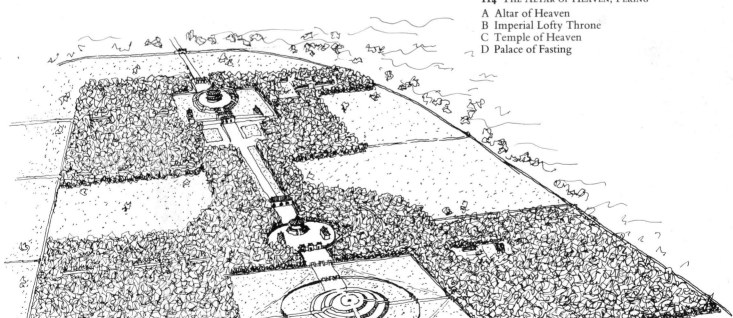

116

THE MING DYNASTY marks the high point of Chinese imperial landscape, reaching a climax of building under Yung Lo (r. 1403–24). Among many monumental works, he converted the **Great Wall (116)** from earth to stone, incorporating imposing fortress architecture on its twisting line. Yung Lo's greatest landscape conception was the complex of his own tomb and those of his future dynasty. The site, some three miles by two, is twenty miles north-west of Peking and was chosen by geomancy, against the mountains and close to the·Great Wall. The design was traditional. The approach is along a **spirit road (117)** of giant animal and human sculpture, passing through a monumental gatehouse to the Emperor's walled enclosure. The culmination is the tree-planted **artificial hill (118)**, about half a mile in circumference, within which the tomb lies inaccessible. Twelve later tombs of the dynasty were added in the vicinity.

117

118

8 Japan

Environment 43. The three main islands that constitute Japan lie across latitude 30°–40° north. They are approximately 1,000 miles from north to south and 150 miles wide. To the east is the comparatively shallow Sea of Japan, separating the main island from Korea. To the west is the very deep Pacific Ocean, from which emanate typhoons. Earthquakes are thought to be produced by the tension of the Pacific 'plate' grinding on that of Asia. The scale of the landscape is small but varied. Rounded mountains and adjoining valleys form the spine, the highest volcanically shaped being Mount Fuji (12,395 feet). Only about one-eighth of the land can be cultivated, the staple food being fish. Rivers are plenteous, broad and short, at times no more than beds of pebbles and boulders. The climate is humid, but varies from north to south, the average temperature in Kyoto being 56 degrees F. The average annual rainfall is about 1·5 metres, with 215 days of sunshine. Snow throughout the winter is heavy in the west, brought by winds from Siberia, but slight in the east. The soil is generally rich. There is no permanent grass, and the principal indigenous trees are oak, wild prunus, wild vine, sumach, maples, birch and zelkova. Cherry and plum blossom luxuriantly in spring, to be followed by wistaria, azalea, iris, peony and lotus; in the autumn the chrysanthemums. Many species have been introduced from China.

Social History 44. The Japanese are probably Mongolian stock from Korea. Society has always been aristocratic and military, the emperor being recognized as divine. Japan was never conquered militarily between primitive and modern times, the only invasion in AD 1281 by Kubla Khan being heroically repelled. Culturally it was at first overwhelmed by China, from whose more ancient civilization all culture was derived. The first Emperor is assumed to have been Jimmu, AD 662, but during the whole of the Japanese feudal period (eighth-nineteenth centuries) his power was replaced by that of the *shogun*. Buddhism was introduced about AD 550 and the energies of the country were soon directed to the building of monasteries as much as palaces and mansions. When the capital was at Nara (AD 707–81) the arts are said to have absorbed one half the total government expenditure. Kyoto became the capital in AD 784, remaining the administrative and cultural centre until this moved to Tokyo in 1869. Kyoto was destroyed by war in 1467 and again by fire in 1788, but remained the national shrine of historic Japanese landscape architecture.

Philosophy 45. On islands where the immensity of sea and sky was dominant, the basic Japanese religion, Shinto, has been concerned with the elements of the universe as a whole. The primitive Japanese worshipped the sun, the moon, the sea, the earth, the mountain, wells, springs, stones and rocks; the deities of thunder, wind, rainstorm and fire; and those of the terrifying earthquake. He worshipped the serpent and other animals and, in due time, the emperor himself. Buddhism, tinged with Chinese Taoism, later joined with Shintoism to make life and landscape a conscious religion. The tea ceremony, with its pavilions, was religious in origin. Zen Buddhism went further and set out intellectually to reach infinity and achieve enlightenment on the meaning and purpose of existence through meditation and the contemplation of landscape. It considered this force to be greater than the power of words. The reasoning was as follows: (*a*) the universe was conceived as a void in which floated material substances existing in time; (*b*) the mind reflected this, being a void in which floated worldly events; (*c*) the quartz sand garden, reflecting both universe and mind, was the medium that linked the two: the rocks the worldly events, the quartz the void.

Expression *46.* Because of the enormous land mass, the Chinese outlook on landscape was extrovert and in breadth. In Japan, because of the tight and hostile sea boundary, it was introvert and in depth. As in China, the garden landscape was a microcosm of the natural landscape, which all Japanese equally loved and worshipped. House and garden were indivisible. The objective was to live and move in the abstractions of a painting, as well as in the contemplation of it. But whereas in China the outer landscape could be 'borrowed', in Japan the frame, however invisible, was in principle always present. This sense of enclosure forced attention upon the inward minutiae of nature and the discovery and enjoyment of worlds not normally reached by the senses. The art of analogy and symbolism, continuing from that of the Sung dynasty in Hangchow, reached its climax under Japanese Zen Buddhism, relying upon the highly disciplined imagination of the beholder for personal interpretation. In its intelligible and popular form the art centred round a recognizable subject or story, such as the allegory of man's passage through the world expressed through the shapes of rocks.

Architecture *47.* Buildings, similarly constructed of timber as in China, have tended to survive, firstly because of the political stability of the country and care in maintenance, and secondly because of strict reconstruction (or regeneration) in the original style; the ancient Imperial precincts at Ise have been rebuilt on alternate sites continuously every twenty years. The more monumental groups of buildings under Chinese influence tended to be symmetrical, with internal courts, apparent in the landscape as a complex of long low lines marked by a great pagoda. Domestic dwellings in principle were single storeyed, able to ride an earthquake but not fireproof. Their shape evolved from landscape design, to which they were at all times subsidiary. House and garden interlocked but were complementary inasmuch as the one was asymmetrically geometric and the other organic. The house, timber framed, was planned on a mathematical module with movable partitions which were translucent when they formed the outer walls; in the long summer they were opened to verandas, often round three sides. Within the interior were sometimes wall-paintings echoing, and therefore introducing, the external landscape.

Landscape *48.* Successive phases can be detected. I. In the beginning an empty gravelled courtyard for Shinto rites and court ceremonies is gradually transformed with the introduction of the primary elements of the natural environment: water, rocks and trees, followed by little hills, islands and bridges. Chinese influence is overwhelming, creating symbolism in use of natural materials and symmetry in monumental groups and town-planning. II. (Kamakura AD 1185–1332) Period of unrest and civil strife. The Buddhist paradise garden, a mandala of specific symbolism, provides an escape into religion from a temporarily hostile environment. III. (Muromachi 1333–1573; Momoyama 1573–1615) The secular garden revives and reaches its highest level under the influence of the Chinese Sung. Zen Buddhism evolves the temple landscapes of (*a*) the separated ceremonial tea pavilion, and (*b*) the static gardens of contemplation. IV. (Edo 1615–1868) The secular 'stroll' garden develops from the stepping-stones of the tea pavilion to become a garden of movement. To the primary elements are now added stone lanterns and lavers (hand-rinsing basins). V. The secular garden expands aesthetically. The 'borrowed' landscape appears; plants are clipped like rocks or as pure abstract form; the proliferating small urban garden, intent on tradition, calls for a miniature within a miniature; tiny gardens are made in receptacles with live dwarf trees.

THE VOLCANIC LANDSCAPE OF THE SETO INLAND SEA (**119**) epitomizes the basic Japanese religion, Shinto, which was concerned with the elements of the universe as a whole. Within this turbulent scene of sky, sea and land – a microcosm of Japan as a whole – the human race survived and prospered. Space available for agriculture and human habitation was limited, enforcing efficiency and, therefore, instinctive mathematical planning. The overall indigenous Japanese scenery became one of wild mountains with pockets of geometry in the lowlands; a landscape they loved. **Mount Fuji (120)**, the 'perfect' mountain seen across the strip fields, was itself symbolic of the majestic dominance of nature over man, his works and his art. His art in landscape became a microcosm of the whole, and sprang from such purely functional scenes as the **ricefields and villages (121)** near Lake Biwa, above Kyoto, set against mountains. From this it ultimately developed into the sophisticated 'garden of the borrowed landscape' of the **Shugaku-in Imperial Villa (122)** (1655), where the eye passes across Kyoto in the middle distance to link with the mountains beyond. Between these two extremes of thought lies all the inward-looking sacred and secular work of Japanese landscape design.

119

123

124

THE SACRED LANDSCAPE: unlike the churches and monasteries of the West, Japanese religious buildings include, but transcend, the world of nature. The *torii*, or gateway, of the Shinto **Itsukushima shrine** (**123**), dating from AD 811, extends the shrine over the water in a way that is consistent with the conception of the divinity of both sky and earth. The coming of Buddhism via China in the seventh century introduced new forms to Japan, but they were soon given a distinctively Japanese character. Chinese desire for symmetry normally placed the pagoda (descended from the Indian stupa) on the same central axis as the Buddha hall, but Japanese preference for asymmetry placed them side by side, as at the **Horyu-ji monastery, Nara** (**124**). Later temples relegated the pagoda to beyond the confines or dispensed with it altogether, the Buddha hall becoming dominant. At Nara, aloofness from the material world is suggested by enclosing walls, at Itsukushima by the water, and at the **Kiyomizu temple, Kyoto** (**125**), by a sense of inaccessibility. The building, a seventeenth-century reconstruction of a ninth-century original, extends from the tree-clad slopes on a gigantic substructure of un-nailed timber. In the distance is modern Kyoto.

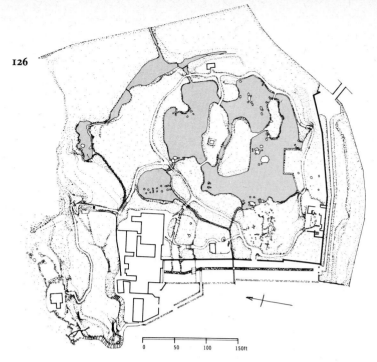

126

127

THE PARADISE GARDEN was evolved between 1185 and 1332 as part of a return to contemplative Buddhism. The **Moss Garden of Saiho-ji temple, Kyoto (127)**, was made *c.* 1350 and is composed of more than a hundred species. The **plan (126)** is basically original. In *The World of the Japanese Garden*, Loraine Kuck writes:

Saiho-ji marks a definite change in garden development, with the disappearance of the old, gay, open Heian pleasure park, while it preshadows the new subjective feeling in gardens of the coming age . . . Saiho-ji was built to express the Jodo concept of Amida's celestial garden, but over the years other feelings have crept in. The curious effect of the moss, the lichen-marked tree trunks, the dark gleaming water with its long reflections, all combine to create a feeling of the centuries rolling over. And with this has come the mood of great tranquillity that Japanese artists call *yugen*. *Yugen* is called into being by atmosphere, one of hazy unreality that creates in a mind attuned to it the feeling of kinship with nature, the sense of one's spirit merging with the spirits of other natural things and the eternal behind them all. This is the basic feeling of Oriental mysticism, fostered consciously by Zen. From this time on, it was to play a large part in Japanese gardens, with the garden artists striving consciously to put it into their work.

By the late fifteenth century, pictorial design technique had become professionalized, reaching its highest aesthetic level. **The Golden Pavilion or Kinkaku-ji, Kyoto (128)** (1394, rebuilt after a fire in 1950), was designed under Chinese Sung influence as a place of contemplation for a retired nobleman. The building appears to float above the water. The **lake (129)** is divided in two parts by an island: that beside the pavilion being enlivened with lesser islands and tortoise-shaped rocks, the further being placid. This skilful play on optics induces vision from the pavilion to focus on the foreground complexities, allowing the water beyond the island (seen through the stems of trees) to melt into imaginative distance. **The Silver Pavilion or Ginkaku-ji, Kyoto (130, 131)** (late fifteenth century), is a composition of water, rock and delicate plant form and foliage attributed to the painter Soami.

128

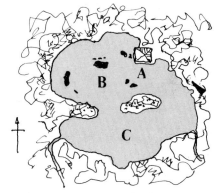

129 THE GOLDEN PAVILION, KYOTO
A The Golden Pavilion B Foreground lake with islands C Distant lake

130

131

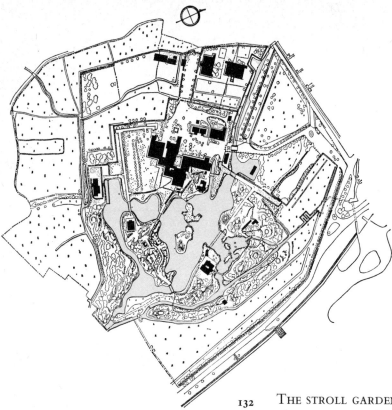

132

THE STROLL GARDEN has been so called to suggest a landscape in which the observer or participant is in movement, in contrast to the static garden of contemplation. The climax of this, and of ordered confusion, was the **Katsura Imperial Palace, Kyoto** (*c.* 1620). The **plan (132)** and the **air view (135)** show how the comparatively small area of eleven acres has been given a sense of boundlessness by being turned in upon itself to become a complex microcosm of nature. A path of 1,760 symbolic stones circuits the garden from and to the palace. Basically, the garden is traditional and at least two ancient symbols (both of longevity) survive in the land forms: the tortoise-shaped island and the flying crane-shaped lake in which it is set. To these have been added the newly introduced ceremonial tea pavilions and other innovations. The **path of stones (133)**, each with its own formidable personality, leads through various incidents to cross a **stone bridge (134)**, passes the **tea pavilion (136)** and continues through a **moss garden (137)** until finally it reaches home. The experience of this circuit, as was intended, is mystical.

133

134

135

136   137

THE ARTIST designed all gardens according to fixed principles, but within these there was scope for individual originality. The **Sento Gosho gardens, Kyoto** (1634), were made soon after Katsura and, although apparently similar, are different in feeling. They seem less tender and more sophisticated, as suggested in the **view over the bridge (138)** towards the tea pavilion. The designer was Kobori Enshu, and his materials, such as the Muromachi flat-topped stones, were traditional. An innovation was the **long beach (139)**, where every pebble was individually chosen.

THE PHILOSOPHER reached into more profound depths, creating in the theological Zen Buddhist gardens the allegory of man's passage through the world to eternity. The inspiration appears to have come from paintings of the Muromachi period (1338–1573), such as that by the artist **Sesshu (140)**, himself a Zen monk and, therefore, primarily a theologian. The picture represents man's spiritual life, his struggle upwards as a pilgrim and his pause for rest and contemplation. So far he is still part of nature. This symbolic scene was translated into rock landscape that formed the first part of the allegory, as at **Daisen-in (141)** (c. 1513), within the precincts of the Daitoku-ji monastery at Kyoto. The rocks were chosen and placed with extraordinary care for this symbolism. From here, the hazardous passage moves into the second part, the world of the infinite as expressed in earthly form. This is the pure Zen Buddhist garden of contemplation.

140

141

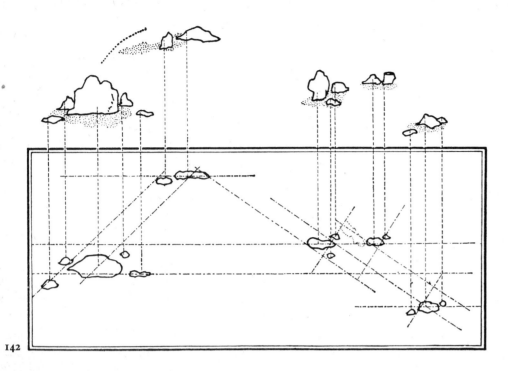

142

OF THE ZEN GARDENS OF CONTEMPLATION that of **Ryoan-ji** (**143**, **144**), within the precincts of Daiju-in monastery, Kyoto, made *c.* 1488–99, is the most profound. The philosophy is described in paragraph 45 on p. 85, but the true interpretation is left to each beholder. The scene is contained within a rigid frame, one side of which is the veranda for contemplation. The floor is luminous quartz from the river-bed (not sand as generally recognized) and no one is permitted to walk on it except the raker. There are fifteen rocks in five groups of five, two, three, two and three each. The groups are composed within themselves. The **diagram** (**142**) shows, at the top, the stones seen in elevation and, below, their projection on plan. What seems a haphazard arrangement is in fact governed by mathematical relationships, conveying to the subconscious an actual sense of harmony and repose that, in the contemplation of nature itself, such as the Seto Inland Sea (**119**), exists in the imagination only.

143

144

9 Pre-Columbian America

MEXICO AND CENTRAL AMERICA
Environment and Social History

49. The two connected areas lie between latitudes 23° and 13° north. The central Mexican landscape consists in general of a plateau crossed by mountain ranges, the southern boundary being an active volcanic belt. The valley of Mexico was a natural metropolitan centre (altitude 6,500 feet, mean temperature 63 degrees F with no extremes), interspersed with lakes and shaped roughly as a circle one hundred miles in diameter; temperate forests, mainly coniferous, clad the mountain slopes. In contrast, the Maya country, east and south of Mexico, rose gradually from low limestone and savanna grass in the east, across tropical forests (mahogany, ceiba, palms, saprodilla; rich in colourful bird life) to the volcanic Guatemalan mountains; despite high rainfall the eastern area was arid through bad natural drainage. Before 10,000 BC a mongoloid people crossed the Bering Strait from Asia, colonizing the Pacific seaboard, and between 6000 and 2000 BC the population of Mexico became dense and agricultural techniques were perfected. The earliest high civilization was the Mayan (*c.* AD 100–900), based on a religious hierarchy dominating an agrarian population, which ultimately revolted. The centres of Monte Alban and Teotihuacan also flourished at the same time. In the 10th century the Toltecs established a warrior society in the valley of Mexico, followed about AD 1300 by the Aztecs, whose balanced and confederated society of warriors, priests and laymen was destroyed by the Spaniards in 1519.

Philosophy and Expression

50. Civilization was based on the worship of the sun for its power to create fertility. The Mayas were preoccupied with time rather than with present activity, in which they were unpractical and uninventive. They evolved a calendar that enabled them to look backwards over a million years and to calculate such future movements of the heavens as eclipses. They believed that celestial influence could frustrate their endeavours to bring order out of chaos on earth, and the choice of the proper day for the commencement of a new project was of primary importance. The conception of the gods was that jointly with humans they were responsible for fertility and that without human blood to keep them refreshed, they would perish. Under the Mayas the gift of human blood to the gods appears to have been voluntary, but under the Aztecs it was achieved by the sacrifice of prisoners and slaves. To maintain and express this partnership with the gods, the Mayas built huge ceremonial centres, uninhabited except for the priesthood and ruling officials, and designed to impress externally: an ordered and geometricized microcosm of the surrounding mountains and valleys.

Landscape Architecture

51. The earliest settlements in the Mayan zone were sited on rivers or lakes in forest areas, moving in the fifth century AD into the forested zone away from the rivers. The conception of an ordered earthly cosmos was given physical form only with stone tools and without knowledge of the true arch; but labour spared from agriculture was unlimited and the earthworks were stupendous. Mayan buildings had heavy corbelling to carry the stone roof, and this required additional thickness of walls, which could thus be deeply sculptured. The pyramids were stepped, faced with cut stone, and furnished with one or more ceremonial stairways leading to temple or sacrificial altar at the summit. The mounds or pyramids were part of a comprehensive space design, and the voids between were modelled and contained altars and stelae to record the passage of time. Under later Toltec influence architecture became more refined, but the original conception of space design became less apparent.

PERU
Environment and Social History

52. Peru was the only seat of an ancient high civilization to lie wholly south of the Equator (latitude 0°–20° south). The Pacific seaboard is paralleled by the Andes, a continuation of the mountain spine that spans the continent from north to south. Beginning about 4000 BC the Peruvian civilizations matured in the narrow fertile river valleys between mountains and sea, watered by streams from the Andes and separated one from another by desert. This lowland landscape contrasted with that of the mountains, in which the Incas founded their capital Cuzco in the eleventh century, occupying a strip of highland averaging an altitude of 10,000 feet. In 1438 this hardy people had conquered their western neighbours each in turn and established an empire that stretched along the seaboard for about two thousand miles. Without horse, wheel or knowledge of writing, the Incas controlled their elongated empire through a system of roads not dissimilar in principle to that of the Romans. Society was highly organized and communal under an absolute monarchy, collapsing when the divine ruler was captured and eliminated by the Spaniards in 1532. The conquest finally extinguished the indigenous civilizations of the Americas, which thereafter received no recognition, until the present day, for any contribution they might have to make in the evolution of landscape design.

Philosophy and Expression

53. In direct contrast to the theocratic civilizations, the Incas were perpetually concerned with survival and therefore practical. Food had to be extracted from mountainsides as well as narrow valleys, and even at the height of empire their eastern flanks were vulnerable to invasion from the jungles. They worshipped the sun, and submitted totally to the king as representative of the sun on earth. They venerated the mountains in which they were enveloped, in parts if not in all of which they saw supernatural forces. The earlier and superior lowland civilizations which they conquered accepted Inca administration but not its religion, for the environment was dissimilar: the region was well watered but rainless, and would have been dried up by the sun had it not been for the mist from the sea which alone made agriculture possible. Inca constructive energy was directed towards food terraces and fortifications rather than the building of monuments, and the grandeur of this engineering work lies more in harmony with its stupendous environment than in aesthetic and architectural skill. The Incas were not themselves creative in the arts and crafts, which they inherited from the lowlands.

Landscape Architecture

54. The pre-Inca cities of the lowlands were built of clay. The sites were relatively level and town-planning designs were composed of rectangular geometrical groups placed closely together, each regulated to topography and therefore not necessarily parallel one to another; change of angle seems to have been sought rather than avoided in all early American landscape design. There were no monumental thoroughfares that would bind the whole into a manifestly co-ordinated design. In the lowlands the influence of topography was gentle and the result subtle, but in the mountains and under the rough Incas it was overwhelming: at Machu Picchu it is almost mystically impressive. The forts and food terraces that are scattered along the valley slopes as seen today throughout the highlands are more romantic than aesthetic, but all have the engineering quality of relation to site. Stone, quarried directly from the mountains and venerated (which clay was not), was re-created in building form by skilful techniques in cutting, shaping and fitting together. It is quality and use of stone that almost alone lifts Inca building into primitive sculpture, if not into architecture.

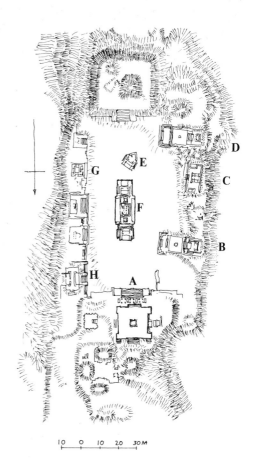

THE SUCCESSIVE CULTURES OF MEXICO produced sacred cities, ceremonial centres, unlike anything in the West. The oldest and most grandiose was **Monte Alban,** capital of the Zapotecs from about 600 BC to AD 900. The **plan (145)** shows the complex about AD 700. Spread over a hilltop at the junction of three valleys, its central area is a crude rectangle of monuments developed over the centuries. North of the main court was a smaller ceremonial area separated by a mound barrier. The mound as a decisive element of ancient American landscape architecture was now established. The **view (146)** looks south, with 'System IV' in the immediate right foreground. **Teotihuacan (147)** (c. AD 100–750) lies twenty-eight miles north-west of Mexico City. The plan is geometrical and classical inasmuch as the monuments are placed along an axial central way, 130 feet wide and about one and a half miles long. The view is towards the Sun Pyramid. According to one interpretation, the complex was a ceremonial centre for the rituals of the agrarian calendar, part of its function being to observe the relationship of earth to sun. The Sun Pyramid itself is so sited that the sun, on the day of its zenith passage, sets on the axis of the pyramid, by which the siting of all other buildings was governed.

Some thousand years later, c. 1350, the Aztecs founded their capital on the present site of Mexico City. The **plan of Tenochtitlan (148)** was published in Nuremberg in 1524 and, despite inaccuracies, conveys the character of the city built on an island in Lake Texoco, a maze of waterways linked to the mainland by stone causeways and an aqueduct bringing pure water from Chapultepec. The monuments remained basically traditional, but the sacred precinct was now a walled square set in a thriving outer city. The scene of a high civilization is described in detail in H. M. Prescott's *The Conquest of Mexico.*

10 0 10 20 30M

145 MONTE ALBÁN
A North Mound Barrier   B System IV
C Danzantes Mound   D Group M   E Mound J
F Mound H   G Mound S   H Ball court

146

147

148

Prescott writes: 'The great street facing the southern causeway, unlike most others in the place, was wide, and extended some miles in nearly a straight line . . . through the centre of the city. A spectator standing at one end of it, as his eye ranged along the deep vista of temples, terraces and gardens, might clearly discern the other, with the blue mountains in the distance, which, in the transparent atmosphere of the table-land, seemed almost in contact with the buildings.' The avenue was lined with the houses of the nobles, mostly one-storeyed and often with gardens on the roofs or on terraces between the buildings. The palace of Montezuma II was surrounded by 'extensive gardens filled with fragrant shrubs and flowers, and especially with medicinal plants. . . . Amidst this labyrinth of sweet-scented groves and shrubberies, fountains of pure water might be seen throwing up their sparkling jets.' The royal garden at Iztapalapan contained a botanical garden with plants of the Mexican flora scientifically arranged. Outside the city, the lake was dotted with floating islands, called *chinampas*, 'fairy islands of flowers, overshadowed occasionally by trees of considerable size, rising and falling with the gentle undulation of the billows'.

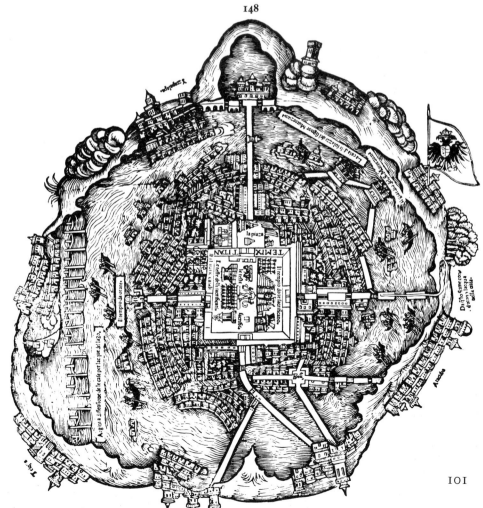

101

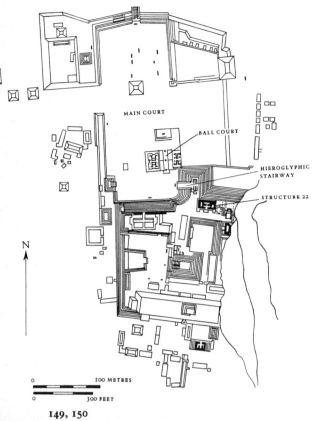

MAIN COURT

BALL COURT

HIEROGLYPHIC
STAIRWAY

STRUCTURE 22

N

0   100 METRES

0   300 FEET

149, 150

OF MAYAN RIVER CITIES in Central America, **Copan** (**149**) (*c.* AD 600) is probably the most assured in its composition, ground modelling and relationship between void and solid. For its execution over two million cubic yards of soil were imported in baskets. The **view** (**150**) shows the concept of design, and in particular, the play on angles. To the right is the steep hieroglyphic stairway. In the centre is the court for the ball game, probably played as a symbol of the diurnal passages of the sun. The standing *stelae* punctuate space and record the priestly computations of historical time and astronomical events; the human figures represent warriors, rulers, priests or god impersonators. **Palenque** (**152**), approximately contemporary, is an exhilarating and volcanic composition of mounds, dominated by the palace. **The palace** (**151**, foreground) is unusual in having two internal courts and a sewage system of running water from an underground stream connected by conduit to the River Otolum. Behind the palace are three of the temples, of the Cross, the Foliated Cross and the Sun.

151, 152

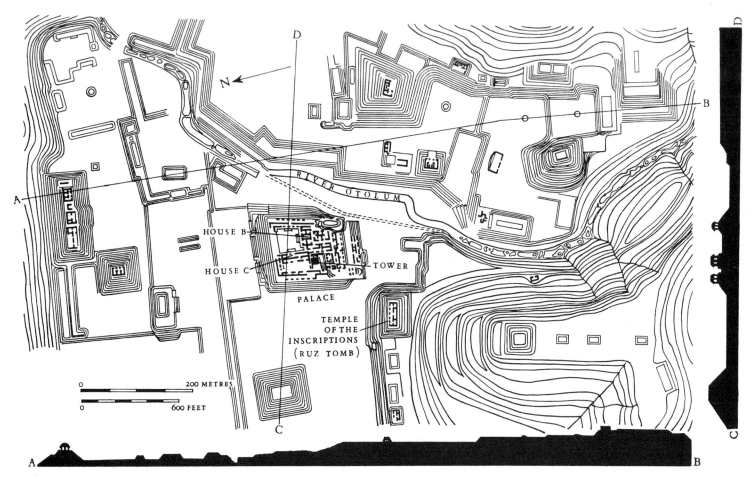

N

RIVER OTOLUM

HOUSE B

HOUSE C

TOWER

PALACE

TEMPLE
OF THE
INSCRIPTIONS
(RUZ TOMB)

0   200 METRES

0   600 FEET

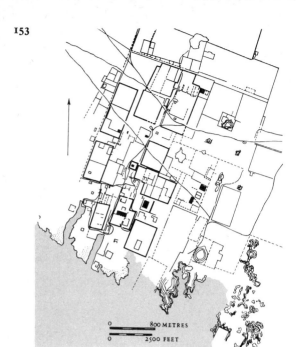

THE CIVILIZATIONS OF PERU lay along the narrow coastal belt, spreading, after the rise of the Incas, to the uplands of the Andes. On the coast the land was mainly level and the town plan was usually gridiron or rectangular. At **Chanchan (153)** (thirteenth to fifteenth centuries), near Trujillo in northern Peru, the city was composed of the individual rectangular walled enclosures of the palaces, not necessarily parallel one to another but seemingly a coherent whole. The Inca cities of the Andes set out to be gridiron or rectangular, but geometry was distorted by the overwhelming topography. The extreme example is **Machu Picchu (154)** (*c.* 1500), a citadel among the mountains with an almost sheer drop of some two thousand feet to the River Urubamba. The **plan (155)** shows the organic disposition of the parts. To the south are some of the descending agricultural terraces; to the north-west are the religious precincts and in the centre places of assembly; to the south and east, the town proper, the richer houses grouped round courtyards, the humbler in parallel terraces. Subsistence was from the terraces, fed by water channels, and consisted mainly of maize, cocoa and peppers. The **stonework (156)** is unique to the Incas. Each stone was treated individually with either a convex or concave curve to fit its adjoining stone, presumably to resist earthquakes.

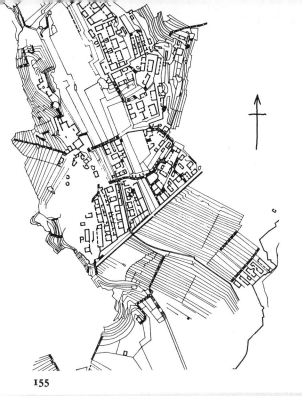

155

156

70

60

70

60

Oslo
Stockholm

•Novgorod

•Rostov

Moscow

Durham
Rievaulx
York

Clonmacnois

Warsaw

Copenhagen

50

Amsterdam

London
Stonehenge

Bruges

Prague Cracow

•Kiev

50

Mt St Michel

Chantilly
Paris

Heidelberg

Vaux-le-Vicomte

Versailles

St Gallen

Carnac

Vézelay

Venice

Richelieu

Vicenza

Nîmes•

Genoa

Florence

Danube

BLACK SEA

CASPIAN SEA

ARAL SEA

Volga

Rhine

Loire

Rhône

Tivoli

Rome

Salamanca

Monte Cassino

Constantinople

Samarkand

Madrid

Pompeii

Meteora

40

Fronteira
Seville

Palermo

Delphi

Pergamon

40

Olympia

Athens Miletus

Baghdad

Delos

Palmyra

Tigris

M E D I T E R R A N E A N   S E A

Knossos

Baalbek

Euphrates

Alexandria

Jerash

30

Gizeh

30

Thebes

Abu Simbel

RED SEA

20

20

Nile

10

10

0

0

10

10

THE WESTERN CIVILIZATIONS:
from Egypt to the Renaissance

The Western civilizations comprise the nations of Europe with Russia; ancient Egypt stands somewhat apart. The cradle was the congenial and diverse landscape of the Mediterranean, from which the civilizations spread slowly to the far north. The parents were Greece and Rome. Until AD 1700 there was almost continuous conflict with the Central civilizations for territorial possession of the Mediterranean and since the Western civilizations were composed of highly independent states, there was constant conflict also among themselves. With the aid of geography, these circumstances of conflict created energy, sharpened the wits, enriched the culture, and ultimately enabled the European family of nations to outstrip by far any rival civilization.

The area of the Western civilizations, showing latitude, mountain barriers and selected place names.

10 Egypt

Environment

55. The Nile rises in the equatorial lakes of Central Africa, which guarantee evenness of volume in its upper reaches, and is joined at Khartoum by the violently seasonal waters of East Africa. Ancient Egypt lay along the rest of its course as a linear civilization for nearly a thousand miles, mainly between latitudes 20° and 30° north. Between cataracts the river is placid and navigable. With a summer rise of over twenty feet, control by irrigation and a guaranteed annual replenishment of soil made the adjoining lowlands highly productive; at its peak the water carries with it some eight cubic yards of silt per second. In Upper Egypt the narrow valley is bounded by red, pink and white granite cliffs, often sand-blasted into sculptural forms; in Middle Egypt by limestone; in Lower Egypt the landscape is flat. On each side lies desert. The climate is cloudless with a prevailing north wind assuring a reasonable temperature. The original natural vegetation included the palm, sycomore, fig, vine, reed and lotus; because of inundations there were no forests. The concept of environment was one of absolute stability, based on an annual repetitive cycle of natural events.

Social History

56. In prehistory both change of climate and animal devastation of park-and-grassland in North Africa created the desert and forced the nomad to the fertile Nile Valley, where he became agriculturalist and settler. As in Mesopotamia, the family and tribe proved too small a unit to undertake the irrigation works which were recognized to be necessary, and the river authorities amalgamated in the common interest. A central government emerged, maintaining its authority by the navigability of the river. In due time a single individual, the Pharaoh, became virtually sole owner of all Egypt, ruling supreme from 3200 BC onwards. The society that supported Pharaoh was aristocratic and military, with a powerful priesthood. Slave labour, imported or indigenous, was a resource of manpower that could be put to work on unproductive building in the off-season of agriculture. The deserts were at first a natural protection against foreign invasions: during the period of the Old Kingdom (2686–2181 BC) there were none. After the Middle Kingdom (2133–1786 BC) the land was invaded and ruled by the Hyksos (1674–1567 BC), a nomad race from Syria. After expulsion of the foreigner, the New Kingdom (1567–1085 BC) opened as an age of accomplishment and of conquest as far as the Euphrates. An Assyrian invasion took place in 671 BC and from 525 BC Egypt was mostly under the Persians until the conquest by Alexander in 332 BC.

Philosophy 57. Egyptian religion was polytheistic and gods were innumerable. The intellect of man and the physique of the beast were combined in the god-like enigma of the Sphinx. The greatest of the gods was the sun god, Ra, who created the Nile and whose passage across the sky from east to west was symbolic of life, death and resurrection. The Pharaoh was accepted as the son of Ra on earth and therefore himself a god. The philosophy that life on earth was an introduction to a similar but eternal life came about through an environment that is unique for its constancy and dependability. The Egyptian was contentedly incurious as to the causes of natural events and his considerable mathematical accomplishments were therefore empirical rather than deductive. Because of the predictability of natural events, economic security and comparative freedom from interruptions such as invasions, he was able to give attention to a future that embraced not only the visible world but also a hereafter envisaged as an eternal extension of the present. He became totally preoccupied with this conception. The spiritual link between the eternal life and the present was the *ka*, or soul, which was conceived to be within Pharaoh and to a lesser extent in his subjects. The physical links were the great monuments that were created to stand midway in scale, thought and timelessness between this world and the next.

Expression 58. The aesthetic was visual rather than literary and, except in the Delta, daylight was more significant than the sky at night. The sense of crisp shadowed form was everywhere. The monuments were inspired by mountains, especially by the granite cliffs whose face was in constant and restless change in the moving sunlight. Whether temple, monument or tomb, the scale was superhuman to express an idea greater than life: in the incised hieroglyphics that everywhere perpetuated the temporal glories of the Pharaohs the scale was interchanged between great (the god) and small (the mortal). Within the frame of metaphysical monuments there is evidence of a high civilized life in house and garden. All representative art, even domestic, was disciplined to basic geometry, seeming to petrify the earthly life force.

Architecture 59. The homes of the upper classes were low, flat-roofed and made of temporary materials such as clay and timber, and therefore ephemeral. The monuments were granite or limestone, symbolic and virtually indestructible. The pyramid was the eternal mountain; the twin pylons guarding the entrance to the temples were the right and left cliffs of the valley; the temple columns were bundles of papyrus or forests of palm or lotus plants; the obelisk, its apex tipped with gold, was (according to Pliny the Elder) a petrified ray of the sun. All were formed from a profound knowledge of solid geometry; the golden mean, later absorbed by the Greeks, seems to have underlain all proportions. Because of the clear light there were few windows and solid predominated over void to give wide expanses of wall surface. These were enriched either by the texture of natural hewn rock or by a profusion of finely carved incised patterns, images and pictures.

Landscape 60. The gardens of the rich, of which nothing remains, were highly cultivated geometrical enclosures. They formed only a small part of the brilliantly coloured linear pattern of irrigated agriculture that lay within the narrow valley and outlined the Nile. There was no natural green landscape. Punctuating this linear landscape were the great rock monuments, the temple on the east bank and the tomb always on the west. The pyramids at Saqqara, Dahshur and Gizeh are the earliest, the simplest and still the grandest symbols on earth of human aspiration as seen through abstract geometry. Yet except as a source of awe and speculation, this tremendous river scene, reaching from Gizeh to Abu Simbel, has as yet had little influence upon the world's landscape design, for it reflects a philosophy of life and death which subsequent ages have found unacceptable.

157, 158

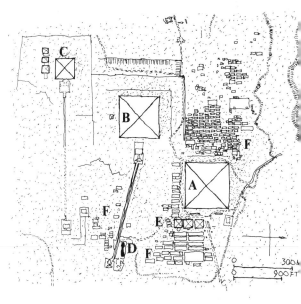

159 Gizeh

A Pyramid of Cheops B Pyramid of Chephren
C Pyramid of Mycerinus D Great Sphinx
E Pyramids of the three queens of Cheops
F Cemeteries

THE PRIMORDIAL GEOMETRY OF EGYPT reflects a view of the world in which every object and every being had its allotted place, which could never change. **The pyramids at Gizeh (157, 158)**, sepulchres of IVth-Dynasty pharaohs (2613–2494 BC), are perhaps the simplest and most fundamental form in all architecture. In the lower view the Sphinx is seen across the inundation between the pyramids of Cheops (right) and Chephren. **The general plan (159)** shows how the pyramids are related asymmetrically one to another, yet precisely orientated to the cardinal points, thus 'making clear beyond question the interplay between pyramid and cosmos' (S. Giedion). Around them are clustered the tombs of the nobility. Between the Delta and the Second Cataract, the **Nile (160)** formed a continuous metaphysical linear landscape. The annual flooding meant stability; the regularity was a sign of divine order and permanence. Parallel with this cycle of nature went the cycle of human life, death and resurrection; hence the monuments on its banks, the temples to the living always on the east and the mortuary temples on the west, following the sun. Far to the south, and in eternal contemplation of the river, were seated the four **colossal statues of Ramesses II** (1304–1237 BC) **(161)**, carved *in situ* before the temple of Abu Simbel – seen here before it was raised above the new water level. Timelessness is achieved through abstract geometry and impressiveness through superhuman scale.

160

161

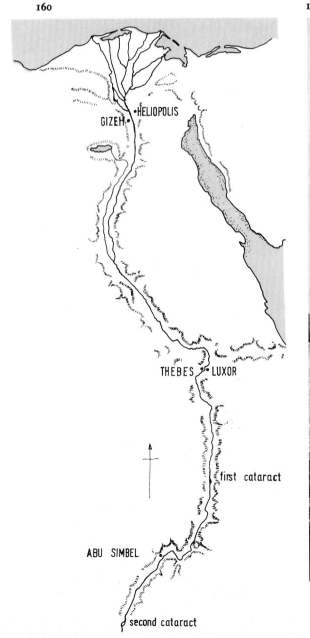

162

THE CREATION OF THE UNIVERSE as conceived by the Egyptians was that out of the first chaos, consisting of primordial water, there emerged a primordial hill. In Heliopolis in historic times and later at Thebes, this was symbolized by a 'sand-hill' with a stone of conical shape on top – probably the prototype of the obelisk. Obelisks and pylons flanked the entrance to temples, as at **Karnak (162)**, the one probably symbolic of procreation, the other of the mountains on each side of the Nile.

Within the tombs of the nobles are often garden scenes, which indicate the high standard of living of the upper classes. The owner thus perpetuated his garden in order to find in the next world the same pleasures he had enjoyed in this: a tomb inscription reads, 'May I wander round my pool each day for evermore; may my soul sit on the branches of the grave garden I have prepared for myself; may I refresh myself each day under my sycomore.'

The garden scene from a tomb at Thebes (163), XVIIIth Dynasty, depicts the elegant and ephemeral nature of domestic architecture and the decorative use of plants such as the vine trellis and the pomegranate. Wall-paintings and fragments of funeral wreaths indicate the enrichment of the native flora, by that date, through importations such as apple, almonds, jasmine and myrrh. Large gardens would have water tanks for angling and reclining in awning-covered boats, but the **plan of a garden (164)**, also XVIIIth-Dynasty Thebes, suggests the wealth of interest that could be contained in a very small rectangle. The garden is surrounded by a wall, probably tile-capped, and divided into unequal portions by low walls, about two feet high, of dry stone or baked mud, with painted wooden gates. The entrance from the tree-shaded canal-walk passes a grandiose porter's lodge; the house is reached by a path under the central vine trellis. On both sides of the house are pavilions overlooking flowers and pools planted with lotus and teeming with wild ducks. Inside the surrounding wall is a screen of date-palms, doum palms and smaller trees.

163

164

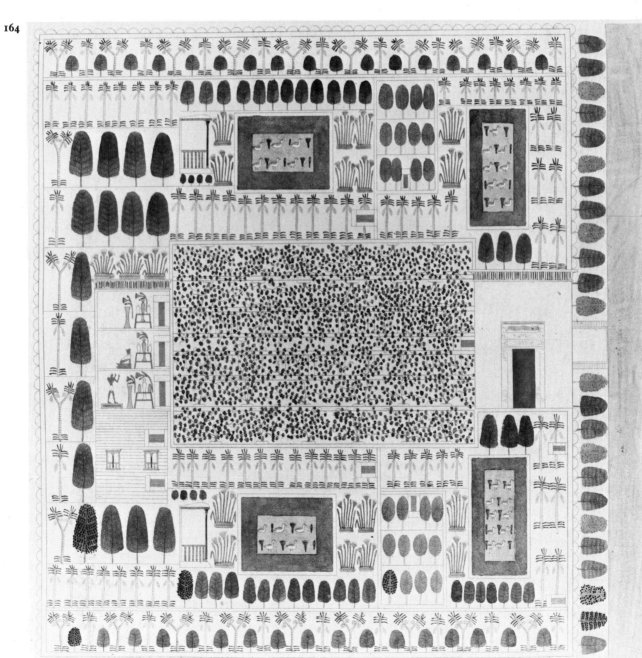

THE PATH OF THE SOUL from this world to the immortal realm of death is symbolized in the Egyptian sacred landscape, which is one of progression, of movement in a straight line from space to space and level to level. The vastest of these landscapes, that of Thebes, reached its zenith under Ramesses II in the XIXth Dynasty, comprising **Karnak and Luxor** on the East Bank of the Nile and the **Tombs of the Kings (166)** among the mountains on the West. On the plains stand the 'colossi of Memnon', and the whole majestic complex is linked in idea by the avenues of sphinxes.

There were two directions for sacred progressions: north–south between Karnak and Luxor by an avenue of sphinxes or on a barge along the river; and that which followed the course of the sun to carry the dead Pharaoh to his tomb and, regularly each year, the image of the god Amun to 'pour water for the Kings of Upper and Lower Egypt'. The **avenue of ram's-head sphinxes at Karnak (165)** points directly to the **mortuary temple of Queen Hatshepsut (167)**, XVIIIth Dynasty (1503–1482 BC), whose terraces were originally planted with myrrh trees and whose unusual design had been inspired by the adjoining XIth-Dynasty temple of King Mentuhotep.

165

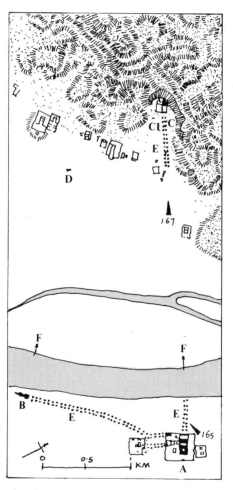

166 KARNAK AND LUXOR
A   Temple of Ammon, Karnak
B   Temple of Ammon, Luxor
C   Tomb of Queen Hatshepsut
C1 Tomb of Mentuhotep
D   Colossi of Memnon
E   Avenue of Sphinxes
F   Crossings of River Nile

167 ▷

II Greece

Environment *61.* Classical Greece includes the mainland, the Peloponnesus, the Aegean archipelago of islands and the western coast of Anatolia; geographically part of the east–west global upheaval of the earth's 'plates'. In comparison with the Himalayas or Alps the scale is small and comprehensible, even though the heights are often concealed in mist. On the mainland, ridges and peaks run individually to the sea, separating one small plain and its seaboard from another. The sea encouraged navigation through favourable winds and the natural havens of a deeply indented coastline, but was hazardous with sudden storms, fogs and hidden obstacles. The atmosphere was clear, soft and bracing, with a mean but very variable temperature in Attica of 63 degrees F. Unlike her rival Sparta in the Peloponnesus, who was self-sufficient, Athens in the sixth century B C was the flourishing centre of an area previously denuded of the humus of trees and now unable to supply its needs. In the light soil it was more profitable to cultivate the olive, fig and vine, and exchange these for cereals imported either from foreign nations or from the colonies that had been planted as far apart as the mouth of the Rhône and the eastern end of the Black Sea.

Social History *62.* Parallel with the Mesopotamian and Egyptian civilizations, and probably commercially linked with them, there existed from 2100 to 1600 B C a society in the island of Crete which was unusually free-thinking and liberal, a race of sea-bred individuals and adventurers. From Crete the early Mediterranean civilization passed to Mycenae in the Peloponnesus. After successive invasions from the north, the city states of Greece proper emerged, to reach maturity by the sixth century B C: self-contained in their plains; loosely federated and at guaranteed peace only during the Olympic Games; in turn tyrannical, oligarchic and democratic, but all respectful of the Delphic oracle, and dependent for existence on maritime commerce. The hereditary enemies of all Greece were the Persians, against whom the conquered Greek cities of the Ionian coast revolted in 499 B C and by whom Greece itself was unsuccessfully invaded in 490 and again in 480 B C. Thereafter Athens became head of a Delian league to ensure combined maritime defence, reaching its climax of power and prosperity under Pericles (490–429 B C). In 404 B C Athens was defeated in war by Sparta, and soon after, control of Greece passed to Philip of Macedon and his son Alexander the Great (356–323 B C). In the second and first centuries power passed to the Roman Empire.

Philosophy *63.* Sparta's economic self-containment within her mountains created an extreme way of thought that was defensive, illiberal and eventually sterile. Athens was the reverse. Just as she challenged the accepted axiom of material self-sufficiency, risking all on a navy, so she challenged the accepted axioms of life itself. There emerged the philosopher of pure reason, concerned with truth based not on myth, but on the scientific collection of facts from which he could intellectually deduce general rules. Although the idea of a pantheon of the gods inherited from Mesopotamia continued to appeal to popular imagination, it became less significant as the inquiring mind expanded. Plato (d. 347 B C), mystic and mathematician, taught that universal essences or truths had an existence apart from the visible world of matter, man and time, and that here lay God. Man was always striving towards this perfection, the way to which lay through the constant and eternal principles of mathematics; Plato was profoundly influenced by the basic geometry of the Egyptians. Aristotle (384–322 B C), logician and biologist, put more stress on understanding the world, and the human mind, as it actually existed. Plato was the artificer, Aristotle the ecologist, in a world in which individual and thinking man had arrived.

Expression 64. The search for perfection through geometry began with Pythagoras of Samos (sixth century B C), who first discovered a relation between spatial and musical proportions. Plato considered that cosmic order and harmony were comprehended in certain numbers which contained, in Rudolf Wittkower's words, 'not only all the musical consonances, but also the inaudible music of the heavens and the structure of the human soul'. The temple was the pure manifestation of the search for proportion, secure and serene in its sense of cosmic order. It was a microcosm of the order of heaven brought to earth, and in its aloofness was primarily an object to be seen and not used, except by the priests. No Greek building attempted to dominate the landscape, but rather to be associated with it as though the elements, wild though they might be, yet had some unrecorded harmony. The search for landscape perfection as something beyond perception and outside this world deteriorated under Philip of Macedon, who ushered in an age of planning rationalism that was to lead to the materialistic works of the Roman Empire.

Architecture 65. The Greek temple of the fifth century grew from an earlier timber form and is based on the simplicity of post upholding lintel, the size of its parts determined by the capacity of the material. The shape was a rectangle, for this could easily be spanned to support a sloping weather-proof roof. There was no adventure in structure. From this primeval shape there grew, almost imperceptibly over the centuries, an architecture that was to establish standards in Western civilization. In the Parthenon the white Pentelic marble appeared jointless, like monolithic sculpture. Every part was modelled for a purpose, either to counteract optical distortion or to allow the eyes to make stereoscopic appraisal, or to pick up the light of sun. Light reflected upwards from pavings illuminated the sculpture in the shadows. Yet essential though such techniques were to convey an idea, they remained techniques only. The Greeks took a common box and, by abstract geometric proportions alone, lifted it almost mystically into the sublime, reaching towards that perfection through mathematics that was Plato's ideal.

Landscape 66. There were no fortifications in Crete: palaces were open to the landscape. Life was domestic and there were pleasure gardens. In Mycenae and later throughout Greece, gardens were either patios, or planted for fruit, or confined to public or semi-public places such as sacred groves, sacred springs and teaching academies; Plato particularly recognized that an ordered landscape was sympathetic to learning. But such incidents were subsidiary to a broader, unplanned and intuitive conception which reached its climax in the fifth century B C. The landscape of Greece was one of mountains, hills and islands that stood out in recession with clarity of form, each small plain having its own *genius loci*. The temple would usually rest on either spur or outcrop of the containing hills or mountains, from which it had been quarried and with which it still seemed to be in harmony. There was no axial approach to anchor it to the man-made surroundings over which it presided. The essence of intuitive Greek site-planning was that all architecture, whether temple, theatre, agora or dwelling, was subsidiary and composed to natural landscape. The angle view of architecture was fundamental. The change in these natural values began with the intellectual town-planning of Miletus and its subsequent development under Hellenism.

170

GREEK CLARITY OF THOUGHT, which gave birth to science, mathematics and philosophy as we understand them, was the product of a slow evolution through Minoan and Mycenaean cultures. This evolution is reflected in landscape. Crete was the first Aegean civilization, developing its own art and system of writing soon after 2000 BC. Its palaces combine Egyptian and Asian influences – the result of trade links – with a preference for domesticity rather than monumentality. Because of natural sea protection, there were no fortifications, and as at the capital, Knossos, the buildings at **Phaestos (168)** are grouped round a central court from which broad stairways lead into a lower court or theatre (right of picture). After the collapse of Crete in about 1400 BC, power in the Aegean passed to **'golden' Mycenae (169)** on the mainland, a city that more than any other inspired the future with myths and legends of an heroic age. The view is across Grave Circle A looking towards the Vale of Argos, which sweeps to the seashore from which Agamemnon, Homer's hero-king, set sail for Troy.

Between the fall of Mycenae and the emergence of Greece proper about 700 BC, Greek mysticism was evolving parallel with rationalism. This sense endowed a landscape with metaphysical qualities that lay solely in the imagination. The barren square mile of rock of **Delos** was thus transformed into the mystic floating island that Zeus moored in the Aegean to become the birthplace of Artemis and Apollo; **archaic lions (170)** overlook the filled-in sacred lake towards Mount Cyntha. The earth beneath the crust was endowed with similar qualities, as at **Cumae (171, 172)**, earliest of the Greek colonies in Italy. The photographs show the entrance and the seat of the Sybil, whence the oracle apparently issued from the depths far below.

171, 172

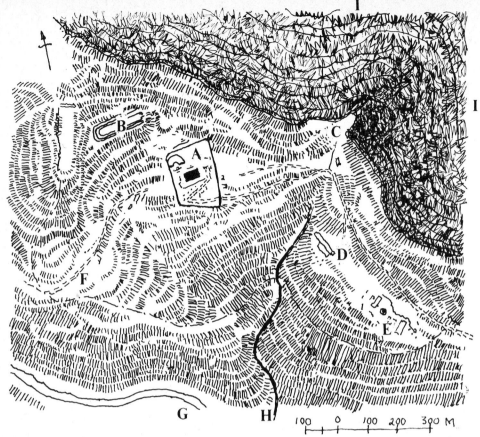

173 DELPHI
A Sacred precinct
B Stadium
C Castalian fountain
D Gymnasium
E Marmaria (antechamber to sacred precinct)
F Sacred Way
G River Pleistus
H Castalian stream
I Mount Parnassus

100   0   100 200 300 M

174

175

176

177

THE SANCTUARY OF DELPHI, legendary centre of the world and home of the Oracle, symbolized the religious unity of all Greece. Twelve miles from the Gulf of Corinth, it appears to cling to the lower slopes of Mount Parnassus. Immediately dominating it are the Phaedridae (the 'shining rocks') from between which emerge the sacred waters of the Castalian spring. As a place of pilgrimage it was inaccessible and deep among the **echoing mountains (176)** where the gods abode. The **plan (173)** shows the drama of the **first view (174)** to the pilgrim from the so-called ante-chamber. The **theatre (175)** (fourth century BC) lies behind the Temple of Apollo (530 BC), and the **stadium (177)** is isolated higher still on suitable terrain. The shape of the enclosure is crude, the treasuries are chaotic and architecturally often brash, and the theatre is awkwardly placed. Although the scene is given apparent cohesion and high purpose by the Temple of Apollo, the overall unifying influence is that of the stupendous *genius loci*, expressing as it does the structure of the world.

178

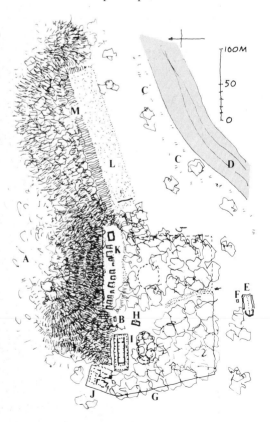

179 Olympia, c. 476 BC

A Mount Kronos B Spring C Marshlands
D Conjectural course of Alphaeos E Council
house F Altar of Oaths G Wall of sacred
grove H Altar of Zeus I Temple of Hera
J Prytaneion (political centre) K Treasuries
L Stadium M Slope for spectators

THE GENIUS LOCI, the recognition and expression of the spirit of particular places, has been the most enduring legacy of Greece in landscape design. Architecture stood for universal order. The existing landscape was in general without apparent order and the Greeks not only harmonized two seeming opposites, but gave to the whole a significance which civilization is only now beginning to accept as not pertaining to Greece alone.

The site of the Games at **Olympia** (**179**) is placid and so was its purpose. The first games were held in 776 BC and during their progress there was common agreement among the city states that there should be no war and that the festival should be one of body, mind and spirit. The **panorama** (**178**) looks across the shady Altis or sacred grove, beyond which, lying modestly against the hills, is the stadium. On the left Mount Kronos, against which the treasuries were placed; on the right, the River Alphaeos; in the distance, the mountains of Arcadia. The victors were crowned with leaves of olives, which grew wild. Other trees were evergreen oaks, white poplars and planes; today, Aleppo pines cover many of the hillsides.

The placing of the Temple of Poseidon (440 BC) on **Cape Sounion** (**180**) emphasizes Greek dependence on the seas, proclaiming a majestic order and security amidst an environment both dangerous and unpredictable. In contrast, the theatre at **Epidauros** (**181**) (350 BC), is protectively modelled out of a north-west slope. The sun is upon the players and the theatre is an almost perfect instrument of sight, sound, player-audience association and landscape affiliation – the climax in form of the Greek philosophy of the unity of all things.

180

181

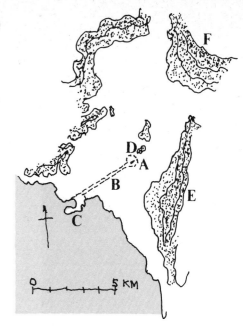

THE ACROPOLIS OF ATHENS, originally a strategically sited royal fortress, became a sanctuary dedicated to the national goddess, Pallas Athena, and a legendary king of Athens, Erechtheus. This sanctuary was destroyed by the Persians in 480 BC and rebuilt in the short period of twenty-three years. Whether seen from afar, as in the sea approaches to the Piraeus, or at close quarters from the city itself, the complex is uniquely composed within itself and in its relation to the mountains enclosing the Attic plain. The composition was not accidental. The name of Pheidias is associated with the Parthenon sculpture, but the presiding genius was clearly Pericles. Unlike other Greek compositions, which were purely intuitive and not always successful, the creation of the Acropolis was both intuitive and intellectual. It is possible to re-create the evolution of this masterpiece of landscape step by step. The **map of the Attic plain** (182) shows how the city takes its place within the silhouette of the mountains and the open sea, and the **restored plan of Athens** (183) the critical western arc of vision, lit by the afternoon and evening sun. The **reconstruction plan and sections** (185, 186) show the Acropolis as completed in 429 BC.

PHASE I The city is re-fortified after 480 BC, the south wall of the Acropolis below the Parthenon and the Nike bastion (begun 468 BC) being rebuilt and the summit extended with infilling. Long walls connect city to Piraeus (completed 458 BC). Aesthetic ideas are germinating for the Acropolis rock and its relation to the city, the plain and the sea approaches. Designs for the Parthenon are perfected.

PHASE II *454 BC* The Doric Temple of the Parthenon is sited on the highest point and work begun. The colossal bronze statue of Athena (29 feet 6 inches) is placed on the western brow of the contours in a position of maximum visibility from the western arc of vision.
438 BC Parthenon completed.
437–432 BC The Doric Propylaea, parallel to the Parthenon but not obstructing the view of it from the sea, is built on the original site, the only possible place of entry.
432 BC The Ionic Temple of Nike Apteros, small in scale and following the idea of perimeter building, complements the Propylaea.
431 BC The Ionic Erechtheion is commenced on the perimeter to balance but not rival the Parthenon and to triangulate the space round the statue; left incomplete owing to the Peloponnesian War (429–404 BC). End of creative period.

The general **view from the south-west** (184), taken after midday, shows the dominance of the Parthenon above the new wall; to the left is the Propylaea, in front of which is the little Temple of Nike. The sectional drawings indicate only one aspect of the knowledge of optics which informs the whole design.

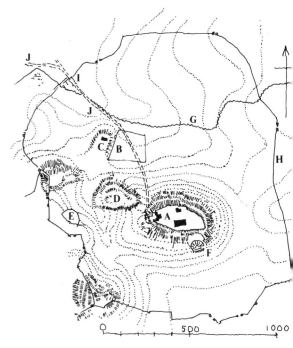

184

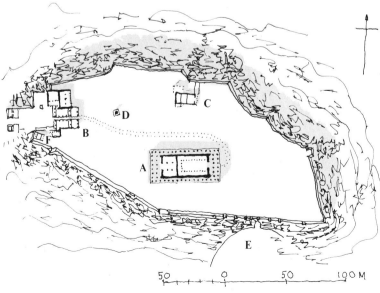

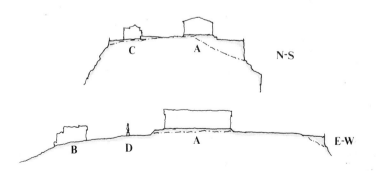

185, 186 Acropolis: plan and sections (N–S and E–W)
A Parthenon (the dotted line indicates the
original contours)
B Propylaea
C Erechtheion
D Site of statue of Athena
E Theatre of Dionysus
F Temple of Nike Apteros

187

EXPERIENCING THE ACROPOLIS: seen **from the Areopagus (187)**, meeting place of the Superior Council, the buildings form a unity with the natural rock. As the Panathenaic procession approached **the Propylaea (188)** it would wind past **the Temple of Nike (189)**, where rock and architecture are in direct association. Passing through the Propylaea the procession would see the **sacred precinct (190)** at a glance: to the right, the Parthenon; to the left, the caryatid portico of the Erechtheion; in the centre the statue of Athena (no longer existing). The whole precinct is a study in interlocking views **(191, the Erechtheion from the Parthenon)** and of the **play of light (192)** upon architectural form.

190

188   189

12 The Roman Empire

Environment 67. In AD 100 the Roman Empire extended from longitude 10° west (Spain) to 45° east (Tigris and Euphrates) and from latitude 25° (Philae in Egypt) to 55° (Hadrian's Wall in England). No other empire has comprehended in a single geographic unit such variety of landscape, climate and people. Italy itself was centrally placed in the Mediterranean and, unlike Greece, had few natural harbours but comparatively easy internal communications. The central area was divided by the Apennines, to the west of which lay the fertile coastal plains occupied by the Etruscans. Further to the south lay the Greek colonies. Indigenous trees were oak, chestnut, ilex, cypress and stone pine. The Etruscans appear to have introduced the olive and vine. Rome lay beside the Tiber on its seven hills or undulations, with a flat *campagna* that stretched on three sides between ten and fifteen miles to the hills and on the west about sixteen miles to the port of Ostia and the sea. The climate of the plains was mild in winter but hot in summer and this induced summer retreat to the hills. Building materials were plentiful and included marble, stone, clay for terracotta and brick and timber; concrete, which revolutionized construction, was invented by a mixture of *pozzolana* (sand) and lime.

Social History 68. The Romans first appeared in history as a small tribe under the Etruscans, themselves proud builders who may have come from Asia Minor. In 509 BC Rome emerged as an independent republic; by 270 BC she had conquered and absorbed all Italy south of the Po; in 146 BC she finally destroyed Carthage from whom she had learned much about agriculture; and under Trajan in AD 116 had reached her full magnitude of empire. The *Pax Romana* and the age of grandeur began with Augustus (made emperor in 27 BC) but two centuries later the power of Rome began to decline, breaking into two empires east and west in AD 365, the latter being finally extinguished in AD 475. Strength and economic stability were based in Italy on a policy of treating the conquered as allies and taxing them heavily. Gold and slaves, in tribute as well as commerce, poured into the capital. Decline was due to internal misrule, corruption and perhaps most of all to the elimination of the family farm unit. Small farms were converted into large estates owned by a single landlord and worked by slaves; land was redistributed compulsorily among the returning military; the army abroad declined in discipline and sense of purpose; and inevitably the Empire fell to the barbarians of the north and pressure from Asia.

Philosophy 69. The original Roman sense of duty and obedience arose from the discipline and beliefs of the plebeian family unit. The father was absolute master, although the women were held in deep respect. The collective gods were those of agricultural fertility, but each individual recognized within himself a protecting 'genius', and sacrificed to it at a domestic altar. Public religion on the other hand was largely maintained by the conservative ruling classes as a matter of state policy, the emperor (after 27 BC) receiving divine honours to confirm authority. In achieving great wealth and the maintenance of a stable order, the upper classes established law as the basis of civil and military administration. This powerful materialistic society produced little philosophy of its own, relying upon Greece for its education. Nevertheless, in the Augustan poets Virgil, Ovid and Horace there is an original creative appreciation of the beauty of landscape that was indicative of the sensitivity that existed below the surface of imperialism. During the Dark Ages, and associated with the turbulent rise of Christianity, the Platonist philosopher Plotinus (d. AD 270) taught the new religion, that beauty, natural or intellectual, was the channel through which to approach God.

Expression   70. Hellenistic national town-planning and landscape materialized under Alexander the Great (conquest of western Asia 338 BC), superseding the instinctive and irrational planning of the Greeks and laying the foundation of Roman ordered planning. Landscape design reached its zenith in the Augustan age and beyond, creating for generations centuries later the myth of a golden age of luxurious living and enjoyment of the fruits of the earth. The gardens of the rich were immense; all buildings, whether sacred, public or the homes of the wealthy, echoed in principle the universal form of the Greek temple. Although the relation to a natural landscape was in general one of total domination, a harmony of opposites between order and wild nature was demonstrated in small landscapes such as that of the Temple of Vesta at Tivoli (AD 205); in the splendid cities of the deserts; and in the great engineering feats, especially aqueducts, themselves monuments of architecture. The symbol of Rome was the road, a straight line drawn across the map. The principles of proportion and of unity within a building were derived from Greece, but the Romans went beyond the Greeks in complexity of architectural form and the organization of external urban space.

Architecture   71. The Romans were primarily engineers. Being unsatisfied with the limitations of column and lintel, they developed the arch and through the invention of concrete were able to increase the range and form of buildings. In principle, and in contrast to Greece, the architecture was that of the wall, pierced as necessary by the void. The basis of the design remained the rhythm of the parts, but columns tended to become decoration, for their work could now be better accomplished by piers supporting an arch. Arch and lintel were often placed in tiers, to create complex horizontal rhythms. Massive structures such as theatres and baths were in general superimposed upon the landscape, the ground if necessary being remodelled for their accommodation. Individual 'group' design of buildings, such as the Fora or Hadrian's Villa, was masterly, but in general the juxtaposition of these groups was haphazard and fortuitous.

Landscape   72. Gardens were a decisive extension of architecture. They first sprang from the farms round Rome, the tradition of the small garden being continued in the courtyard gardens of Pompeii and elsewhere. With the emergence of the wealthy and travelled landowners such as Lucullus, and with knowledge of the gardens of Hellenistic Alexandria and south-west Asia, the importance and magnitude of the country villa grew phenomenally. The younger Pliny (AD 23–79) has left detailed descriptions that convey the sense of architectural formality, the special value of shady promenades and of views of sea or countryside, cool porticoes with romantic wall-paintings that integrated house and garden, of sculpture, clipped hedges, box parterres, topiary, water and grottoes. Flowers were collected from all parts of the Empire, as was much of the statuary. The estate, however vast, remained balanced between garden and farmlands, being maintained by unlimited slave labour. Rome itself became a city of parks extending along the Tiber, contrasting so much with the adjacent slums that first Julius Caesar (d. 44 BC), and later other emperors, gave estates as public parks.

193

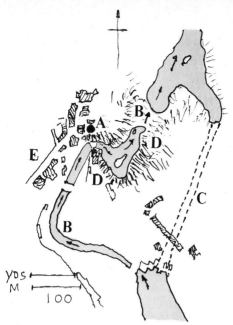

194 TIVOLI
A Temple of Vesta B Old course of river
C Water tunnel of 1831 D Area of gorge
E Town of Tivoli

THE GOLDEN AGE OF CLASSICISM can be set around 27 BC, when Augustus was proclaimed emperor. Under the patronage of himself and his wife Livia, art flourished in its own right and not, as under later emperors, as an instrument to express imperial power; and through his trusted minister and son-in-law Marcus Vipsanius Agrippa (62–12 BC), he encouraged the synthesis of engineering, architecture and natural beauty into a single art of landscape. Both the sites shown here are associated with this partnership. As *aedile* of Rome, Agrippa began in 33 BC to transform and enrich the capital with works ranging from temples and aqueducts to public gardens. Little of this survives, but almost certainly initiated the sacred landscape of Tivoli (27 BC) and he is recorded as the builder of the Pont du Gard at Nîmes (19 BC). Both are masterpieces of the imagination: the one an origin of all future romantic landscape, the other a demonstration that pure structure informed by poetry is among the grandest of man's achievements. The **Temple of Vesta at Tivoli (193)**, a favourite resort of Augustus, is poised as a symbol of the divine order above the River Aniene whose waters (before their diversion in 1831) plunged with fury into the gorge over three hundred feet below. The **present waterfall (195)** is a token only; the site is reconstructed in the **diagram (194)**. The **Pont du Gard (196)** is part of a thirty-one-mile aqueduct that brought water to Nîmes at a gradient of 1:3000. It is 317 yards long and 160 feet above the river, is designed in mathematical proportions and built of squared stone without mortar. The structure is laid out on an **imperceptible curve (197)** and despite its massiveness gives an unequalled impression of weightlessness, **movement and flight (198)**.

196, 197

198

The domestic life of the well-to-do Roman was fully matured by the first century AD, ranging from the enclosed urban homes of the pleasure resorts to the great open villas of the very wealthy. At Pompeii and Herculaneum, both overwhelmed by Vesuvius in AD 79, the objective was a totally enclosed landscape increased in size by imaginative space. There were no external windows to the noisy streets. The shape of each house varied according to site, but the principles of axial integrated open and closed space-planning remained constant. Sculpture and water, sometimes in the form of a short canal, were the permanent elements, enriched by such flowers as violets, poppies, peonies, pinks, marigolds, cornflowers, lavender, martagon and madonna lilies, pheasant's eye narcissus, wallflowers and several species of rose and iris. Acanthus, periwinkle, quince, pomegranates, box, bay, cypress and planes were used in larger gardens. **Frescoes (202)** depicted extraordinary and thought-provoking worlds of landscape, creating a sense of unlimited space. The **court (200)** and **sculpture (201)** of the House of the Vettii (after AD 62) is typical.

The huge open complex of the country villa is exemplified and described in the **Laurentian Villa (199)** of Pliny the Younger. The plan is a conjectural reconstruction by Robert Castell in 1728.

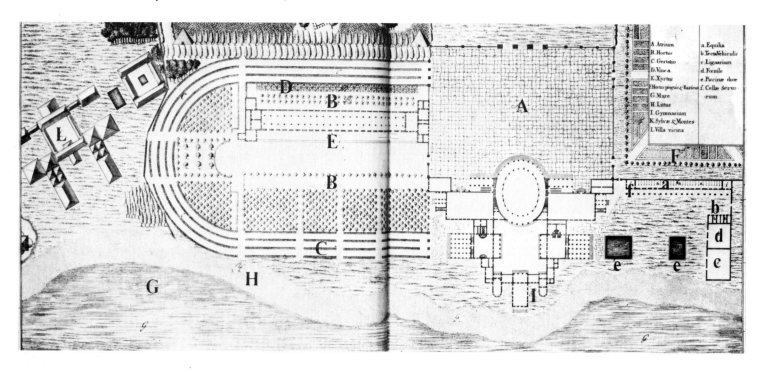

199 Laurentian Villa
A Entrance hall
B Garden
C *Allée* for exercise
D Vines
E Ornamental garden
F Kitchen garden
G Sea
H Seashore
I Gymnasium
L Neighbouring villa
a Stables
b Vehicles
c Woodshed
d Hay loft
e Two fishponds
f Servants

One dining-room runs out towards the sea; so that when a south-west wind drives the sea shoreward, it is gently washed by the edge of the last breakers. On every side of this room there are either folding doors or windows equally large, by which means you have a view from the front and the sides, as it were of three different seas . . . and by another view you look through the portico into the atrium, from whence the prospect is terminated by the woods and mountains which are seen at a distance. . . . At the back of the villa is another dining-room where the sea roaring in tempest is not felt, but only heard . . . it looks upon the garden and the *allée* which surrounds the garden. The *allée* is encompassed with a box-tree hedge, and where that is decayed, with rosemary. . . . Between the garden and this *allée* runs a shady walk of vines, soft and yielding to the tread, even when you walk barefoot. The garden is thickly planted with fig and mulberry trees. . . . In this place is a banqueting room, which though it stands remote from the sea, enjoys, however, a prospect nothing inferior to that view: two apartments run round the back part of it, whose windows look respectively upon the entrance of the villa and into a well-stocked kitchen garden. From hence a gallery (*cryptoporticus*) extends itself. . . . It has a range of windows on each side. . . . When the weather is fair and serene, these are all thrown open; but if it blows, those on the side the wind sits are shut, while the others remain unclosed. . . . Before this gallery lies a terrace perfumed with violets and warmed by the reflection of the sun from the gallery. . . . The whole coast is beautifully diversified by the joining or detached villas that are spread upon it, which, whether you are travelling along the sea or the shore, have the effect of a series of towns.

Pliny, Letter to Gallus.

200   201

202

203

THE IMPERIAL LANDSCAPES began sensitively under Augustus, continued romantically under Tiberius at Capri and Sperlonga, and thereafter appeared to be consistently overbearing. The Palatine itself was gradually converted by infilling and retaining walls from three small hills to a flat-topped rectangle laden with tightly compacted palaces of the several emperors. **Hadrian's Villa near Tivoli** (AD 118–38: **the model (203)**, a reconstruction by Italo Gismondi) is an exception to this siting, for it was built on open land to become, for the Renaissance, the most influential of the landscapes of antiquity. In fact, the complex of nearly 750 acres is a sequence of beautifully planned internal spaces with no relation one to another and little to the external landscape. As architectural episodes they are imaginative and glamorous. In particular, (A) on the model is the '*Marine Theatre*', the Emperor's inner island retreat. The titanic *Pecile* (B), with its colonnaded promenades, may have been used as a hippodrome. The *Canopus* (C) was called after the canal of Serapis, the sanctuary near Alexandria in Egypt. Top left is the romanticized landscape of the Vale of Tempe, significantly inspired by that of adjoining Tivoli (**193–195**).

The **Acropolis of Pergamum** in Asia Minor is in direct contrast. Originally an independent Hellenistic city, it reached its zenith in the second century BC, when it was bequeathed to Rome. The **dramatic site (206,** looking south), with its summit already crowned with sacred buildings and a theatre carved out of the precipitous mountainside, appealed to imperial instincts of domination of landscape by structure. The **plan (205)** and **reconstruction (204)** by M. Collignon show the original Hellenist grouping to have become Romanized by such structures as the Caracalla temple and terrace in the foreground and the Trajaneum on the summit. Unlike Hadrian's Villa, the parts were co-ordinated by the mountain shape; the second-century-AD climax must have appeared magnificent across the countryside.

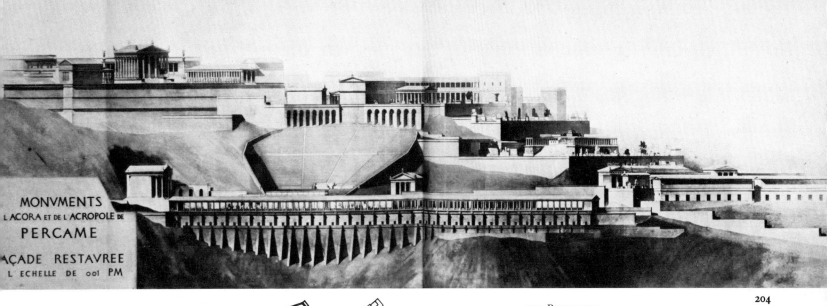

MONVMENTS
L ACORA ET DE L ACROPOLE DE
PERCAME

AÇADE RESTAVREE
L ECHELLE DE oo1 PM

204

205 PERGAMON
A Citadel gate
B Trajaneum
C Temple of Athena
D Theatre
E Caracalla temple
F Terrace
G Altar of Zeus

206

207

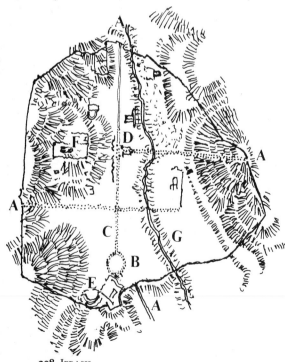

208 Jerash

A Gate B Peribolos C Great Street of Columns
D Basilica E Theatre F Great Temple
G River valley

COLONIAL ROME gave opportunities for town-planning that were denied to metropolitan Rome itself, a city of cramped accretions. New cities founded as trading centres sprang up in the deserts of the expanding empire, designed for commercial impressiveness with all the Roman genius for magnificence, law and order. The sites were spacious and usually unencumbered; stone always to hand. **Jerash (208)** in Jordan dates from the first and second centuries A D and is a completely unified town conventionally planned about axis and cross axis. The Great Street of Columns was terminated by the oval **Peribolos (207)**. The **cross axis (209)** connected the Great Temple with a main gate; the Basilica stood on the cross roads. The **theatre (210)** replaced the stage back-cloth of the surrounding scenery, usual in a Greek theatre, with a formidable architectural façade.

Baalbek (212) in Syria, founded in the first century A D on the caravan route between Damascus and Tyre, had no orthodox town plan. For impressiveness it relied upon the sheer might of its sacred buildings. Even today, with only six colossal columns (sixty-five feet high, seven feet in diameter), standing on a seventeen-foot podium of huge stones each weighing up to five hundred tons, the **Great Temple (211)** (A D 131–61) dominates the landscape. The stones were quarried on the adjoining hillside and gravity-borne to the site. The Temple of Jupiter, seen behind, was erected later, in A D 273.

209, 210

211, 212

13 The Middle Ages in Europe

Environment   73. The Alps and Pyrenees divide the Continent into two climatic regions: Mediterranean and Atlantic. The former was congenial to man and the ancient growth of cities, whereas the land north of the Alps was colder and would have been disagreeably so but for the warm, humid south-west wind from the Atlantic and its Gulf Stream. Extremes of temperature were avoided, and navigation encouraged, by the interpenetration of water and land. The northern sky was cloudy and the weather uncertain. Hardwoods everywhere had displaced pre-ice conifers, and the first agriculturalists cultivated wheat in small villages in clearings segregated one from another. The densest populations were in or around Belgium, for here were open plains. To the north lay Scandinavia with its long dark cold winters and its mountain ranges. To the east across the inaccessible Pripet Marshes, beyond the reach of the warm winds, lay Russia with its northern forests and southern plains. Throughout France and as far north as the Tyne in England (latitude 55°) were the remains of the straight roads and classical townships of the departed Roman civilization.

Social History   74. Christianity, the motive force of the Middle Ages, was established in AD 323 as the state religion of the Roman Empire. The capital was moved to Byzantium, but internal disputes caused disintegration into East (Greek Orthodox Church) and West (Roman Church). The Greek Church expanded northwards from Byzantium (taken by the Ottoman Turks AD 1453), reaching Kiev in the eleventh century. In the West the Franks from the forests east of the Rhine finally expelled the Romans from Gaul, (AD 496), themselves embracing Christianity. Thereafter medieval Europe slowly took shape, France and England becoming rival monarchies, while Germany, after a brief period under Charlemagne (AD 768–804), disintegrated into small states. Parallel with worldly conquest, monasticism spread from the Middle East and Italy throughout all Europe, establishing itself powerfully enough in remote Celtic Ireland (AD 400–800) to rival the Papacy in Rome. Spain was continuously at war with the Muslims. By the eleventh century western Europe had so far progressed as a Christian entity no longer on the defensive that it was able to undertake the unique Crusades to the Holy Land. As commerce and learning increased and universities were founded, so the temporal sovereigns became restless of the authority and cost of the Papacy in Rome; similarly, feudalism began to crumble before the new classes created by commerce. By AD 1400 Flanders had outstripped the Italian republics to become the centre of commerce of a new class, that of bourgeois merchants, whose independence and cultural civilization were above all others in northern Europe.

Philosophy   75. Christianity introduced the new and essentially simple idea of kindness and love of man for man. It preached of a future world and thus captured men's minds at a time when the decline of the Roman Empire meant chaos and misery in the present world. Individuals fled from society to contemplate in remote and wild landscapes. Soon they coalesced to form a distinct class, the ecclesiastical and monastic orders that were to preserve civilization throughout the Dark Ages. In the early centuries, lay people – even kings – were not expected to read or write. The great philosophers of the period were the Christian St Augustine (354–430), who described the 'City of God' as opposed to the city of man; Averroes (1126–98), the Muslim of Cordova, who interpreted and transmitted the philosophy of the Greeks; and the Christian St Thomas Aquinas (1225–74), who reconciled Aristotle with Christian theology. The illiterate, who far outnumbered the literate, were taught by an international and brilliantly organized religion to believe blindly that the good life led to heaven and the evil to the fires of hell.

Expression 76. The age was one of Christian faith and expressed itself in direct opposition to the worldly classical serenity and land geometry of the Romans. Silhouette in the dull northern light was important. Except where they were dominated by castles, towns and villages made their presence visible in towers and spires which rose above the huddled dwellings like fingers pointing to heaven. Man did not wish to project his personality over the landscape, but rather to grow from it and thus be part of it; the influence of upward forest growth was apparent everywhere. Cultivated gardens, mainly of vegetables and medicinal plants, only existed within the precincts of buildings, but the open-field system provided a pattern found round all habitations, whether walled or open. Across this landscape, and beyond, the bells would summon the labourer to prayer in the huge sanctuaries of the church that could contain at any one time the greater part of the population. In Russia, where medievalism continued long after the Renaissance elsewhere, the monastic silhouette changed after 1483 to become one of joyous and childlike exuberance, a fortress for the human spirit against the rigours of climate and famine.

Architecture 77. The seeds of Christian architecture were the underground caverns, catacombs and secret places of Rome, not emerging above ground before the fourth century. In the West the progress was one of continuous evolution of one form or 'style' into another. 'Early Christian' was in principle an adaptation of the Roman basilica, merging into 'Byzantine' whose domes were the heirs of those already evolved in Rome and Persia. The Greek Orthodox Church remained basically Byzantine. Christian architecture was later transplanted north of the Alps, retaining the classical arch but otherwise showing the first characteristic of an independent Gothic arch suitable to a northern light and psychology. Roofs of all structures became pointed to throw off snow and rain; windows were enlarged to draw in light. Partly through Muslim influence, but mainly because it reflected a spiritual urge, the pointed arch was evolved out of small stones (thirteenth century). The art and science of thrust and counter-thrust in structure reached a climax in French Flamboyant and English 'Decorated' (fourteenth century) and thereafter the initiative passed to English Perpendicular (fifteenth century), when massive and complex fan-vaulting seemed suspended like a canopy of trees above the lightest of tracery.

Landscape 78. Garden art was confined either to the cloister garden, whose antecedents in the West can be traced through the cloisters of Tarragona in north-east Spain to the Muslims, and thence to the Persian paradise garden; or the small enclosed domestic or castle garden rich with raised beds, fountains, pergolas and such delights, that may also have come from the East. Apart from gardens, the landscape arts of the age were intuitive rather than conscious design and the contemporary appeal lay largely in the message of symbolism. Cross or calvary in the open air, such as were numerous in eighth-century Ireland or fifteenth-century Brittany, endowed a whole countryside with a sense of purpose and meaning to the common man whose Bible it was. This age of emotional rather than intellectual landscape influenced the future in two principal ways: (*a*) as an inspiration for the romanticism of the eighteenth and nineteenth centuries, and (*b*) as an aesthetic standard or guide for asymmetrical composition, whether based on that of farm, monastery, castle or town, which persists today.

213

214

CHRISTIANITY was first expressed in landscape by the basilica and campanili such as those of Ravenna in the west and the mushroom domes of Byzantium in the east. The Latin Church was to develop rapidly, but the Eastern, or Greek Orthodox, remained traditional until destroyed by the Ottoman Turks. The **Brontocheion Church, Mistra (214)** (*c.* AD 1300), overlooking the plain of Sparta in Greece, was typical of churches scattered along the Mediterranean as far as Venice.

Even before the collapse of the Roman Empire and the subsequent chaos, individual Christians had sought sanctuary and contemplation in the remote wilderness. Single hermits then united to form groups and from these sprang a new force in European civilization: monasticism. Extremes of seclusion were reached in such sites as **Meteora (213)** in north-west Thessaly, Greece (fourteenth century), and **Skellig Michael (216)** off the west coast of distant Ireland, where an independent Christian Celtic society flourished from the fifth to tenth centuries. **Clonmacnois (215)**, founded 541 on the Irish mainland in Co. Offaly, was typical of the many open monasteries whose round tower was the sole protection against attack. A teaching Cross of the Scriptures, such as often sanctified the open landscape, is seen with others against the background of the River Shannon.

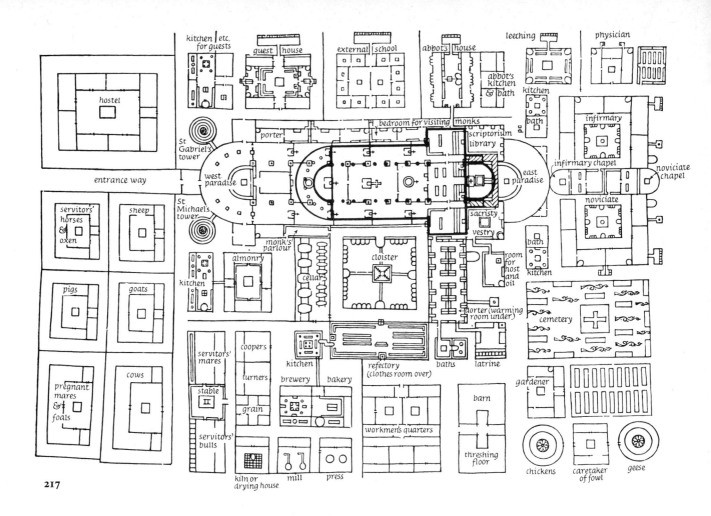

kitchen etc. for guests · guest house · external school · abbot's house · leeching · physician

abbot's kitchen & bath · kitchen

hostel

St Gabriel's tower

bedroom for visiting monks

porter

scriptorium library

infirmary

bath

entrance way

west paradise

east paradise

infirmary chapel

noviciate chapel

St Michael's tower

servitors' horses & oxen · sheep

monk's parlour

almonry

cloister

sacristy

noviciate

vestry

pigs · goats

kitchen

cellar

room for host and oil

bath

kitchen

pregnant mares & foals · cows

dorter (warming room under)

cemetery

servitors' mares · coopers

turners

stable

kitchen

brewery · bakery

refectory (clothes room over)

baths · latrine

gardener

servitors' bulls

grain

barn

workmen's quarters

threshing floor

kiln or drying house · mill · press

chickens · caretaker of fowl · geese

217

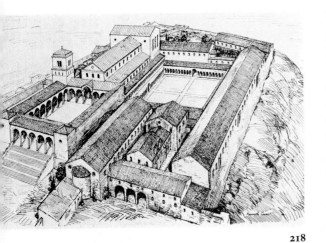

218

UNDER MONASTICISM, the ideal of planning and order no longer applied to the world at large but to the enclosed world of the community. The rule of St Benedict (founded in the sixth century), which was to be the basis of Western monasticism, established a precise timetable for the religious life and a precise physical setting in which that life was to be lived. A drawing of about 830 preserved at **St Gall, Switzerland** (**217**, a modernized version) – an ideal model rather than the record of an actual monastery – already contains all the elements that were to become standard throughout the Middle Ages. In the centre is the cloister garden for perambulation and contemplation. The physic garden was the prototype of specialized flower-growing, with separate beds for each kind of plant. St Benedict's own monastery was on **Monte Cassino** in central Italy (**218**, reconstruction, as existing in the eleventh century, by Professor Kenneth Conant).

The Cistercians, in reaction against the growing laxity of the Benedictines, returned to strict austerity. The sites chosen for their settlements were in remote rural areas where there was land to exploit, for a return to manual labour was a special feature of their life. They became the great farmers of the Middle Ages, introducing and popularizing many improvements in agricultural methods. **Rievaulx Abbey** (**221**), founded in 1131, follows the orthodox pattern. There was apparently no conscious attempt to design the setting aesthetically – the course of the river was changed for agricultural reasons – yet its **siting** (**219**), composition and adaptation to local climate and topography was so much part of the countryside as largely to inspire the English school of landscape design in the eighteenth century. A **view from the north** (**220**) shows the ruined transept within the arc of the wooded hillside.

220

221

219 RIEVAULX ABBEY, YORKSHIRE

A Abbey
B Gateway
C Bridge
D Previous course of river
E Present course of river
F Hanging woods
G Eighteenth-century terrace by Capability
   Brown overlooking abbey landscape

222

223

MONASTIC EXPANSION reached to the furthest limits of Christendom and encouraged the extreme exploitation of Romantic landscape architecture. The composition of **Assisi (222)** (1182) in central Italy, the birthplace of St Francis, with the town and its many churches, the hills and the plain, and the little hermitage where the saint went into retreat, is the greatest sacred landscape in Italy outside the cities. In Russia, the Monastery of **St Joseph, Vokolamsk (223)** (fifteenth to seventeenth centuries), near Moscow, follows the plan of a Roman fortress, but the internal asymmetry gives externally a glorious complex of coloured forms patterned against sky and snow. Off the coast of Brittany in northern France, the Monastery of **Mont St Michel (224)**, founded by the Benedictines in the tenth century, converted a rock island in 1203 into an object of landscape architecture that is unrivalled. The *flèche* and belfry were added in 1870 to complete a composition that seems to have grown organically to become a culmination of Gothic scenery.

224

225

227, 228

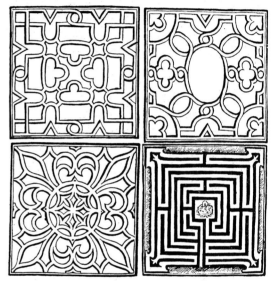

226

229

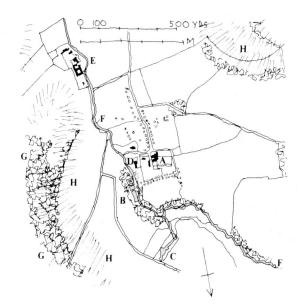

230 Bingham's Melcombe, Dorset

A Manor
B Fishponds
C Mill pond
D Church
E Farm
F River
G Hanging woods
H Hillside

232

231

233, 234

THE EVOLUTION OF HOMES AND GARDENS virtually began afresh after the Dark Ages. Only the monasteries were a link with a now fabulous classical past. 'A goodly gardeyn to walk ynne closed with high walls embattled' was the medieval ideal. It was symbolic, as depicted in the **Paradise garden** (**227**) of a Rhenish master of the fifteenth century. A scene such as this from a manuscript of the **Roman de la rose** (**225**) is typical and did not materially change for a hundred years. Pieter Brueghel's **Spring** (**226**) shows the culmination of the medieval garden and, in detail, the first influences of the Italian Renaissance. In England, the Elizabethans were fascinated by formal hedge-clipping which ranged from **knot patterns and a maze** (**228**) (from Lawson's *Countrie Housewife's Garden*) to the **topiary** (**229**) that can be seen at Levens Hall, Westmorland (1690).

In the critical period between medievalism and Renaissance, Tudor England created through its smaller and less fashionable manor-houses a landscape art that was both indigenous and intuitive. The sketch of **Bingham's Melcombe, Dorset** (**231**), shows the 'flowered rooms' contrasted with the new lawn extending to the countryside. The **plan** (**230**) shows the composition with the surrounding hills. The series of spatially separate units includes the **entrance court** (**232**), two **'flowered rooms'** (**234**) with the dovecote beyond, and **the bowling green** (**233**) with its ancient yew hedge that has crept across the terrace walk.

THE CITY was as powerful a symbol as the garden. St Augustine used it as an image of the divine order, the **Civitas Dei** (**235**: an illustration from a manuscript of that work) – unified, enclosed, dominated by the Church. A few medieval towns still survive with this strong power of evocation. At **Vézelay, Burgundy** (**236**), the middle-distance road is modern, but otherwise the scene is close to history. Leadership lay in the Church, which preserved learning and created the arts of civilization, while in immediate contact with realities. Peasant, craftsman, merchant, scholar and theologian were held together by spiritual collectiveness rather than material gain. Homes were individual and most had small gardens within the walls. The habitat was necessarily compact and set cleanly in the landscape from which it drew its materials for food and shelter. Collective peace of mind was assured, provided dogma was not questioned.

Durham (**237**) stands like a sentinel on a narrow peninsula of the River Wear. Town, cathedral and castle form an historic and aesthetic unity. The castle faces north to Scotland, but the cathedral overwhelmingly predominates in the landscape.

235

236

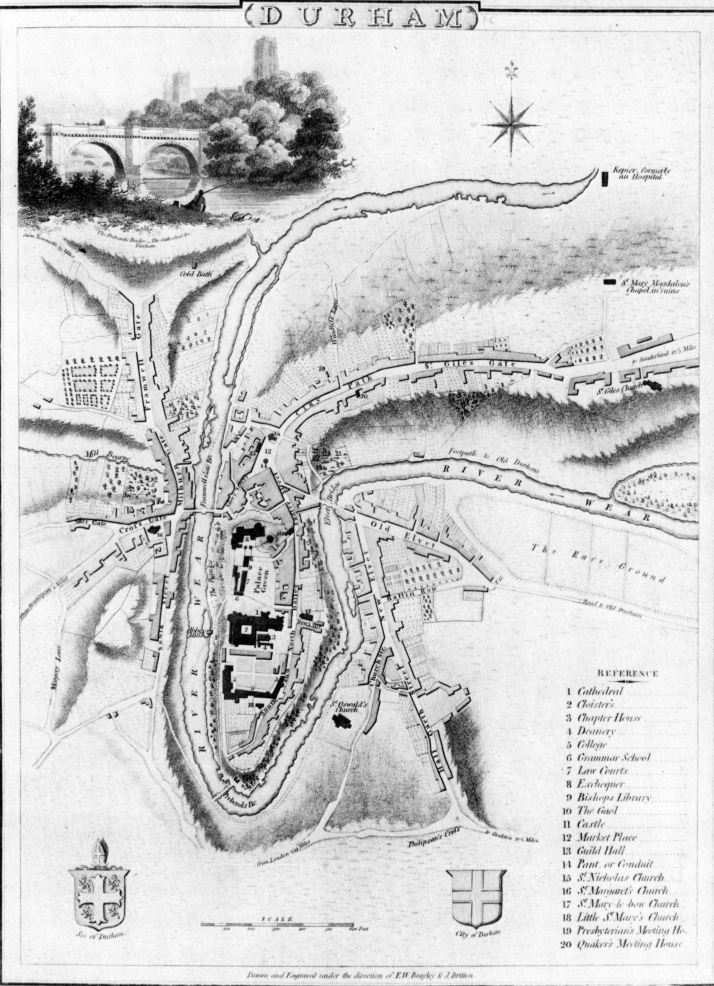

237

DURHAM

Kepier, formerly an Hospital

St Mary Magdalen's Chapel in ruins

The Prebends Bridge — The Cathedral &c Durham

Cold Bath

to Sunderland 12½ Mile

St Giles Gate

St Giles Church

Framwell Gate

Mill Dean

Feetpath to Old Durham

RIVER WEAR

The Race Ground

Milbourn Gate

Framwelgate Br

Elvet Bridge

Old Elvet

Miller Gate

Cross Gate

Palace Green

Rattin Row

Road to Old Durham

Mivery Lane

RIVER WEAR

St Oswald's Church

Prebends Br

Philipson's Croft

from London 250 Mile

to Stockton 20½ Miles

REFERENCE

1. Cathedral
2. Cloisters
3. Chapter House
4. Deanery
5. College
6. Grammar School
7. Law Courts
8. Exchequer
9. Bishops Library
10. The Gaol
11. Castle
12. Market Place
13. Guild Hall
14. Pant, or Conduit
15. St Nicholas Church
16. St Margaret's Church
17. St Mary-le-bow Church
18. Little St Mary's Church
19. Presbyterian's Meeting Ho.
20. Quaker's Meeting House

See of Durham.

SCALE

City of Durham.

Drawn and Engraved under the direction of E.W. Brayley & J. Britton.

Engraved by J. Roper, from a Drawing by G. Cole.

In accompany the Beauties of England and Wales.

238, 239

THE CITIES OF THE NETHERLANDS in the fifteenth century were the richest and most independent in Europe. Among the arts, landscape painting was in advance even of contemporary Italy. The detail of the **Adoration of the Lamb (238)** painted in 1432 by Hubert and Jan van Eyck as an altarpiece for St Bavon's Cathedral, Ghent, portrays a realistic composition of hills, groups of trees, glimpses of cities, and distant views that came to be translated into English landscape, for intellectual reasons, some three hundred years later. Neighbouring **Bruges** remains basically medieval in form, with a romantic appeal that has ever since been overwhelming. It was both City of God and city of intelligent man. The unity of the one was enriched by the intricacies of the other, and the blend created the visible picturesque with its accidental and ever-changing scenes. The detail from a **bird's-eye view (239)** as it was in 1578 indicates the domestic nature of the city, packed tightly round its open spaces and churches and threaded by canals. The old **Customs House (240)**, 1477, terminates one of the entrance canals. The **Béguinage (242)**, founded in 1245 for 'pious women', may have influenced the English Garden City movement. **Massive gateways (241)** break the encompassing fortifications, which gave protection from wind across a flat countryside and incidentally provided sites for windmills.

240

241

242

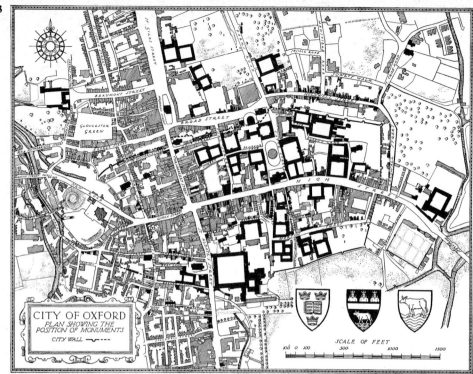

243

244

246

245

247

ORGANIZED LEARNING outside the monasteries began in Italy in the ninth century. The internal quadrangle as a form was adopted almost universally, from **Cracow in Poland (245)** to **Salamanca in Spain (244)**. Although the shape is similar to the entrance atrium of an early Christian basilica, its real source was the secluded monastery cloister, which itself can be traced to the four-square enclosed Persian paradise garden. It was a powerful symbolic shape that encouraged learning, meditation and discourse, as well as being severely practical. It was so self-centred that its general adoption at **Oxford (243)** and **Cambridge (246)** created two cities whose independent quadrangulated colleges jostled one another indiscriminately for position. Oxford was compact; Cambridge followed the graceful curve of the river. Externally, the complex silhouette of towers and spires proclaimed beyond doubt the ascendancy of Christian faith over learning. The developing science of ecology was furthered by the Botanic Garden at Oxford in 1621, which followed the **Orto Botanico at Padua (247)** (1545: seen against the basilica of S. Antonio).

14 Italy: the Renaissance

Environment *79.* Both climate and topography were irregular. To the north were the flat plains of Lombardy, chilled by the Alps; in the centre were river valleys and plains that were mild in winter but hot in summer; and in the south the climate could be tropical. Landscape design developed in three distinct areas: Tuscany, Rome, and across the north from Genoa to Venice. The Tuscan landscape was composed of small hills and valleys enriched with farm buildings and the textured irregular patterns of olive and vine plantations, punctuated with hardwood trees such as ilex and cypress – a domestic scene of green and grey foliage penetrated by the yellow Arno. The Roman *campagna*, in contrast, was a wide flat plain of poor farm- and marshlands crossed by the remains of ancient aqueducts and roads, such as the Via Appia, all leading to a walled medieval city built round and upon classical ruins. In the Tuscan hills water was adequate; in the hills round Rome it was active and abundant; in the northern landscapes of the lakes and Venetian lagoons it was spacious, passive and reflective.

Social History *80.* Italy emerged from the Dark Ages as a series of independent states under lay princes owing allegiance to the Pope and constantly quarrelling among themselves. Early in the thirteenth century Frederick II of Hohenstaufen, monarch of the Holy Roman Empire in Germany and of Sicily, defied Papal authority and was duly excommunicated. Opposition to the Pope's political power was never absent in Italy, and thus encouraged a certain freedom of thought in theology and morals, especially in places like Venice which were relatively immune from ecclesiastical control. The individual thinker first emerged as individual man in Florence where the Medici family had assumed control in 1400 and under whose influence the arts of an elegant mercantile and domestic civilization first appeared. After exile in Avignon the Papal civilization itself returned to Rome in 1420 and thereafter embellished the city continuously until the sack by the Spanish and Germans in 1527. During the fifteenth century the revival of classical learning (humanism) dominated intellectual life and was not considered incompatible with the glorification of the Church. These two ideas came together in the works of Pope Julius II (1503–13). Throughout Italy during this period the larger cities tended to absorb the smaller, but without destroying their identity. The northern cities developed spontaneously from medieval beginnings, Venice with her Eastern contacts being one of the most cosmopolitan and liberal.

Philosophy *81.* The struggle for men's minds continued unabated after Frederick's revolt. The same Papacy that had sanctioned the mendicant orders of St Francis and St Dominic, a few years later instituted the Inquisition (1233). The Church remained ruthless in its defence of existing theology, resistant to the criticism of moral behaviour that led to the Reformation, and unmoved by geological and astronomical discoveries. Frederick II, moving freely within a Sicilian society based on four civilizations (Italian, German, Byzantine and Muslim), had liberally encouraged the arts and sciences, founded the first university, and can be said to have initiated the greatest of all discoveries, that by man of himself. Within himself man found a mixture of the noble and the ignoble. Dante enshrined the whole medieval world system in his mystical vision, *The Divine Comedy*; Petrarch and Boccaccio stood more outside that system, developing a type of psychological awareness that heralds the modern world. Plato displaced Aristotle in man's new and determined search for contact with the infinite, but the only major philosopher of the age itself was Machiavelli (1467–1527), who divorced politics from moral considerations and taught that the end justified the means. For good or ill, man now regarded himself as the centre of the universe.

Expression *82.* The eye that had previously looked inward upon an eternal world, now looked outwards to see the physical world and to find it good; Petrarch is said to have been the first Western man to climb a mountain for the sake of the view. The change was one of symbolism to worldliness. To enhance these newly found pleasures, the house extended itself into the open air, creating what were defined spaces whose links were as important as were the internal doorways between salons. Views of the countryside were part of the design, rather in the manner of the classic frescoed wall; it was not until later that garden and landscape were physically more closely integrated. The fundamental purpose was to create shapes that responded to the intellectual mind searching for order, tranquillity and stimulus, giving dignity and status to the human himself. In principle, the sites overlooked the mother city from adjoining slopes or hillsides. The Florentine villa remained domestic, in spirit associated with its rural surroundings. The Roman villa was almost solely humanistic and heroic, the purpose being to reincarnate the spirit and grandeur of antiquity.

Architecture *83.* The ruins of classical Rome were now examined with new attention, and at first inspired architectural form of all kinds, religious and domestic. Preoccupation lay in the rediscovery of the secrets of mathematical proportion. The Greeks had established that there was a harmonic relation between geometry and music and felt that they had found the universal law that lies behind all things. The Roman writer Vitruvius (*c.* AD I) enunciated the relation of the human figure to the circle, elaborated and developed by the architect Alberti (1404–72). Palladio (1518–80) carried the theory of Platonic geometry to finality, giving harmonic proportions not merely to a single three-dimensional room, but to a series of rooms, which, though not visible *in toto* at any one time, would strike the mind as a single harmonic chord. These proportions were absolute, stable and finite and were the climax of the Renaissance search for perfection. It was to break out of this purist world that Mannerism arose, manifesting itself at first in the internal design of churches, where it began the search for a new concept of space, that of infinity. Out of Mannerism grew Baroque.

Landscape *84.* The garden was made for man and dignified him. The proportions gave him peace: the form was therefore crucial. The interior of the house thrust itself outwards, levelled to the rising or falling site, the shapes made more by intuition than by mathematical calculation. The sites were usually on hillsides, because of view and climate; the descending terraces were carved out of the ground and harmonious with it; the long shapes were genial to contemplative perambulation. The contents were basically evergreens, stone and water – materials that were permanent rather than ephemeral. They included box parterres, clipped hedges, the dark cypress and groves of ilex; sculpture, stairways, pergolas and arbours; water in repose and in fountains. Flowers played little part. The architectural details were tactile and friendly through the emotional curves of mouldings, nosings, balusters. The wide versatility of design, especially in Tuscany, was caused by the endless combinations possible between the personality of the owner, of the architect and of the site. Vignola (1507–73) lifted landscape design into the sublime at the Villa Lante, subordinating architecture to an ancient and universal idea of cosmology. This conception of landscape marked the end of an era; parallel to it in date, Palladio evolved the wholly self-centred Villa Rotonda, eliminating the orthodox garden and preparing the way for the harmony of geometry with natural form that was to be the basis of the eighteenth-century revolution in England.

248

FLORENTINE HUMANISM was an intellectual awakening that looked to Greece and Rome rather than to the Church for authority. Lorenzo de' Medici and his circle saw themselves as the heirs of the Platonic Academy and tried to re-create for themselves the cultured life about which they read in Horace and Pliny. At the same time, they could not at once rid themselves of the conventions of the Middle Ages. The early Medici Villa by Michelozzo Michelozzi at **Cafaggiolo** (**248**) (1451) is still essentially a medieval fortified house with compartmented garden. A few years later, however, at the **Villa Medici at Fiesole** (**251**), the same architect created the first true Renaissance villa. The idea was similar to that of the Generalife at Granada, made by the Moors some century and a half previously (**45–49**). The house is projected along the hillside into the open air. The gardens are still formal and regular, but the surrounding countryside has been brought into the design. The **upper terrace** (**250**), artificially formed by a huge **retaining wall** (**249**), looks out over Florence. Below lies a traditional pergola. No longer in any way symbolic, the garden has become a setting for pleasure and philosophical debate.

249

250

251

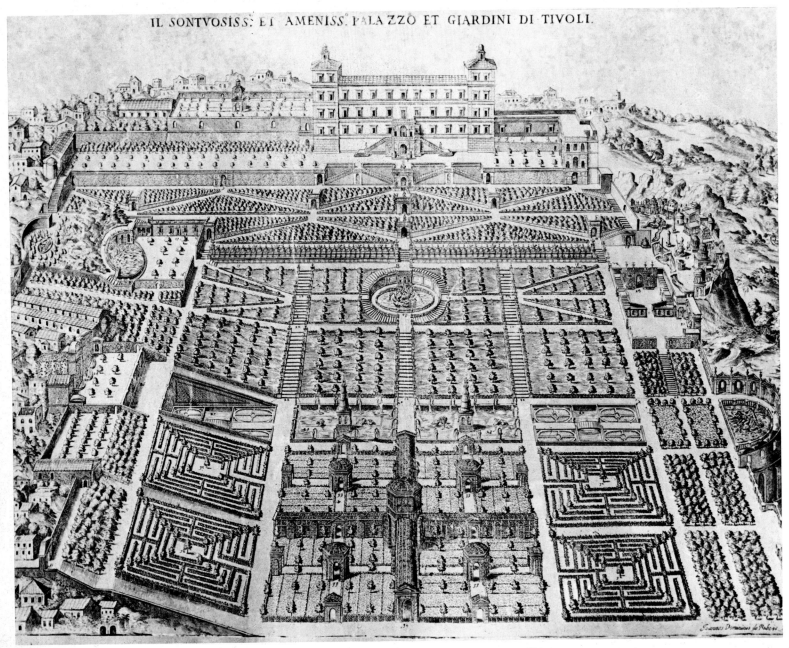

IL SONTVOSISS: ET AMENISS. PALAZZO ET GIARDINI DI TIVOLI.

252 253 254 255

256

257

THE VILLA D'ESTE at Tivoli (**252**), shown in the contemporary print by Etienne du Pérac, is the most spectacular and sumptuous of the gardens of the High Roman Renaissance. Made in 1550 by Pirro Ligorio, the conception is based on antique Roman – not only the nearby Hadrian's Villa (from which sculpture was taken) but also Ligorio's own re-creation of the classical **Temple of Fortune at Praeneste** (**257**). The plan is accomplished, the modelling on the steep hillside firm, the detail robust and the transition between gardens and landscape clearly defined; over all is the sense of Roman domination of landscape. The **central vista** (**256**) looks north-west across the Tiber to the Sabatina Mountains. The **triumphal arch** (**253**) that terminates the upper terrace looks towards Rome. Below this is the Rometta, or 'little Rome', with its models of antiquity. The gardens – now shady with cypress trees – everywhere echo to the sound of water, diverted through a conduit from the River Aniene and spread lavishly and musically through the garden: the **water organ** (**254**) with its reflecting fish-pools, the **terrace of a hundred fountains** (**255**) and through many other equally refreshing devices.

258
259

260

261

THE IDEALS OF CLASSICAL SPACE COMPOSITION were brought to a climax in painting by Perugino and Raphael, in landscape architecture by Vignola, and in architecture by Palladio. The search was for perfection in divine harmony between man and the universe, of which man assumed himself to be the centre. **Christ giving the keys to St Peter (258)**, painted by Perugino in 1503 for the Sistine Chapel, shows the same principles of composition as the **Villa Lante at Bagnaia (259)**, designed by Vignola in 1566. The climax of the one is the centripetal temple, of the other, the similarly centripetal **water gardens (260)** with central figures by Giovanni da Bologna. Both have evolved from an outer landscape, the one by suggestion from the sky, the other from the woods by water intricacies such as the **fish rill (261)**. Painting and garden together seem to foreshadow the idea of the distant Taj Mahal at Agra (77).

FROM ORDER DISPLAYED TO ORDER CONCEALED: the Villa Lante was an exercise in geometry – **a house divided into two parts, each a square (262)**. Vignola was preoccupied with translating ideas into architecture and then projecting them into the landscape. But Palladio, the more influential architect, was concerned with architecture only as pure, self-contained geometry, standing aloof from any designed environment. In a building such as the completely symmetrical **Villa Rotonda (263)**, built *c.* 1550 on a low hill near Vicenza, classical abstract thought can go no further; it nobly and decisively marks the end of an era in landscape design. Yet, paradoxically, this very unconcern opened the way towards a new conception of the landscape required by an ideal building, and already the painters were exploring such landscapes as backgrounds to their own conventional architectural scenes. The detail from the **Castelfranco Madonna (264)**, painted by Giorgione *c.* 1500, foreshadows those romantic landscapes whose order was concealed and whose translation into reality was to be such a future preoccupation, particularly for the English school.

262

15 Italy: Mannerism and Baroque

Environment

85. The new attitude which had so powerful an effect upon all Italian art, and therefore upon landscape design, was now concerned not so much with man's relation to his immediate surroundings as with his relation to the universe as a whole. The sea route to the East was discovered in 1486 and America in 1492, but the immediate effect of these was remote from Italy and apparently little appreciated except by Venice, from which trade was diverted. The visible universe, however, was of immediate moment. Early in the fifteenth century Copernicus published statistical evidence for the hypothesis that the earth was not a fixed point in space, but one of several planets that both turned on their axes and revolved round the sun. Galileo supported this theory by observation and experiment. In 1609 Kepler proved that the planets moved round the sun in ellipses and thus destroyed another profound assumption: that all heavenly bodies moved in circles. How and why they retained their positions remained obscure until the following century, when Isaac Newton (1642–1727) showed the solar system to be in equilibrium, subject to uniform laws of gravitation and thus intelligible to pure reason.

Social History

86. After the sack of Rome in 1527 the influence of the Papacy declined and Italy politically became a pawn, first of Spain and subsequently of more liberal France. The only surviving free commonwealths of any size were Genoa and Venice, and Italy ceased to have a political history of her own until the beginning of the nineteenth century. Internally, the Papacy was struggling to reform itself (at first with austerity), but it was not until the Council of Trent (1583) that the Counter-Reformation began to overcome Protestantism. Thereafter the Catholic Church consolidated its position in Europe as the Church Triumphant and expanded to the Far East. During the seventeenth century the power of the Papal States increased while that of Venice declined. The domestic life of the country continued independently of changes in foreign masters, of whom the mass of the people were probably ignorant. It is significant that the most prolific period of villa- and garden-building lay in the theologically disturbed second half of the sixteenth century and that the predominant builders were the officers of the Church.

Philosophy

87. Astronomical discoveries, combined with the questioning of religious dogma, had thrown doubt upon the very foundations of the existing order and beliefs. Individual and thoughtful man found himself groping for something beyond his understanding; common people as a whole still remained intensely religious and it was this passionate emotion that the Counter-Reformation was determined to capture and exploit, through art as well as teaching. The assault was led by the Jesuits, whose understanding of the conflict in the human mind was acute. They conceded that man might have an influence upon the shaping of his own destiny – a fundamental break with medieval theology. They accepted the change in man's relation to the universe, and that all things were in flux; and set out in church architecture to create emotional environments that would answer subconscious yearnings and overcome all reason. From the staggering revolution in church design sprang a new conception of space that was to spread to all realms of art, especially of landscape design and town-planning.

Expression

88. The second half of the sixteenth century was a transition from one philosophical concept to another: from the classical finite to the Baroque infinite. The expression of the finite is factual, that of infinity can only be imaginative. The mind and not the eye takes charge, and it was on the creation of imaginative space and movement that Baroque art depended. It was technically based on illusion and the newly found art of the theatre. In church interiors, the space volumes followed one another in progression, culminating in the great painted vision of the heavens that blasted away the confining ceiling. Architecturally the parts were in constant and imaginative movement, symbolized by curve chasing curve. Externally, and most notable in landscape design, an awareness that man was now only a part of a swirling complex that embraced rocks and water as well as the heavens, established the idea that an object was not an object in itself but related to others in an infinite chain. All these objects, and not man alone, now inspired his design. From rocks he finally created the abstract forms of the Trevi Fountain (1735), probably the most symbolic achievement of the age; from water and shells he created countless shifting abstract forms; from the movements of the sea he made the Salute Church in Venice; he joined heaven and earth with the water's reflecting mirror. The synthesis of the environment as a whole entity and as a part of infinity had now begun.

Architecture 89. In 1544 Michelangelo had begun the Capitol in Rome, a forerunner of the Baroque sense of urban space. In 1551 and onwards the Nuova Strada in Genoa (now the Via Garibaldi) created imaginative space in a sumptuous but narrow street by means of vistas from fixed viewpoints, through palace forecourts, to what in reality were very small gardens climbing the hillside behind. Baroque art reached its zenith under Bernini (1598–1680) and Longhena (1598–1682). The fixed viewpoint remained but the eye was directed through illusion with such subtlety as to appear to be free; spectator, object (whether architecture or sculpture) and environment all appeared to be part of one scene. Bernini was involved in the making of the scenographic Piazza del Popolo in Rome which came to influence French design, but his masterpiece is the apparently simple Piazza of St Peter's. Roman space design was townscape rather than landscape, but Longhena's Salute Church emphasizes that over the centuries Venice, by reason of its water spaces, had been in continuous evolution as a city of open landscape. The Salute itself organizes its own space, both internally and externally, according to Baroque principles; in the grand scenery of the lagoon, its domes respond to others that are either Venetian-Roman or Venetian-Byzantine.

Landscape 90. During the period of transition romantic artificialities such as rocks, grottoes, giants and secret fountains were often incorporated in a ground design that continued the basic geometry of the Renaissance. They represented the struggles of Mannerism (as the style was known) to escape from the classic frame, a thoughtful culmination of which was the Villa Gamberaia at Settignano (c. 1610) echoing as it seemed to do many parts of the individual human mind. With the Baroque, the garden finally became theatrical, designed for unfolding drama in which people were players rather than philosophers. The organization of country space could go far beyond the constrictions imposed by urban planning. Freedom of choice of site gave inspiration to originality of design, the site usually determining the major axis of the composition. If it were a hillside with abundance of water and a view, the garden might emerge as a giant cascade artificially planned for perspective, with terrace upon terrace for spectacle. The sense of strong composition was paramount; the detail was often coarse. From this lyrical and experimental use of land sprang many of the ideas of future town-planning; the Villa Dona dalle Rose at Valzanzibio in Venetia was in itself a maquette for a small town for human rather than imperial habitation, having its co-ordinated open and closed spaces and its main axis determined by the shape of the hills rather than the location of the house.

265

After Classicism, with its world of order and harmony, came an era of tension, ambiguity and fear. The macabre park of the **Villa Orsini, Bomarzo**, is the exclusive product of the new Mannerism, of individual rumination as opposed to universal thought. The valley complex is peopled by **primitive giants (266)** determined upon the destruction of human order. Architecture, that ancient symbol of balance, is **thrown askew (265)**. A Christian *tempietto* on high ground alone gives assurance of salvation from these terrible forces.

The **Boboli Gardens** of the Pitti Palace, Florence, are a mixture of Roman Renaissance, Mannerism and Baroque. The **grotto (268)**, designed by Buontalenti about 1550, shows the Mannerist escape from reality into a grotesque world of imaginative space where nothing any longer seems secure: the paintings have no consistent perspective; rocks grow into men or animals; Michelangelo's slaves are themselves emerging from solid stone. On the other hand, the **gardens (267)**, by Ammanati, link classical Rome splendidly to the France of Le Nôtre. The amphitheatre was modelled from an existing quarry and the whole dramatic shape with its *tapis vert* and upper terraces is carved out of woodlands, as they were to be in France. The age of the theatre had arrived and with it the art of spectacle; optics and perspective now became a science.

266

267, 268

THE SMALLER GARDENS of Tuscany and elsewhere were varied and inventive, expressing a particular rather than a collective mind and drawing unending inspiration from the site. Two gardens that are each a masterpiece of domestic Mannerism are the Villas Capponi and Gamberaia, overlooking Florence from each side of the Arno. The **Villa Capponi, Arcetri (269)** (*c.* 1572), combines traditional compartmentalism with the open terracing of the Villa Medici at Fiesole (**251**), and is thus suited to the maximum changes of climate and mood. The **plan (270)** shows, on the right, the lemon garden and the view along the terrace and over the *giardino segreto*. In the centre is the exposed grass terrace, probably used for bowls. To the left is suddenly revealed the flowered and fragrant *giardino segreto* in compartments on two levels. The **upper garden (273)** is entered by a tunnel direct from the house (until recently the only entrance) and is **windowed (272)**; the lower is reached by a **gateway and garden stairs (271)**.

270

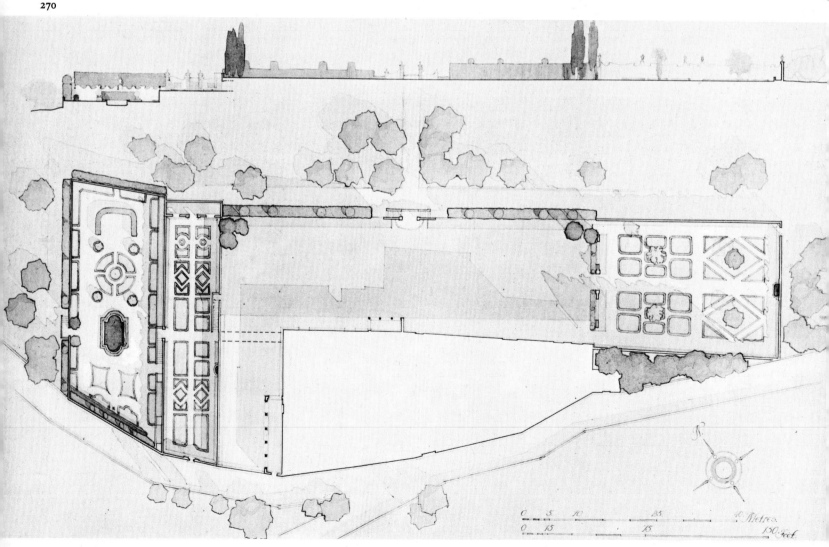

274

275

276

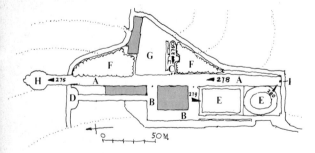

277 GAMBERAIA

A Long alley
B Grass view terrace
C Grotto garden
D Entrance drive
E Original water garden
F Bosco
G Lemon garden
H Cypress garden
I Statue on viewpoint

THE PLAN OF THE VILLA GAMBERAIA, Settignano, appears to have evolved mainly during the seventeenth century. It is perhaps the most thoughtful of the Mannerist garden designs, for it has accepted the challenge of the many moods of man, translated them into physical form and co-ordinated them on an awkward site into a single unified whole. There seems to have been no single master designer. Excluding the house itself, there are some nine units of composition shown in the **perspective (274)**. The composition can be analysed from the **diagram (277)** as follows: the plan structure is the **long alley** (A) **(278)** or bowling green, to which the house is axially fastened by means of the grass view terrace (B), by the arched extensions of the east wall of the house, and by the **grotto garden** (C) **(276)**. Embraced by these are the spaces that include the entrance drive (D), the modernized **water garden** (E) **(279)**, the two dark ilex *boschi* (F), the raised lemon garden (G) and the mystic **cypress garden** (H) **(275)** at the north end of the long alley. Terminating the south end of the alley is **a statue (280)**, behind which are seen the olive groves of the Arno Valley.

278, 279 280

281

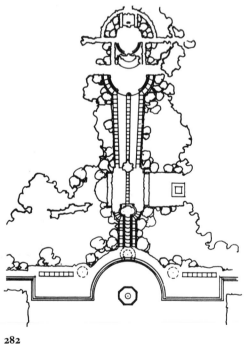

282

BAROQUE LANDSCAPE was based on a sense of movement and of expansion beyond the finite boundaries that governed the space design of the Renaissance. In urban planning, these objectives were principally achieved through the straight avenue, introduced for military use as well as for spectacle. The avenue, with its designed rhythms, led the eye either out of the picture frame to infinity or towards fragmentation on such a non-directional object as an obelisk; but rarely to be halted by a flat surface or façade. These elements are to be found in the **Piazza del Popolo, Rome** (**281**) (mainly the work of Sixtus V, 1585–90), whose three radiating avenues and central obelisk were to be the source of much future garden design. In the country, there was more room for expansion. The **villas behind Frascati** (**283**), all looking towards Rome, formed an almost continuous experimental ground of landscape design. The **cascade of the Villa Aldobrandini** (**282**), designed by Giacomo della Porta 1598–1603, is based on ingenious perspective to increase the illusion of steepness by bringing the distance telescopically closer to the high *loggia* from which it is seen. But even more opportune were the cool climate and mountainous settings of the northern lakes. The **Isola Bella** (**284**) on Lake Maggiore was made 1630–70 by Castelli and Carlo Fontana. The original intention was to geometricize the whole island, giving the impression of some monster galleon drifting across the lake. The island is perhaps the greatest single surviving achievement of the Baroque art of romantic affinity to environment. The **drawing of the plan** (**285**) is by Georges Gromort.

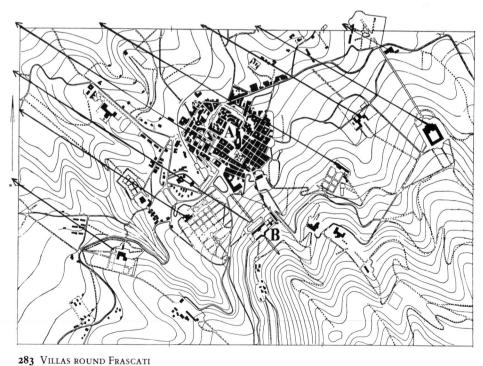

283 VILLAS ROUND FRASCATI
A Frascati   B Villa Aldobrandini   The diagonal lines show the sight-lines of seven of the villas towards the dome of St Peter's

284, 285

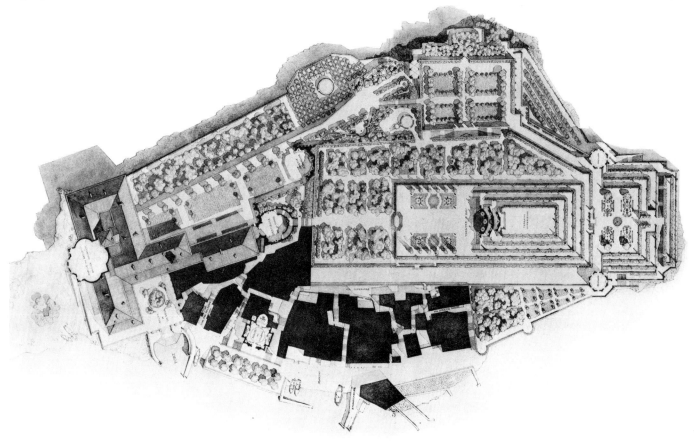

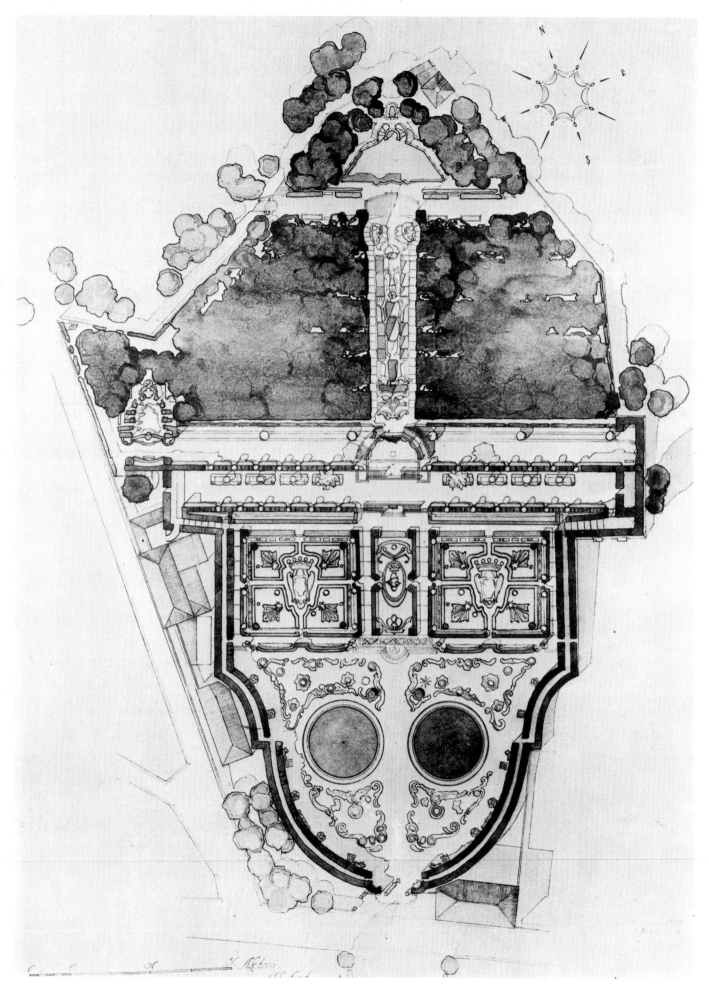

174   ITALY: MANNERISM AND BAROQUE

287

BAROQUE SPECTACLE in landscape reached a climax in the gardens of the **Villa Garzoni, Collodi**, near Lucca, made in 1652. The gardens are independent of the house, as shown in the **perspective** (**288**), but' the lower parterre is seen from the windows and merges into the background. The upper garden, with its tiny open-air theatre and shady *boschi*, would be domestic. The **view from below** (**287**) is pure scenery. The **plan** (**286**) is technically and aesthetically brilliant.

288

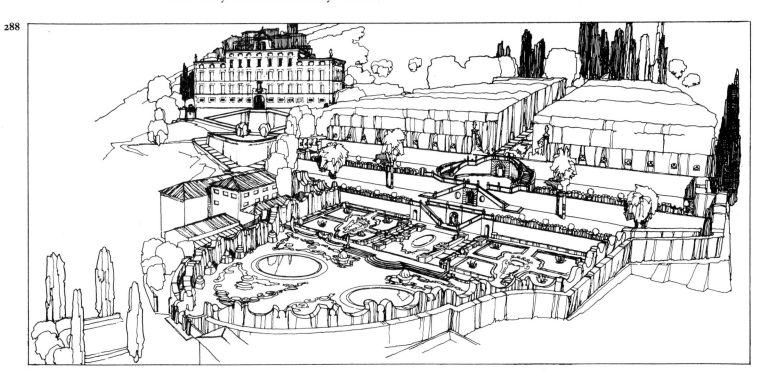

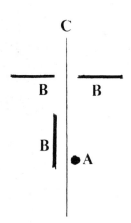

289 Tintoretto's 'Susannah and the Elders'
A Susannah
B Trellis screens
C Green arch

THE SHAPE OF VENICE (**290**) had been determined by the movement of water; its boundaries were the surrounding lagoon; its light was luminous; it was ruled by an oligarchy and not an absolute monarchy; and it was cosmopolitan and liberal-minded through its commercial relations with the East. From the beginning, therefore, it had all the elements of the ideal Baroque city which it was to become. The canvas was immense and capable of absorbing and harmonizing all periods of architecture. The **painting by Canaletto** (**291**) shows, from right to left, the Doge's Palace (1309–1424) with the Campanile behind, the Piazzetta columns, the classical St Mark's Library (1537) by Jacopo Sansovino and, in the distance, the pure Baroque church of Santa Maria della Salute, begun 1631, by Baldassare Longhena.

As a citizen of this restless, romantic city of unfinished compositions and infinite boundaries, Jacopo Tintoretto was the first painter deliberately to disintegrate classical form and re-create it with a new sense of space. His landscapes were made from models. **Susannah and the Elders** (**292**) was painted in 1556 and is analysed in the **diagram** (**289**): the fixed motifs are Susannah and the screens, around which the landscape moves as restlessly as the Elders. Just as Mantegna in neighbouring Padua had foreshadowed one aspect of landscape design, so Tintoretto appears to have foreshadowed another, far in advance of his age.

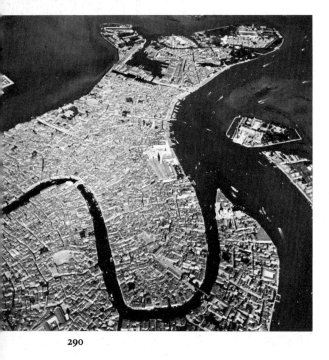

290

291

The Veneto had been dominated by Palladianism with its architectural gardens, but in the Euganian hills the **Villa Donà dalle Rose, Valzanzibio** (**293**) (1669), has close affinity with both painting and landscape-planning. The site lies within an amphitheatre of hills, from the upper centre of which a water axis leads gently downwards to the principal entrance, a ceremonial gateway on the approach canal. The cross axis, originally linked by avenues to the outer ends of the amphitheatre, leads from the villa itself by diminishing perspective (to exaggerate distance). Clipped hedges and shady walks of pleached limes define a plan that includes a maze and a rabbit island. The axes are in balance and raise a technical issue in design: if considered as architectural planning, the major axis is through the villa; but if as landscape-planning, the major axis is that which comes from the hills.

292

293

16 France: Sixteenth and Seventeenth centuries

Environment

91. The Paris basin comprehended the Seine and the Loire and was a natural geographical unit. This focusing on Paris was largely responsible for the centralization so characteristic of French life and history. Similarly, all French classical landscape was focused upon this one unit, for the Loire, with its subsidiary capital at Orléans, was the romantic complement to the Seine. The scenery of the basin as a whole was one of peaceful undulating corn-lands interspersed with cathedral or market towns, with here and there a château set in its canalized moat. Near Paris there were hardwood forests criss-crossed with straight rides for hunting. The climate was Atlantic-European with an average annual rainfall of twenty-four inches and a summer warm enough for vines. Paris itself was a densely populated and thriving city set on lines of continental communications, reshaped in the second half of the sixteenth century by the change of royal residence from the Île de France. Established in the Louvre (original royal residence *c.* 1400) and the Tuileries, the monarchy thenceforth never ceased to be attracted towards the west. In the Touraine lay the source of all the splendid water conceptions of seventeenth-century France.

Social History

92. In 1453 the English were practically expelled from French soil; France emerged as a united nation; and Charles VIII, invading Italy in 1495, experienced the first flush of the Renaissance. Francis I (r. 1515–47) obtained parity of power with Spain, and became the first French king to rule 'au bon plaisir'. Cultivated, elegant and appreciative of the Italian Renaissance, Francis invited eminent Italian artists and craftsmen to his court at Amboise on the Loire; among these were Vignola and Leonardo da Vinci. Following a period of instability, Cardinal Richelieu (1585–1642) came to power under Louis XIII (r. 1610–43) and virtually ruled France from 1624 to 1642, overcoming internal disorders rising from the Reformation, promoting national security abroad, and ruthlessly establishing the foundations of an absolute monarchy. On this basis Louis XIV (1661–1715) ruled for fifty years, shrewdly and efficiently, enlarging French influence abroad to become the dominant power in Europe, encouraging the arts and sciences at home, and creating in his Court at Versailles a civilization of pleasure that has had no equal. The vast expenditure involved was met by taxation from which the nobility and the Church were exempt, an injustice that led to the French Revolution in 1789.

Philosophy

93. Civilization as expressed by the monarchy was superficially one of delightful materialism. In this it differed from that of Italy, where there had always existed a passionate desire that art should convey something of the unknown world that lay beyond the senses. In contemporary France this was not so apparent: civilization centred upon the Sun King and the arts were in principle expressive of the pleasures of living. The acceptance and support by the public of such a monarchy at such a time was only possible because the majority still remained docilely Catholic. The Papacy itself was in general friendly to the French, becoming an agreeable instrument of policy. The philosopher whose theories were studied and put into practice, especially by Richelieu, was the Florentine Machiavelli: that princes were absolute, and that to ensure this the end justified the means. Light writers such as Molière (1622–73) were encouraged, provided they were in accord with the régime. Beneath this façade of uniformity, concern for moral values was expressed by Jansenism (Cornelius Jansen, 1585–1638). Blaise Pascal (1623–62), natural philosopher and mathematician, evolved the transformation of geometrical figures by conical and optical projection, and may thus have encouraged the three-dimensional geometry of Le Nôtre. The great original French philosopher of the period was Descartes (1596–1650), who settled in more liberal Holland.

Expression 94. Few churches were built, the energy being directed towards new country estates for monarch and nobility. The sixteenth century saw the creation in the Loire Valley of an almost total romantic water landscape stretching for over a hundred miles. Thereafter classicism gained control, great country layouts becoming more ordered and symmetrical. Cardinal Richelieu laid out perhaps the first domestic landscape design to comprehend a whole new town, named after himself. Influence continued to filter through from Italy but there was no daring innovation in space design until Vaux-le-Vicomte and the advent of Le Nôtre (1613–1700). His brief for the grand country-house was simple: to organize the landscape into one mighty scene that would express the dignity and elegance of man and delight his senses. All nature should conform. The supreme moments were those of carnival, with barges on the canals, fireworks and countless guests in the gardens. The concept of comprehensive landscape-planning, apparent at Richelieu, was fully realized in the gardens, palace and town of Versailles, which came to symbolize the power of a united nation.

Architecture 95. Sixteenth-century architecture grew from French Gothic with Italian grafted upon it. The moated château gave rise to an imaginative water relationship from which sprang Chenonceau (1515) and later inspired both moated house and independent canal at Vaux-le-Vicomte (1661). Gothic gave way to classic about 1600 but the spirit within was that of monarchist France rather than Italian Baroque. It is not surprising that Bernini's design for the Louvre in 1665 was rejected; although reliant upon environment, Italian Baroque architecture was still violently individual. In France the tendency towards total space organization made the individual building subservient to the whole. The French grouping of buildings might be likened to a military parade where all ranks were properly positioned and moved only on instruction; the Italian to a fashionable party, where eloquent and not so eloquent were in common medley and movement. This concept of the ordered assembly of buildings transformed Paris and inspired town-planning until the present century. It created the vast idea of town, palace and gardens of Versailles whose unity was subsequently impaired by the architect Hardouin-Mansart (1646–1708), apparently unappreciative of the composition as a whole.

Landscape 96. André Le Nôtre revolutionized French garden design, abolishing the idea of compartments and substituting that of totally organized space. The principles of composition were simple: (*a*) the garden no longer to be a mere extension of the house, which itself became part only of a great land composition; (*b*) solid as opposed to two-dimensional geometry based on axiality, related to an undulating site; (*c*) shape as though carved out of ordered woodlands and crisply defined by *charmilles* (clipped hedges); (*d*) the Baroque quality of unity with sky and surroundings achieved by water reflection and avenues leading indefinitely outwards; (*e*) the scale expanding as it receded from the house; (*f*) sculpture and fountains, themselves works of art, to provide rhythm and punctuate space; (*g*) the science of optics to direct the eye firmly without power to roam, and illusionist devices to make distance seem nearer or further; (*h*) the apparent revelation of the whole project in a glance, and the later element of surprise and contrast mainly in intimate woodlands; (*i*) the disposal of all parts, and especially of steps and stairways, for the dignity and enhancement of persons in movement; their scale to be larger than life, and thus to give a sense of being within an heroic landscape of the gods.

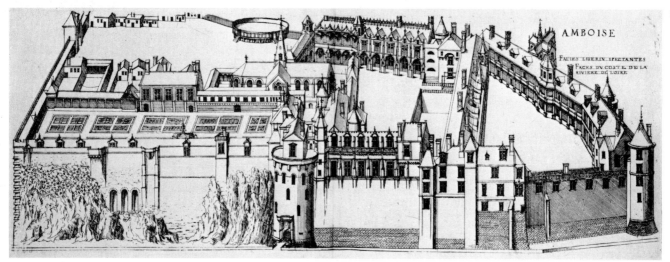

294

AMBOISE

FACIES LIGERIN IPECTANTES
FACES DV COSTE DE LA
RIVIERE DE LOIRE

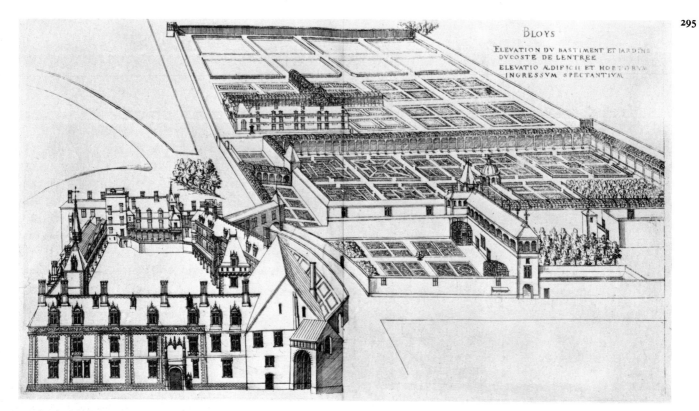

295

BLOYS

ELEVATION DV BASTIMENT ET IARDINS
DV COSTE DE LENTREE

ELEVATIO ÆDIFICII ET HORTORVM
INGRESSVM SPECTANTIVM

296

THE RENAISSANCE IN FRANCE began with the return of Charles VIII (r. 1483–98) from Italy in 1496, bringing with him architects, sculptors and men of letters to his home and birthplace at Amboise in the Loire Valley. The sixteenth century was a period of transition from medievalism to classicism; the essence of the Touraine landscape was the blend of romanticized indigenous Gothic architecture with the slowly maturing classicism. **Amboise (294)** was remodelled in 1496. The only sign of the new Italian influence is the garden extension, surrounded with lattice and pavilions (Italian designer: Pasello da Mercogliano). The gardens of **Blois (295)**, birthplace of Louis XII (*c.* 1500 by Mercogliano), are still medieval in their compartmentation, but their size and independence from the house reflect the growing love of the Renaissance landscape. At **Chenonceau (296)** on the River Cher the water scenery is essentially French in its poetic combination of medievalism and classicism. The castle itself was begun in 1515; the bridge was added by Philibert de l'Orme in 1557 and the gallery over by Jean Bullant *c.* 1576.

297, 298

Marie de Médicis married Henry IV in 1600, giving a superficial impetus to Italian influence upon French culture. A comparison between the form of the Boboli Gardens (**267**), her home in Florence, and the **Luxembourg Gardens (297)** shows a nostalgic similarity. The detail, however, was original and French. The **compartiments de broderie (298)**, for instance, were first introduced here by Boyceau (d. 1638), executed in box, flowers and coloured sands. Cardinal Richelieu (1585–1642), on the other hand, who unified France and laid the foundations of absolute monarchy, ushered in a new and pure French concept of comprehensive planning and space design. The landscape of the **Château de Richelieu (299)** in Touraine was a unified design carved out of woods, with decorative canals arising from drainage, and inclusive of a town as a subsidiary element. The concept, designed 1627–37 by J. Le Mercier, prepared the way for the work of Le Nôtre.

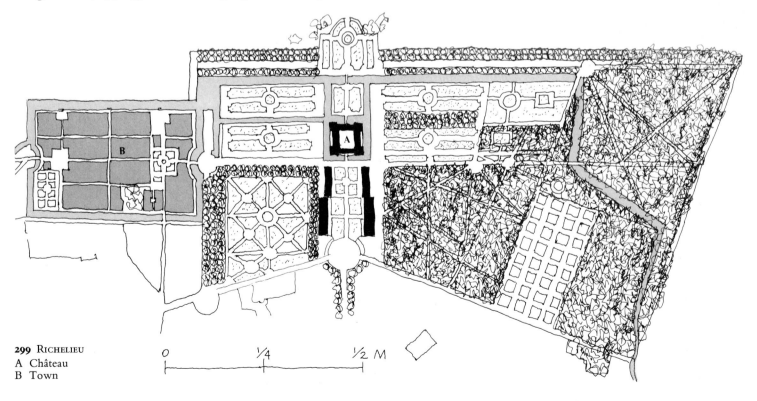

299 RICHELIEU
A Château
B Town

0   ¼   ½ M

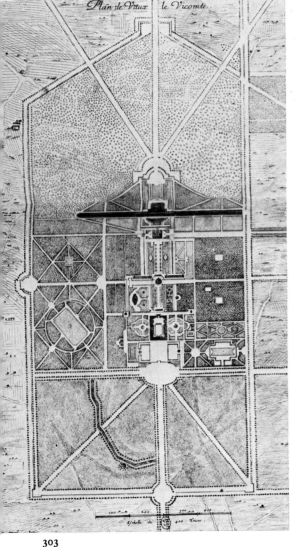

VAUX-LE-VICOMTE, completed 1661 for Fouquet, Finance Minister of Louis XIV, was the first major work of André Le Nôtre. The predecessor of both château (Le Vau, architect) and landscape was Richelieu (**299**), whose simple conception of space was transformed by Le Nôtre into an accomplished work of art. In principle, a single woodland compartment of gently falling and rising land has been sculptured to present at a glance a majestic scene of ground architecture. Apart from the skilful proportioning and subdivision by cross axes that disappear into the woods, and the rich carpeting, the design develops two important new principles: (*a*) architecture is secondary to landscape architecture and the scale expands outwards from the buildings to become heroic rather than domestic; and (*b*) the element of surprise withholds the grandest single feature, the sunk canal, from the first glance.

Many of the elements of the design are a re-creation of tradition, such as the **moat** (**300**) beside the château, beyond which lies the first comprehensive glimpse of the gardens. The **canal** (**301**) and the **retaining buttresses** (**305**) are interpretations of French traditions and on a scale greater than that of the château, as can be seen in the **backward view** (**304**). The masterly sense of landscape form is most easily appreciated when the **plan** (**303**), from an engraving by Silvestre, is studied in conjunction with the **air view** (**302**).

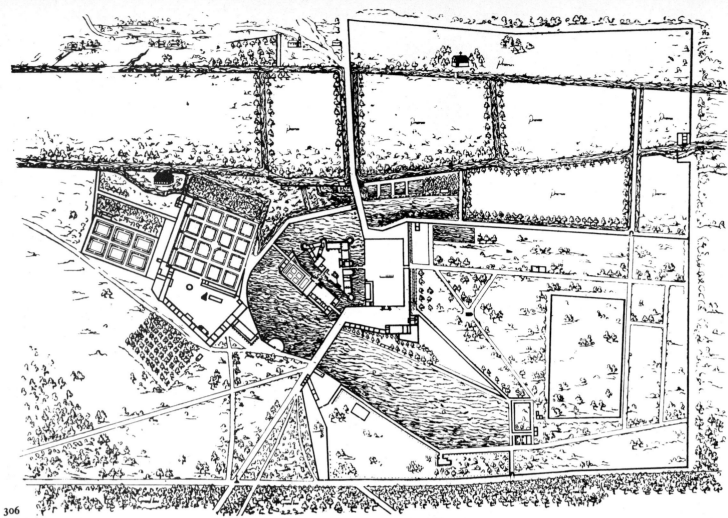

306

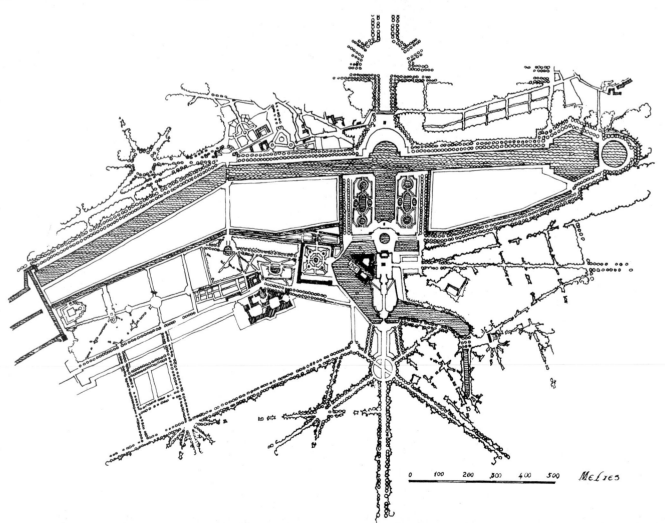

307

0 100 200 300 400 500   MELIES

AT CHANTILLY Le Nôtre carried his principles a stage further than at Vaux. The **original site** (306) comprised an old castle, triangular in plan, surrounded by a lake, without any conscious shaping of the landscape. **Le Nôtre's plan** (307) created a new main axis, but unlike Vaux did not feature the house as the central accent; here the castle has become secondary. A canal, similar to that of Vaux but even larger in dimensions, is again placed at right angles to the axis, but there is no element of surprise. Water embraces both castle and parterre gardens, and the project is primarily one of the spectacle of water pageantry. The scale of Le Nôtre's layout, as can be seen in the **air view** (309), is vast in relation to the historic castle. The two elements – castle and axis – are linked by the equestrian statue of the Grand Condé, for whom it was built. **Looking south** (308), one sees the canal in the foreground, the statue above its flight of steps in the middle distance; the vista is closed by the avenue approach.

308

309

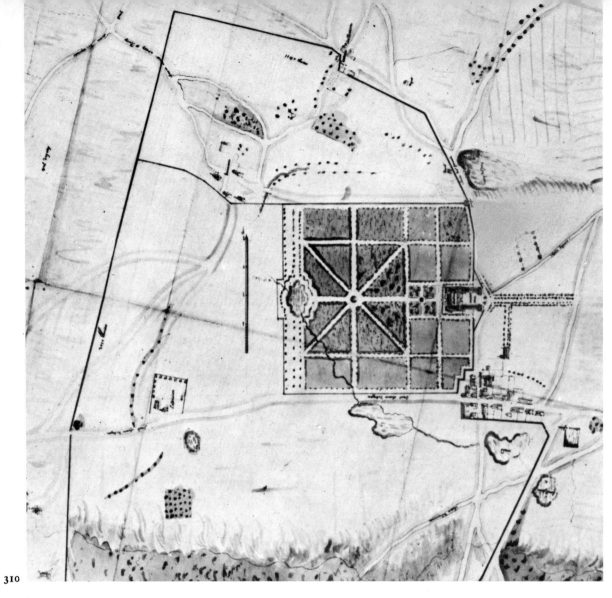

310

311

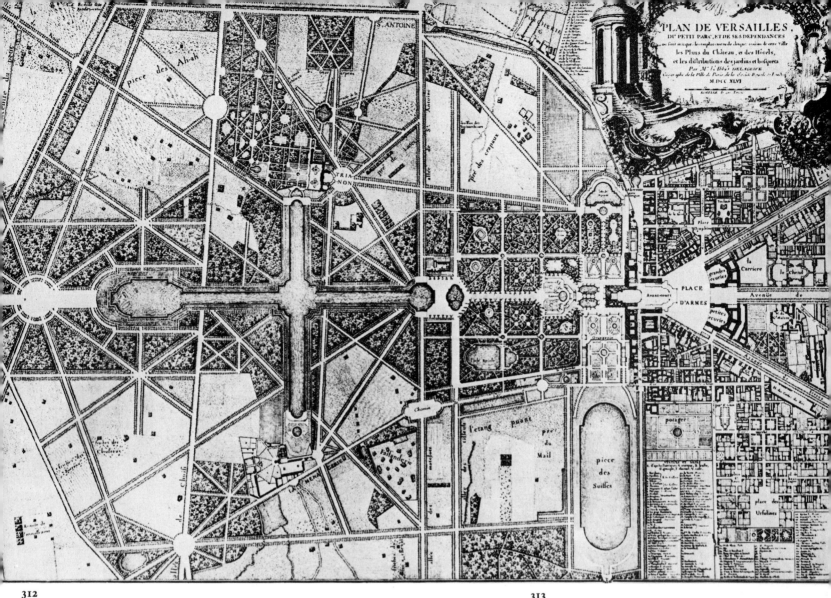

312

ALTHOUGH VERSAILLES WAS THE CULMINATION of the work of Le Nôtre, greatly exceeding Vaux and Chantilly in magnificence, it suffered from a late change in the shape of the palace which proved harmful to the concept of château, town and gardens as a single unit of landscape architecture. The process of evolution was as follows. A relatively modest **hunting lodge** (**310**) was begun in 1624 for Louis XIII. This was reconstructed after 1661 by Louis XIV; the **painting by Patel** (**311**) (*c.* 1668) shows that service wings have been added to the original moated château and that Le Nôtre has developed the main lines of the layout. In 1669 the moated château was embedded in a new front by Le Vau. In 1678 Hardouin-Mansart displaced Le Vau as architect, closed the central elevational recess and added the enormous wings. The **plan of the palace** (**313**) reconstructs the stages. The **plan of 1746** (**312**) made by the Abbé Delagrive shows Versailles as completed by Le Nôtre before 1700.

313

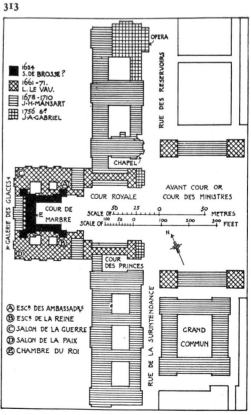

314   315

316   317

318   319

THE MOST SPLENDID EXPRESSION OF ABSOLUTE MONARCHY in history: from **the palace of Versailles (320)**, the distance passes into infinity. The shape is defined by trees and punctuated by sculpture seen against the clipped *charmilles* or hedges. The smaller views show the **grand canal across the fountain of Apollo (314)**, seen from the *tapis vert;* the **fountain of Apollo (315)** in play against the light; and **the cross canal from the Grand Trianon (316)**. Secretly within the woodlands are garden features that were in constant change, among them the **water colonnade (317)** by Mansart, the **obelisk fountain (318)** and the **children's fountain (319)**, behind which is seen a *charmille* in the making. Schools of open-air sculpture and fountain design ensured a consistent standard of detail that has never been surpassed in landscape.

320

321

322

323

324

325

THE TECHNICAL DESIGN OF VERSAILLES can be traced, among other sources, to the Piazza del Popolo in Rome, the Boboli Gardens in Florence, Richelieu, and to experience at Vaux-le-Vicomte and Chantilly. The challenge to landscape authority came when the palace began to expand in size and scale far beyond the original intention. Le Nôtre appears first to have responded by creating the inspired Baroque water cross of the canals. He left virtually unchanged the east–west cross axis, now encroached upon by the advancing palace, as shown in the **painting by J. B. Martin (321)** (*c.* 1745), and in the views of the **Dragon fountain (322)** and the **Neptune fountain (323)**; the eye is confined to the avenue, and the dwarfing by the Mansart wing is apparent only from the parterre. The treatment of the western arm of the cross axis, however, proved a triumph of landscape architecture. **The upper parterre (324)** was extended over a new orangery of noble modelling and architecture. The Swiss lake was enlarged. The colossal **stairways (325)** that flank the orangery on each side epitomize the Baroque art of Le Nôtre: they are large beyond reason; they pass into infinity; and they illustrate his basic conception that landscape should be greater, more heroic, than the buildings it comprehends.

17 Spain, Germany, England, the Netherlands: Sixteenth and Seventeenth centuries

Environment 97. The patchwork quilt of European countries that surrounded France was very diverse in texture. Climate, topography and geology produced one sort of variety; racial characteristics another; and external influences perhaps the most decisive. Without these variations the Renaissance from Italy might well have imposed a standard method of design. West of France, and separated by the Pyrenees, lay Portugal and Spain in a Mediterranean climate. Portugal was influenced by contacts with the Far East; Spain with the Muslim world even after the expulsion of the Moors, especially in Seville. East of France, Germany was a bundle of nervous semi-independent states, a forest country without real unity of structure or physical geographical character. Holland now emerged as a power out of the flat lands adjoining the North Sea to influence its neighbour England, and through England the domestic architecture of the North American colonies (Williamsburg was founded in 1693). England itself was prolifically and competently creating fine geometrical landscapes to fall in with its undulating agricultural pattern. So were the Scandinavians, with adaptations for climate, short summers and mixed topography. Overcoming problems of cold, the new civilizations had now advanced in strength to latitude 60° (St Petersburg founded 1703).

Social History 98. Charles V of Spain inherited the Netherlands in 1506 and the Holy Roman Empire of Germany in 1520, becoming the most powerful ruler in Europe. The age was one of absolute monarchy in the greater countries and of princely autocrats in the lesser, the Papacy endeavouring to maintain a balance of power. In due time the Spanish monarchy came to grief in chaotic Germany, failed against England and lost the Netherlands to allow Holland to make itself a republic by 1609; with all rivals in discord, France rose to predominant power in Europe. The first serious challenge to absolute monarchy as a principle came in England, whose liberal traditions were based on Magna Carta (1215), and which had broken with the Papacy in 1530. Here the nobility and wealthy citizens wished to be free to conduct their lives undisturbed on their country estates, some of which were as large as that of a German princeling. The undercurrents due to the Reformation, the discoveries of science, and enlightenment by the invention of printing, appear to have run independently of the princely diplomacy which settled the fate of nations. In the seventeenth century the condition of the peasant improved and over the period remained comparatively quiescent.

Philosophy 99. While Catholic and Protestant were in theological combat, allowing the lay monarchs to shake themselves free from the power of the Church, a new world of thought was originating from individuals whose ideas transcended nationality. Copernicus (b. Poland 1473), Kepler (b. Germany 1571), Galileo (b. Italy 1564) and Newton (b. England 1642) together form a chain of individual scientists that revealed and established laws of the universe which remained absolute until the present century. Descartes (b. France 1596), Spinoza (b. Spain 1634) and Leibnitz (b. Germany 1646) were founders of modern philosophy. Philosophic liberalism grew up mainly in England and in Holland, which became a haven of philosophic revolutionaries. Early scientific empiricism was based on Descartes's 'I think, therefore I am', which affirmed that each individual reasoned from his own existence and experience rather than from others'. Such an attitude presupposed religious toleration and contradicted the divine right of kings. While it believed in democracy and that all men are born equal, it tended to favour the middle classes and the rights of property. The principles were embodied in the work of John Locke (1632–1704), profoundly influenced thought in England, and subsequently formed the basis of the American constitution.

Expression *100.* Ideas emanating from Italy percolated to all parts of Europe, not being superseded by those of France much before the end of the seventeenth century. They were superficial inasmuch as they were fashionable, but eagerly sought since they expressed the new dignity of man. With few exceptions, the designers or interpreters did not experience the philosophic torments that had created the Renaissance and the Baroque in Italy: they were unconcerned with the movements of the heavens and the effects upon the soul: these things meant little. The arts of this period are a compromise between the indigenous and the Italian, and have more charm than quality and more inventiveness than scholarship. The most prolific landscape design, quantity-wise, was in insular England, where the political climate favoured the building of houses and gardens in the deep country. The great houses were influenced by fashion, but countless smaller manor-houses were designed harmoniously within the local landscape with little more than common sense and intuition.

Architecture *101.* The most exotic style of the period 1500 onwards was the Manueline in Portugal, followed by indigenous styles in Spain and Germany. In England, Tudor charm gave way to Italian purism when Inigo Jones (1573–1651) built the Whitehall Banqueting House. In the new republic of Holland there appeared the first broad urban landscape that was domestic rather than monumental: the geometrical canals were lined with tightly packed and well-proportioned brick houses which never repeated in design and yet were a coherent whole. The gardens were walled extensions of the house, rich in flowers and often with a look-out. The low domestic silhouette of Dutch cities was punctuated by tall church belfries and the land was so small, flat and unobstructed that one complex was visible from another. Between lay a geometrical pattern of fields through which ran the straight canals and dikes. Under this influence, and in opposition to the French, English architecture compromised between the domestic and the monumental, Christopher Wren (1632–1723) making Hampton Court Palace mainly of brick and Greenwich Hospital of stone: each according to its purpose and location.

Landscape *102.* Outside Italy and France the first preoccupation of landscape designers was to develop the garden from the medieval internal court into an external extension of the building. In medieval castles an outward view was obtained by perambulating the battlements or climbing a garden mount. In the new gardens, this idea sometimes reappeared in the form of a raised terrace, which disappeared when gardens grew in size and boundary walls receded. The period represents the emergence of the garden from a series of enclosed boxes to a coherent whole: by the end of the seventeenth century French influence in space design was established but without the mastery of geometry that was unique to Le Nôtre. The English added avenues to their huge rectilinear layouts, which were sometimes interlocked with those of their neighbours and reached such extent across the landscape as to cause a violent revulsion of feeling among aristocrat and commoner alike. England was a land of soft undulations, green grass and luxuriant trees, and in the next century was to reject the imposition of any foreign geometry whatsoever in landscape design.

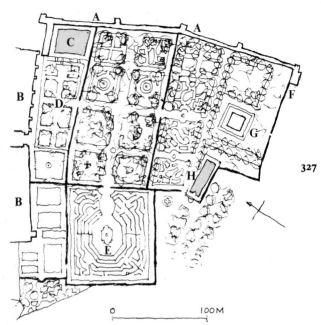

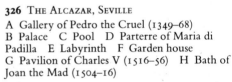

326 THE ALCAZAR, SEVILLE
A Gallery of Pedro the Cruel (1349–68)
B Palace   C Pool   D Parterre of Maria di
Padilla   E Labyrinth   F Garden house
G Pavilion of Charles V (1516–56)   H Bath of
Joan the Mad (1504–16)
328

SPAIN WAS THE MEETING-PLACE of Central and Western civilizations. Christian armies recaptured **Seville** in 1248, but the work added to the Alcazar after that time is still Moorish in character. During the sixteenth century Charles V again enlarged it with buildings in the Renaissance style, combining with the earlier work to produce a curious cultural blend. The **plan of the gardens** (**326**) shows how the periods overlap each other. A **Moorish pool** (**327**) is surrounded by a wall built by Don Pedro the Cruel. The **Pavilion of Charles V** (**328**) is similarly placed in a Moorish setting and owes much to Moorish art. When deprived of this element, Spanish planning is often slight and derivative. In the Americas Spain established new towns, based on principles exactly determined at home, which came to have individuality and charm; but she herself received little cultural fertilization from her Empire overseas.

329

THE PORTUGUESE IMAGINATION, on the other hand, was fired by the Eastern cultures with which Portugal came into contact. Highly inventive architecture and gardens developed from the sixteenth to the eighteenth centuries, among which was **Fronteira**, made at the end of the seventeenth century, a few miles from Lisbon. It consists of three elements, each drawn from a different background. The **parterre** (330) with its clipped hedges is early Italian Renaissance; the rectangular **water-tank** (329) is Moorish; while the gallery is lined with **coloured tiles** (*azulejos*) (331) which are indigenous to Portugal – decorative patterns on the upper part, blue and white equestrian figures overlooking the pool below. The **Baroque pool** (332) is probably eighteenth century.

331, 332

330

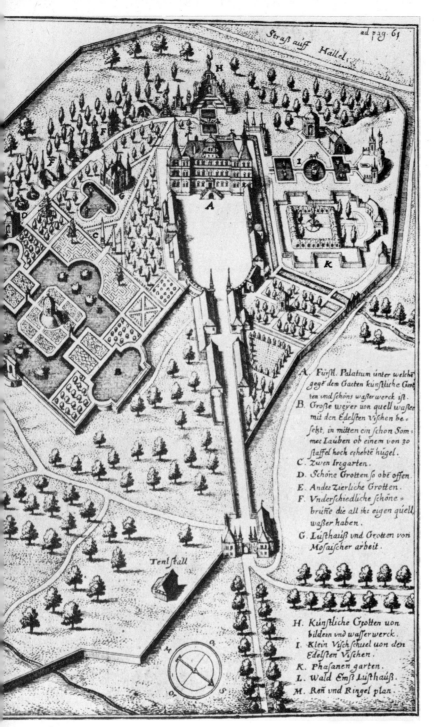

333 HELLBRUNN

A Palace, under which are grottoes and waterworks
B Large fishpond with rare fish; in the centre is a mount with an arbour on it
C Two mazes
D Grottoes
E Other grottoes
F Various fountains, each with its own spring
G Pavilion and grottoes in mosaic
H Grottoes with statuary and waterworks
I Small fishpond
K Pheasantry

334

335

AUSTRIA was the closest neighbour to Italy and the first state of the Holy Roman Empire to feel the influence of the new ideas. **Hellbrunn**, near Salzburg and close to the Alps (**333**), was laid out in 1613–19 for Archbishop Marcus Sitticus in a style that is playfully Italianesque. Water tricks and fantasies abound. The south windows, for instance, look across **water-scenery** (**334**) towards a **dining table** (**335**) and seats with secret jets for guests but not for the host.

GERMANY before the Thirty Years War (1618–48) comprised a number of small states whose rulers vied with each other in the arts and sciences. The centre of culture was Heidelberg, whose university had been founded in 1385, the oldest in Germany. **Heidelberg Castle** itself (**337**) was begun for the Electors Palatine in the thirteenth century, but the principal buildings were erected between 1531 and 1618, when the great garden was completed from designs by Salomon de Caus. The castle stands dramatically 330 feet above the Neckar and the garden terraces are the ultimate expression of a medieval garden. The century was too disturbed for the furtherance of landscape design, but love of flowers and interest in botany continued to grow; the **woodcut by Joachim Sandrart** (**336**) comes from an anthology of plants published in Nuremberg in 1650.

336

337

338
339

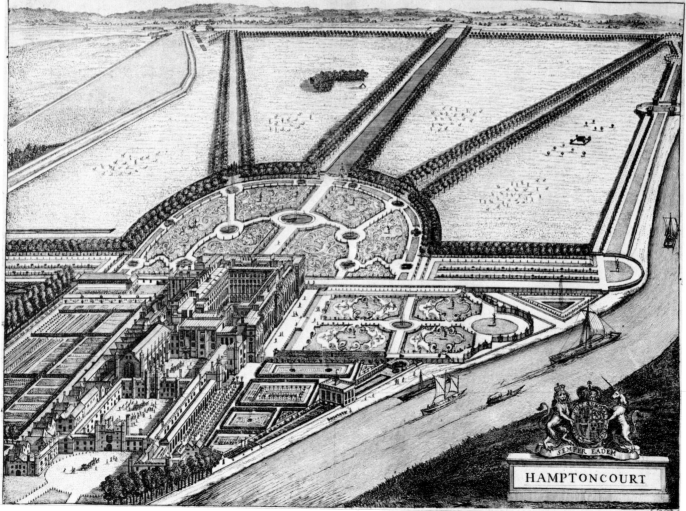

HAMPTONCOURT

340

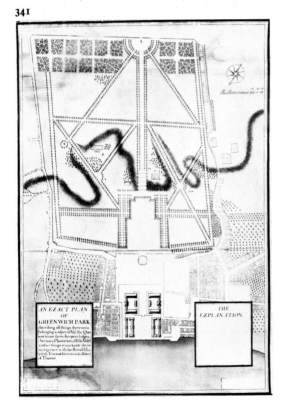

341

ENGLAND in the seventeenth century, despite an inherent love of gardens and interest in horticulture, remained a province of France – and to a lesser extent of Italy – in respect of landscape design. The avenue carved out of the French forests became the open avenue that proliferated across the English countryside. But beside the fashionable layouts of great estates were certain areas that remained wholly English. One of these was the River Thames, bordered by lush meadows, luxurious trees and rich diversification of architecture and gardens from Hampton Court to Greenwich Palace – a river described by Joseph Addison as the noblest in Europe. **Hampton Court (339)** was a Tudor palace partly rebuilt by Wren as an English Versailles in 1699, when the park was laid out by London and Wise. Although the gardens have charm of detail, the layout lacks the mature technique of Le Nôtre. Moving downstream by barge, an early-eighteenth-century traveller would enjoy a gradually unfolding panorama that reached a climax with the **view of the dome of St Paul's (338)**, engraving by Rooker after Canaletto, riding above Wren's post-fire silhouette of towers and spires. Then, after negotiating London Bridge, he would pass on to **Greenwich Hospital (340)**, a complex of different dates and architects, but nevertheless the most monumental and co-ordinated of all English landscape plans. In the centre was the Queen's House (1618–39) by Inigo Jones; to the right, the King Charles block (1661–67) by John Webb; while the remainder was created from 1699 onwards by Christopher Wren followed by John Vanbrugh and Nicholas Hawksmoor. (The painting by A.W.N. Pugin shows the funeral of Nelson.) The **contemporary plan (341)** emphasizes the Baroque principles of outward expansion of space across the river and the subordination of architecture to landscape composition. The Queen's House, very small in scale, becomes a central *objet d'art*, an incident only, within a grand design, punctuated by the twin domes, that extended from Blackheath to the Thames.

ENGLAND 199

342

343

344

THE PAINTERS OF HOLLAND were to have a profound effect on the way Western man saw the world about him. Political freedom allowed scientists and philosophers to develop new ideas, including the realization that man was not the centre of the universe, but a fragment in the totality of nature. Even the most commonplace object now acquired a status. The men and women of Holland themselves lived in neat brick houses where small geometrically enclosed gardens astonished the traveller on the canals with the richness and variety of their individual furnishings, including sculpture and colourful flowers. But the artists made them look outside the planned environment altogether – an attitude that was to lead to the Picturesque and then to romanticism. Hobbema in **The Avenue, Middelharnais (342)**, finds that most classical of features, the symmetrical avenue, but finds it almost by chance, strung along the ditches of a country road. In Jacob van Ruisdael's **View of Haarlem (343)** the town has become only one element in an immensity of land and sky. **Evening landscape with horseman and shepherds (344)** by Albert Cuyp goes further towards romanticism; the scene is more Italian than Dutch, owing something to Salvator Rosa and Claude.

The full significance and inherent beauty of the planet's atmosphere was unconsciously recognized by the Dutch painters of the seventeenth century, far in advance of science.

Part Two

THE EVOLUTION
OF MODERN LANDSCAPE

During the sixteenth, seventeenth and eighteenth centuries, the Western civilizations began to transform themselves from a restrictive to a liberal society. Their classical basis of philosophy and law had enabled them, through scientific inquiry, freedom of enterprise and social mobility, to prosper and expand to a greater extent than the Central and Eastern civilizations with their static basis of religion or ethics. From this time began the universal interchange of ideas that ultimately lifted landscape arts from the level of local and domestic design to the modern concept of comprehensive planning.

THE EIGHTEENTH CENTURY

Environment   *103.* With the exception of Japan, all parts of the civilized world were now in commercial communication. South and Central America had already been partitioned between Spain and Portugal and continued to pour wealth into Europe; North America was almost wholly English-speaking. Discoveries of sea routes round the Cape of Good Hope in South Africa had opened up trade between Europe and the East and colonies were lodged everywhere. The voyages were hazardous, but more manageable than the land routes, and heavily laden ships interchanged both goods and ideas. The monarchies of Versailles and Peking were both keenly inquisitive one of another, but the traffic in ideas was almost entirely from East to West, to have far-reaching effects upon landscape. A global characteristic begins to appear for the first time. Apart from ideas in design, plants were now freely circulated, in due time to multiply, mix with indigenous species, and enrich local scenery beyond the power of natural distribution to do so.

Historical   *104.* By the eighteenth century the unifying force of medieval Christendom had finally vanished and its place as a power been taken by absolute monarchy in small as well as great countries. Following the decline of Spain, the French monarchy under Louis XIV rose to a dominating position in Europe; Germany was a complex of small principalities still recovering from the Thirty Years War; the Papacy, with little influence, was supporting France; and only Protestant England and Holland could act as a counterpoise. As French power declined after the death of Louis XIV, so that of England grew. Britain ruled in India and her colonies, now established throughout the world, so prospered that the most vigorous, that in North America, fought for and won independence in 1783. In Europe, Sweden and Denmark, unable to take advantage of the discoveries of the New World, were reduced in stature though not in culture. Russia under Peter the Great, while looking towards the West, was expanding eastwards almost to the frontiers of the vast Chinese Empire of the Manchus (1644–1912). At the end of the century Prussia emerged as a major power under Frederick the Great and Poland had vanished from the map. It was a merciless European age of the power politics of princes.

Social   *105.* Absolute monarchy remained little disturbed in the East, but in Europe it became increasingly unacceptable; in 1789 came the French Revolution. Opposed to the system of absolute monarchy were republican Holland and the special parliamentary monarchy of England. The English aristocracy preferred a monarch by invitation from overseas who ruled as a symbol rather than one from home who ruled by divine right. The country was ruled by Parliament, and Parliament by the landed gentry whose primary interest lay in the protection of their way of life on a country estate. In France the aristocracy was centred round Versailles, but in England the town-house was no more than a distinguished *pied-à-terre*. In 1700 the poorer classes were seemingly content, but throughout the eighteenth century the wealthy became more so and a new class was thriving on the colonies. The aristocrat had sufficient means and leisure to accumulate knowledge, travel abroad, make collections and yet run his estate so intelligently that he could harmonize his learned classicism with the simplicities of the countryside. At the end of the century the English landscape was formed of a sequence of immense green parks set in an agricultural pattern, whose mansions were veritable treasure-houses of the arts.

Economic *106.* The wealth pouring into Spain following the conquest of Mexico and Peru had upset and ruined the home economy, helping to reduce that country to a second-class power but providing partial benefit to Europe as a whole. In France, the revenue to support monarch, aristocrat and clergy was raised to the limits by taxation of the poor. In England, revenue in principle was raised by the rents of tenant farmers and relations between tenant and landlord were more personal and better adjusted. The traditional system of agriculture was that of strip farming, the peasant working several strips that were normally separated. This was uneconomic use of land and throughout the century Enclosure Acts were passed that erected the hedge and field system of today. Production was increased in this and other ways to the mutual advantage of country and landowner, but to the disadvantage of the peasant class. Towards the end of the century, industrialization in the towns promised a more secure living and there began a migration from the land and an increase of factory population that would soon change the British economy from one of agriculture to one of machine production. Canals were a forerunner of the future urban expansion that was soon to encroach unimpeded upon the countryside.

Philosophy *107.* It was the Age of Reason. By 1700 the Church had lost countenance with the influential and educated classes, who determined that the one true God to be worshipped was not the God of the Testament, but the nation itself. The empiricists John Locke (1632–1704), George Berkeley (1685–1753) and David Hume (1711–76) laid the philosophical foundation for science and cut it finally from revealed religion. It was of special significance to landscape that to help fill a spiritual vacuum which disturbed all thinking men, the philosophers Leibnitz and Voltaire (1694–1778), himself an Anglophile, turned to the newly acquired knowledge of China. The writings of Confucius (*c.* 550–478 BC) were translated and studied, providing a moral rather than a theological attitude to life; and associated with this revolutionary concept of a reasoned rather than a revealed religion were stories of the physical environment of China itself. The stories were exaggerated and idealized, but the ideas percolated into every European country. In opposition to this, but in sympathy with the revolt against the accepted order, was the philosopher Rousseau (1712–78), who advocated the return to nature and the state of the 'noble savage'.

Expression *108.* Three schools of thought intermingled to motivate landscape design: (*a*) Western classicism, which emanated from Baroque Italy or through the Grand Monarchy of France, whom the majority of European states sought to copy and rival; (*b*) China, which the French Court at first seized upon for its frivolity and novelty, not recognizing the inner quality of symbolism. The principles of irregularity of this school became so confused with those of the English as to be known on the Continent as 'Anglo-Chinese'; (*c*) England, which was in revolt against classicism in landscape (though not in architecture) and in favour of the expression of a totally new and liberal age. The aesthetic roots of this school may be traced, through painting, to beginnings in Italy, but the movement was primarily literary and native, already foreshadowed in the writings of Milton (1608–74). By mid-century its influence was felt throughout Europe, intermingling with that of *chinoiserie*.

Italian Influence *109.* In Italy itself Baroque energy in painting and landscape remained vital through such individuals as the Venetian painters G. B. Tiepolo (1696–1770), G. A. Canaletto (1697–1768), G. F. Guardi (1712–93) and the Roman architects N. Salvi (1699–1751) and F. de Sanctis (1693–1740). The Italian influence abroad continued to widen. Austria was physically and emotionally closer to Italy than to France, and the defeat of the Turks outside Vienna in 1683 created an unprecedented exuberance of spirit that for a brief period flowered in Baroque architecture and the landscapes of palaces and monasteries. Inspiration was both Italian and Austrian. The Belvedere at Vienna is a classical Baroque canvas of gardens, city and sky; in contrast the Monastery of Melk is a romantic Baroque composition, based on medieval relation to site. Elsewhere in Europe, with the possible exceptions of Holland and Portugal (Lisbon replanned 1755), classical landscape was mainly influenced by the French, architecture by the Italians; Wilhelmshohe is a freak composite of Italy, France and England. In England the new and revolutionary concept of romantic landscape that had taken the place of classicism, turned architecturally as a compensating and stabilizing factor to the strict Italian Palladianism of two centuries earlier. A hybrid Baroque architecture was introduced into China by the Jesuits for Ch'ien Lung (Emperor 1735–96), together with hydraulic experimental fountains and other delights.

French Influence *110.* French landscape energy was now concentrated at the Court of Versailles, and in the extension of the Tuileries in Paris. Landscape was further to merge into town-planning: at Nîmes a fortress engineer inserted a landscape spine to co-ordinate the town plan as a whole (1740), and in the Place Stanislas at Nancy (1760) pleached limes were an integral and permanent part of the architectural structure of town design. The French sense of the organization of space dominated the era, laying the foundations of an autocratic form of town-planning which created Washington and most major new cities until modern times. Emulation of the Grand Monarch led to prodigious projects by the independent German princes, many of whose landscape estates have since become the basis of a modern town. The declining Spanish monarchy followed the French closely, but the landscape architecture of the Tsars of Russia, who founded St Petersburg in 1703, was more independent and cosmopolitan, being influenced by Baroque Italy and their own Oriental traditions as much as by contemporary France.

Comment *111.* Throughout the century French classical influence mingled with Italian to encourage extension of formal space through geometry. The main elements were the closed avenue with open spaces and these turned easily from the green walls of clipped *charmilles* into the streets and squares of city-planning. Germany rather than France established the conditions for landscape expression of all kinds, sometimes to the point of freakishness. Originality and inventiveness appeared in innumerable landscapes and gardens, foreshadowing the German outburst of philosophy and art at the end of the century. The development of the concept of landscape-planning as an extension of parks and even town-planning, may have been due to land claustrophobia. Potsdam, for example, was an expression of the aspirations of a monarch, Frederick the Great, who founded the greatness of the Hohenzollern dynasty; in the plan and its universal elements was the mark of an enlightened autocrat and brilliant administrator whose territorial ambitions extended far beyond his own limited boundaries.

The Monastery of Melk, Austria (345), symbolizes Counter-Reformation confidence, projecting it into the new century. It was begun in 1702, to the designs of Jakob Prandtauer. In its triumphant use of the steep site overlooking the Danube it is a proclamation of the same spirit that created Durham (237) five centuries previously.

FOR RESIDENCE AND ENTERTAINMENT ON THE GRAND SCALE, **the Belvedere Palaces** in Vienna, designed for the national hero, Prince Eugene of Savoy, by Lukas von Hildebrandt, were begun in 1700 and completed in 1723. The gardens were laid out in collaboration with François Girard. The **print (349)** shows the complex of palace gardens: on the left is the Lower Belvedere for summer residence and above is the Upper Belvedere for entertainment. The gardens of the lower are compartmented, domestic and shady; maple is trained to make meticulous green walls twelve inches thick and twelve feet high. The upper gardens are larger in scale, open and, together with the lower, could accommodate up to six thousand guests. Despite disparity of ideas, the two parts are integrated into a single design. Unlike the concepts of Le Nôtre, the gardens appear from above to be architectural and finite, but the siting and sky reflections as seen from the upper terrace in relief extend the gardens beyond their rigid boundaries. The **painting by Bernard Bellotto (346)** in mid-century is from the upper palace overlooking the city. On the right, the Salesian nunnery and the low-roofed Lower Belvedere; in the centre, St Stephen's Cathedral; on the left, the Schwarzenberg Palace (begun 1697) by Fischer von Erlach. The **view up the central axis (347)** shows the unity of architecture and landscape. There is no obvious central path, for the line of circulation between the palaces, punctuated by **ramp-stairways (348)**, has been divided and relegated to the boundaries.

346

347

348

349

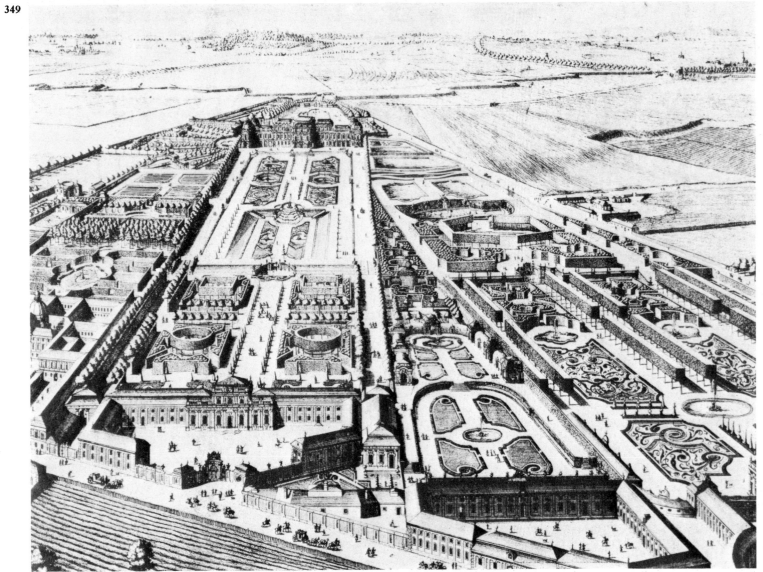

THE AUTHORITARIAN IDEAL of classicism was taken to extremes in the small independent duchies of Germany, which, by originality and boldness, tried to out-Versailles Versailles. Two such were Karlsruhe and Wilhelmshohe. **Karlsruhe (350)**, built to the glory of Margrave Karl Wilhelm of Baden-Durlach, was begun in 1709. From the palace, with its octagonal centre, radiate thirty-two avenues, those at the back dividing the park and those in front forming the skeleton of the new town. The proposals for **Wilhelmshohe (352)** were even more gigantic for a community with small resources. In 1701 the Landgrave of Hesse, with the advice of a Frenchman, Denis Papin, laid out an avenue of four miles from the centre of Kassel to the centre of an arc of the escarpment of the Habichtswald. On the summit is a great octagon visible from the town above the palace roof. Only part of the **cascade (351)** by the Italian G.F. Guerniero was completed, but even this fragment outdid any single similar feature anywhere. The statue of Hercules is 33 feet high, with room for eight persons within the club. The obelisk below is 98 feet, the cascade itself to the platform below the octagon is 130 feet and the whole is 1,360 feet above the River Fulda at Kassel.

In mid-century and at the beginning of a second stage of fantastic works, fashion changed to romanticism, but with skilful interweaving the basic classic character was retained. Other views show the **avenue from the palace (353)** and the **relation of palace to octagon (354)**.

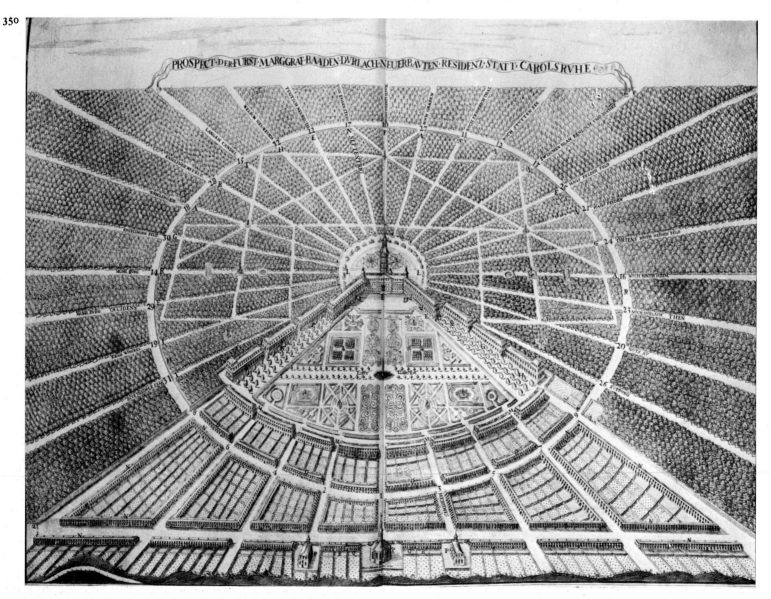

350

PROSPECT·DER·FURST·MARGGRAF·BAADEN·DVRLACH·NEUERBAVTEN·RESIDENZ·STATT·CAROLSRVHE

351

352 WILHELMSHOHE

Classical landscape begun 1701
A Octagon
B Cascade and central axis
C Palace
D Reservoir
Romantic landscape added mid-eighteenth
century
E Reservoir
F Roman aqueduct
G Greek temple
H Lake
I Gothic castle

353   354

355 PANORAMA OF ST PETERSBURG ACROSS THE RIVER NEVA

St Isaac's Cathedral   Admiralty spire
The Winter Palace and Hermitage

The Exchange on Vasilevsky Island

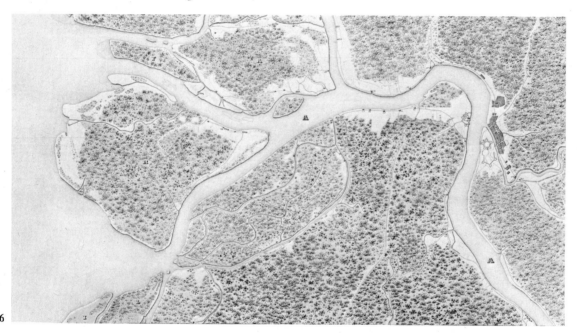

356

357

359 ST PETERSBURG
A Magazine   B Peter and Paul Fortress
C Exchange   D Admiralty   E Imperial
Palace (Winter Palace)   F St Isaac's Cathedral
G Nevsky Prospect

ST PETERSBURG (now Leningrad), founded by Peter the Great in 1703 as a strategic 'window on to Europe' and as the new capital of Russia, illustrates uniquely the evolution of an ambitious classical urban waterscape from an unpromising site. The site is on the Neva delta where it enters the Baltic and is shown in its original condition in the **map of 1700 (356)**. On the right is an abandoned Swedish fortress. The land was waterlogged and unfit for building; materials such as stone had to be brought from afar.

The **plan of 1716–18 (357)** shows the basis of the modern city. In 1703 the Peter and Paul fortress had been built on an island on the north bank of the Neva. In 1704 the Admiralty fortress and shipyards were built on the south bank and the radial roads envisaged but not constructed. Soon after this, A. Le Blond (1679–1719), a pupil of Le Nôtre, planned a gigantic oval city on the Vasilevski Island (between the arms of the Neva) to co-ordinate the two existing centres. The proposals were not accepted and a gridiron plan substituted. Commerce and society generated by the Admiralty now finally established the major city centre on the south bank. The Admiralty spire symbolically remained the visual focus.

The **plan of 1846 (358)** is virtually that of the central area of today. During the eighteenth century the looseness and excessive width of the waterscape

Peter and Paul Fortress

Cathedral of Peter and Paul

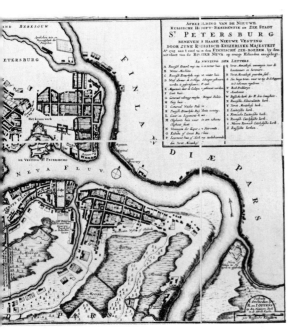

358

360

composition was continuously recognized. The water-front opposite the
Peter and Paul fortress was extended with a wall of palaces and the designer
of the Winter Palace (1754–62), the Italian B. F. Rastrelli, created the distant
domes of the Smolny convent (1748–64, far right in the bend of the river)
with a true Baroque sense of silhouette. In 1804–10 the Exchange (Thomas
de Thomon, architect) was critically sited and built on the tip of the Vasilevski
Island (known as Strelka), to attempt to unify the two sides of the river. In
1818 St Isaac's Cathedral (H. A. Montferrand, architect) was sited inland
as part of the cityscape, the dome alone being visible from the Neva.

The **panorama** (355) looks west from a bridge across the Neva. The
architecture derives from classical Europe, the spires from the Baltic
countries. Although the waterscape was not created with the topographical
skill and assurance that seemed intuitive to the Venetians over centuries,
there is a majesty of size here and in the city spaces that suggests the huge
scale of the Russian land mass. Uncertainty in space design may have been
due to inexperience in classical landscape and reliance on foreign designers.
More assured are the almost accidental scenes of the coloured façades of
classical palaces seen along the canalized streams, such as the **River Moika**
(**360**).

THE PERIMETER COUNTRIES OF EUROPE, until well into the century, were dominated by Italian or French classicism, either calling in foreign designers or employing native talent to interpret the new fashionable styles. The water approach from the Baltic to **Peterhof** (Petrodvorets) (**362**), the palace of Peter the Great outside St Petersburg, was designed by Le Blond in 1717 without the maturity of his master Le Nôtre. The façade of the **Catherine Palace at Tsarskoe Selo** (Pushkin) (**361**) was designed by Rastrelli in mid-century for Peter's daughter, the Empress Elizabeth; but the foreground parterre of red, grey and black stone chippings was French. The park of **Frederiksborg** (**363**) in Denmark was designed by the Danish designer J. C. Krieger *c.* 1720, mainly as a spectacle to be seen from the castle windows. The **original plan** (**365**) is a delightful conglomeration of French and Italian techniques seen through Danish eyes. View (**364**) shows the **castle from the oval pool**.

361, 362

363

364

365

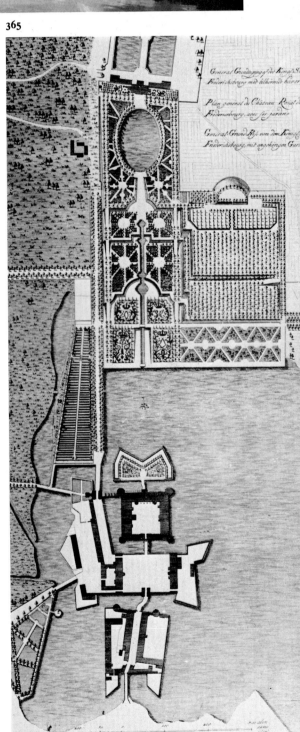

368

369

FRENCH INFLUENCE IN SPAIN predominated in landscape design, only mildly modified by Moorish influence. The **water stairway at La Granja, San Ildefonso (366)**, with its coloured tiled risers, is part of a considerable complex made in 1720–40 by Philip V. Attributed to the Frenchman Boutelet, the design conforms to the romantic configuration of the land but lacks the French sense of total organization. Inspired undoubtedly by La Granja and in direct rivalry with Versailles, Philip's son Charles III, Spanish King of Naples, created the longest and most flamboyant cascade in history at **Caserta (367)**, designed by the Italian L. Vanvitelli in 1752.

In Portugal, the *genius loci* was more powerful, the inclination domestic rather than monumental and cosmopolitan rather than strictly European. French influence was less pronounced and the landscape design that evolved was an original Baroque composite of Italy, France, Moorish Africa and the Far East. In 1755 the centre of Lisbon was destroyed by earthquake. The **map of Lisbon (370)** made in 1785 shows the new plan prepared by Portuguese engineers, uniting town and Tagus in a great riverscape composition; to the immediate right is the ancient labyrinthine Alfama, clustered round the citadel. Near Lisbon are the **palace and gardens of Queluz (368)** made 1758–94 under the direction of the Frenchman J. R. Robillon and the native Mateus Vincente. The **garden canal (369)** is contained within walls topped with classical statues and urns and covered with traditional *azulejos*, or coloured tiles, blue and white on the inside, yellow and white on the outside.

370

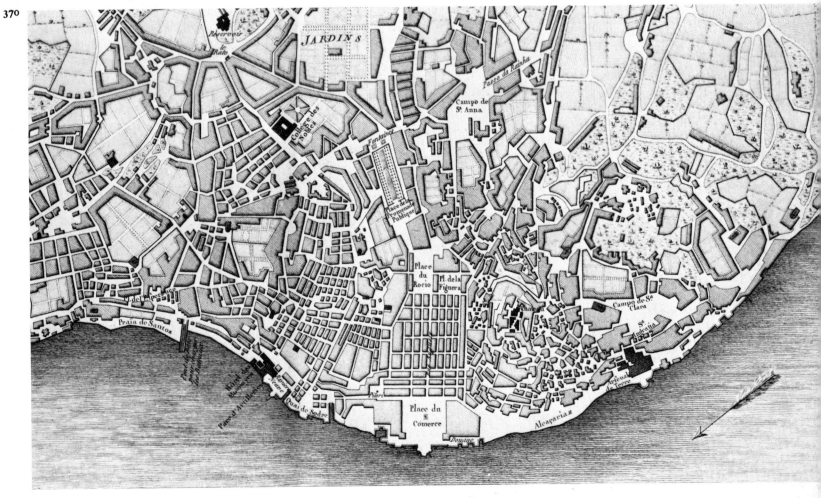

By mid-century the authoritative straight line across the landscape, the ideal of which had been the enclosed tree-lined avenue, began to take note of the environment through which it passed, whether urban or rural. At **Nîmes**, the sacred Roman mountain landscape of the Fountain was converted in 1740 by the Director of Fortifications into the public **Jardin de la Fontaine (371)**. From this extended an avenue and canal to spread a sense of landscape and give classical cohesion to a medieval and Roman city. The **plan of the park at Potsdam (372)**, based on a contemporary print, shows a two-thousand-yard central axis giving cohesion to a landscape environment composed of all current fashionable schools: Baroque, *chinoiserie* and *jardin anglais*. Here the most original contribution of the formidable and catholic-minded creator, Frederick the Great, was his personal conception of the functional **terraces of vineyards (373)**, woven into the architecture of Sans-Souci (1744, G. W. von Knöbelsdorff, architect), unique in Western classicism and a pointer to the future.

371 NÎMES
A Jardin de la Fontaine B Temple of Diana (Roman) C Canal D Tour Magne (Roman) E Maison Carrée (Roman) F Amphitheatre (Roman) G Hanging woods H Original course of river
Inset shows the central area enlarged

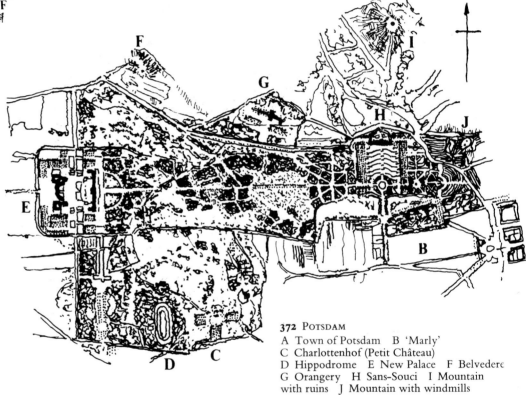

372 POTSDAM
A Town of Potsdam B 'Marly'
C Charlottenhof (Petit Château)
D Hippodrome E New Palace F Belvedere
G Orangery H Sans-Souci I Mountain with ruins J Mountain with windmills

373

374

375

THE NATURAL AND THE MAN-MADE ENVIRONMENT – eighteenth-century man was keenly aware of both, deriving pleasure from juxtaposing them, setting up tensions between them or resolving them into harmony. Nowhere can this be appreciated more clearly than in the Baroque fountains of Rome and the **Trevi fountain (374, 375)** in particular, inspired by Bernini, and erected between 1732 and 1762 from designs by N. Salvi and G. Pannini, architects, and (mainly) Filippo della Valle and P. Bracci, sculptors. This great monument to the papacy and the spirit of man as the centre of the universe is the climax of a struggle to retain the panoply and dignity of classical man in a changing world. The triumph is complete. The designers have created order and harmony out of the apparent chaos of natural rock form, by pure abstract design. The Trevi fountain is a supreme work of classical landscape art. Like the cave art of Lascaux, it is the final statement of a world of ideas whose transformation had already begun in northern Europe, a world in which nature's relation to man was to be one of partnership rather than subordination.

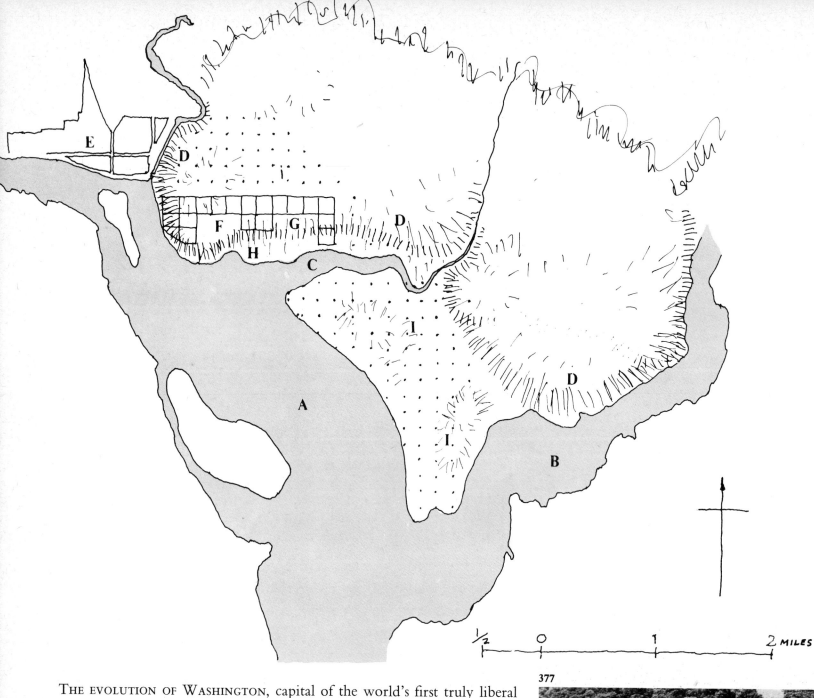

377

THE EVOLUTION OF WASHINGTON, capital of the world's first truly liberal
society, presented the problem of style and form. George Washington, the
first President, had designed his own home in 1785, **Mount Vernon
(377)**, combining monumental English Palladianism with traditional
Virginian domestic charm; the flower-garden, for instance, is balanced with
the kitchen garden, an idea unheard of in aristocratic England. Responsibility
for the new design for Washington was given to Secretary of State Thomas
Jefferson, who travelled widely in Europe to study the relevant shape of
cities. The site on the Potomac was chosen with surprising sensibility for so
immature a nation and **Jefferson's own first sketch**, interpreted above
(**376**), shows his grasp of the elements of landscape design. Although his
inclinations were towards Palladianism, the Capitol and the President's
house were placed charmingly and unclassically side by side overlooking
a long reach of the river, each in an enclave of buildings. The engagement
of a professional town planner was now of primary importance and the
choice fell on a Frenchman, Pierre Charles L'Enfant, partly because America
was at war with England and partly because the tradition of classical
monumental planning for absolute monarchy appealed to Jefferson as being
equally appropriate for a liberal society.

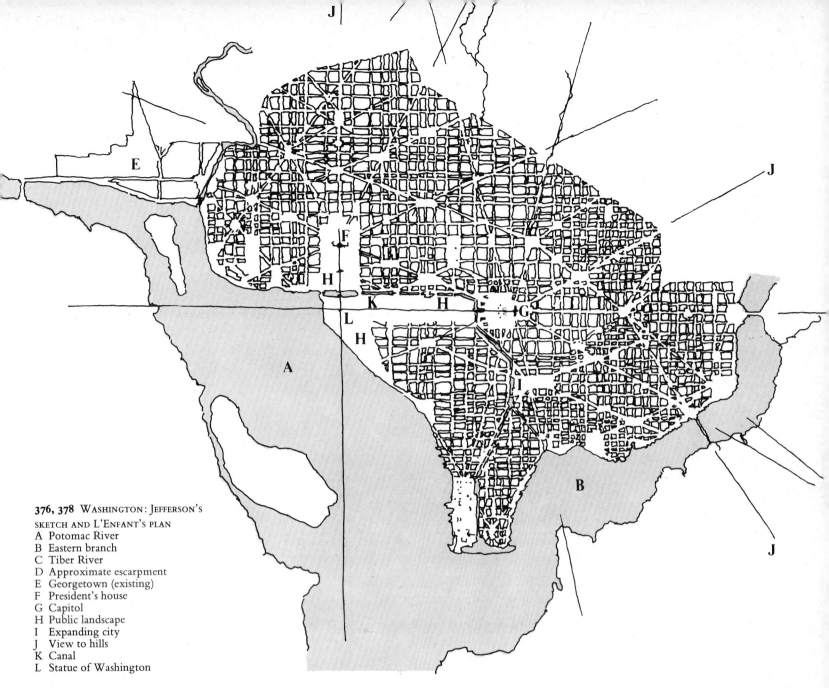

J

376, 378 WASHINGTON: JEFFERSON'S
SKETCH AND L'ENFANT'S PLAN
A Potomac River
B Eastern branch
C Tiber River
D Approximate escarpment
E Georgetown (existing)
F President's house
G Capitol
H Public landscape
I Expanding city
J View to hills
K Canal
L Statue of Washington

L'Enfant's plan of Washington (378) (1791) expanded and superseded that of Jefferson. Although based on formal French principles, the design was so beautifully informed by its setting that in idea at least it was a more enlightened approach to nature than had been shown by absolute monarchy. The Capitol was moved one and a half miles eastwards to an escarpment; two great axes were formed to culminate in the sky-reflecting surface of the Potomac; radiating avenues recalling French forest rides linked the Capitol and the President's house to the surrounding hills, giving dynamism to an already complex gridiron; intersections were explosive and marked with fountains. The search for infinity in this brilliant composition is apparent everywhere, but the superhuman space scale lacked the skill and know-how of Le Nôtre. Supported by Jefferson until his death in 1831, the plan was unrealizable as a contemporary city and intractable to change and growth. The idea collapsed and the new Washington that arose after 1900 was a return to classical as opposed to Baroque principles (**561**).

Tien in ion cciang = Figura del Cielo perfetta.mte dilettevole = Veduta del Tempio dell Idoli, che l. Imp.re colle sue donne adorava. questo Tempio è ufficiato, e custodito notte e dì da molti Sacerdoti dell Idoli, mà questi son tutti Eunuchi. Stà situato sù d'un Isoletta deliziosa—

China

112. Chinese landscape design reached a climax in the Summer Palaces of Peking at the same time as Versailles and with a very similar objective. The style was a continuity of history, but the poetry within it had declined. The conception of the organization of space was in direct contrast to that of the French (whose unified splendour was comprehended in a glance), and was concerned with the breaking down of scenery into compartments that were a succession of unfolding and asymmetrical scenes whose scale was not majestic, but rather that of the tree. The Imperial city itself was an austere series of geometrical boxes, one within another. The Summer Palaces in contrast were composed of artificial valleys, hills and lakes, providing a sequence of self-contained idealized worlds in which the several elements of the Emperor's innumerable family could reside in peace and privacy. Further transformation into fantasy was experienced at the monthly Lantern Festival, when the whole countryside was illuminated. The human scale by which the Emperor sought to come to terms with his huge, self-created environment was echoed in his personal township, described by Father Attiret in 1743 (see p. 225), with a similar purpose to, and antedating, the Hameau of the Petit Trianon.

Europe

113. In France the Chinese classics were first translated in 1687, and in 1697 Leibniz published the *Novissima Seneca*, praising Confucian virtues. While the philosophers were welcoming a conduct of life that seemed to coincide with their antagonism towards monarchy and Church, the Court itself at Versailles also turned, but for a different reason, to the new concepts filtering from the East. The light, fantastic Chinese architecture, an escape from classicism, became merged into Rococo. In England, Sir William Temple published the *Gardens of Epicurus* (1687) wherein he praised Chinese gardens, which he had visited, for their intricate irregularity, giving the name 'Sharawaggi' to those parts 'where the beauty shall be great, but without any order . . . that shall be easily observed'. In 1728 Batty Langley's *New Principles of Gardening* showed *chinoiserie* plans grafted on to the classical, and in 1757 Sir William Chambers published *Designs of Chinese Buildings*. Significant Chinese influence is manifest in England until mid-century, but thereafter is mainly confined to garden details. The new fashion appeared all over Europe and even in the colonies of North America. Sweden, in close commercial communication with China, was perhaps the only country in which the elegant new style took permanent root.

Comment

114. Imitators did not appreciate that the spirit of the traditional Chinese garden was one of symbolism. Probably travellers only saw and described the prodigious works of the contemporary Manchus, from which the true Chinese spirit may have already passed. They were clearly overwhelmed by the novelties presented to the eye, and by the idea that a landscape should respond to moods of awe as well as enchantment and pleasure. Europeans erected countless elegant garden structures, bridges, palings and the like, contrasting these with rocks and grim grottoes. While the English School, reaching full stature in mid-century, acquired its curves from the natural undulations of the land, those of *chinoiserie* were artificially close and serpentine, though for the Chinese, this was part of their way of thought. In general, the response to *chinoiserie* in France, Germany and Russia was highly accomplished, that of England unremarkable and that of Sweden exceedingly graceful. The light structures, as in China, were of timber and thus ephemeral: today it is difficult to imagine the landscape scenes which they punctuated so vividly with colour.

EUROPE LOOKED AT CHINA through the eyes of travellers, who brought back pictures often conveying a first sense of the Chinese scene. In 1713 an Italian priest, Father Matteo Ripa, engraved 36 views for the Emperor K'ang-hsi; they showed the imperial palaces and gardens at Jehol, about 150 miles from Peking, and several copies reached Europe. It was in such drawings that the most obvious aspects of Chinese landscapes were exemplified for the West: the serpentine line, the ingenious use of water, the miniature scale and the all-over pattern of small rounded hills.

THE OLD AND THE NEW SUMMER PALACES were built by the Manchu emperors in the first half of the eighteenth century. About six miles from Peking, they lay against the Western Hills in natural landscape that contrasted with the geometry of the city itself. Both palaces, or complex of palaces, were destroyed by the British in 1860, the New Summer Palace being later restored. Undoubtedly their influence on the course of landscape design was greater outside China than within, for these vast projects were no more than a continuation and climax of tradition. To the traveller from Europe the ideas were a revelation (but it is interesting that the traffic in ideas was not wholly one way: the Emperor Ch'ien Lung (1735–96), for instance, incorporated Baroque designs by the Jesuit Father Castiglione within the Old Summer Palace itself).

One of the palaces within the complex, **Fang Hu Sheng Ching (380, 381)**, is shown in an engraving by Lerouge from a Chinese woodcut. Typically, it is a geometrical design totally subordinate to natural landscape. Unlike the Western conception of a monolithic palace, it exemplifies the Chinese tradition of the deliberate multiplication of small, almost domestic, units. The terraces were marble, the roofs were of gilded tiles and pillars and beams were deep red. Another element of the complex was the **'bay of the Sea of Bliss' (382)**, with the nine-arched bridge and the hamlet in the background, the latter enabling the Emperor to experience the way of life of his subjects. Knowledge of contemporary China reached the West through travellers' descriptions; opposite is an extract from a letter by Father Attiret, a French missionary, to a friend in Paris *c.* 1752:

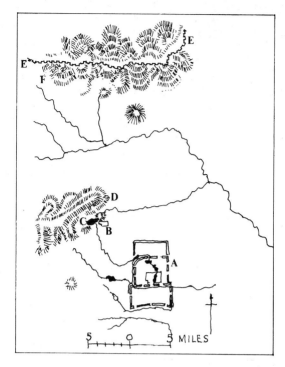

381 THE TWO SUMMER PALACES AND THEIR SETTING
A Peking
B Old Summer Palace
C New Summer Palace
D Western Hills
E Great Wall
F Ming Tombs

380

As for the Pleasure-houses, they are really charming. They stand in a vast Compass of Ground. They have raised Hills, from 20 to 60 foot high; which form a great Number of little Valleys between them. The Bottoms of these Valleys are water'd with clear Streams; which run on till they join together, and form large Pieces of Water and Lakes. . . . In each of these Valleys, there are Houses about the Banks of the Water; very well disposed: with their different Courts, open and close Porticos, Parterres, Gardens, and Cascades: which, when view'd all together, have an admirable Effect upon the Eye. . . .
All the Risings and Hills are sprinkled with Trees; and particularly with Flowering-trees, which are here very common. The sides of the Canals, or lesser streams, are not faced (as they are with us), with smooth Stone, and in a strait Line; but look rude and rustic, with different Pieces of Rock, some of which jut out, and others recede inwards; and are placed with so much Art that you would take it to be the Work of Nature. . . .
On your entrance into each Valley, you see its Buildings before you. All the Front is a Colonnade with Windows between the Pillars. The Woodwork is gilded, painted, and varnish'd. The Roofs too are cover'd with varnish'd Tiles of different Colours; Red, Yellow, Blue, Green and Purple: which by their proper Mixtures and their manner of placing them, form an agreeable Variety of Compartments and Designs. Almost all these Buildings are only one Story high; and their Floors

382

are raised from Two to Eight Foot above the Ground. You go up to them, not by regular Stone Steps, but by a rough sort of Rock-work; form'd as if there had been so many Steps produced there by Nature. . . .

But what is the most charming Thing of all, is an Island or Rock in the Middle of the Sea; rais'd in a natural and rustic Manner, about Six Foot above the Surface of the Water. On this Rock there is a little Palace; which however contains an hundred different Apartments. It has Four Fronts; and is built with inexpressible Beauty and Taste. . . . From it you have a View of all the Palaces, scattered at Proper Distances round the Shores of this Sea; all the Hills, that terminate about it; all the Rivulets, which tend thither, either to discharge their waters into it, or to receive them from it; all the Bridges and all the Groves, that are planted to separate and screen the different Palaces, and to prevent the Inhabitants of them from being overlooked by one another. . . .

To let you see the Beauty of this charming Spot in its greatest Perfection, I should wish to have you transported hither when the Lake is all cover'd with Boats; either gilt, or varnish'd: as it is sometimes, for Jousts, and Combats, and other Diversions, upon the Water: but above all, on some fine Night, when the Fireworks are play'd off there; at which time they have Illuminations in all the Palaces, all the Boats and almost every Tree. . . . There is this Symmetry, this beautiful Order and Disposition, too in China; and particularly, in the Emperor's Palace at Pekin. . . . But in their Pleasure-houses they rather chuse a beautiful Disorder and a wandering, as far as possible from all the Rules of Art. They go entirely on this Principle, 'That what they are to represent there, is a natural and wild View of the Country; a rural Retirement, and not a Palace form'd according to all the Rules of Art.

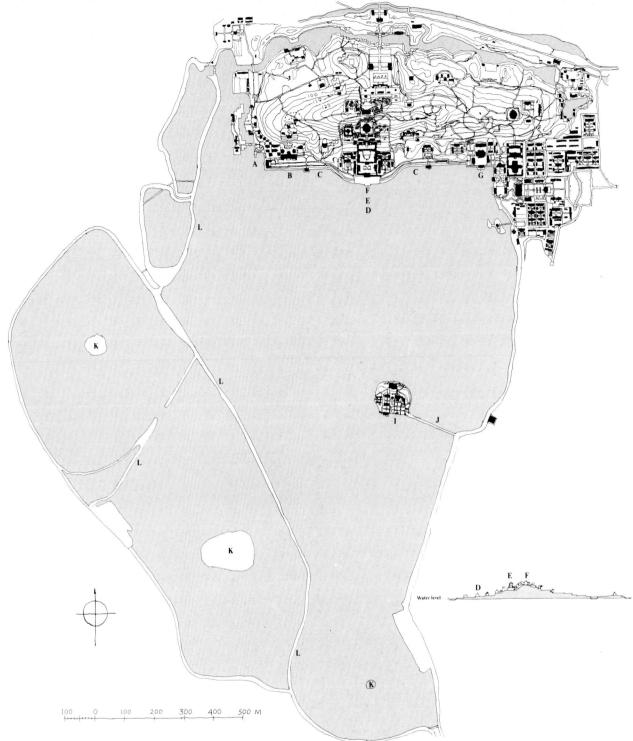

383 The New Summer
Palace, near
Peking: plan and
section through
centre

A Marble Boat
B T'ing Li Kuan (Salon
  for hearing the Oriole)
C The long corridor
D P'ai Yüh Tien (Palace
  of Pushing the Clouds)
E Fo Hsiang Kê
  (Pagoda of
  Buddhistic Fragrance)
F Chih Hui Hai (Sea of
  Wisdom)
G Shui Mu Tzu Chin
  (Intimacy of Trees and
  Water)
H Jên Shou Tien (Palace
  of Benevolence and
  Longevity)
I Island of Nan Hu
J Ch'ang Ch'io
  (Bridge of the
  Seventeen Arches)
K Islands
L Bund or causeway

100 0 100 200 300 400 500 M

384

THE RESTORED NEW SUMMER PALACE comprises 823 acres of artificial landscape, of which four-fifths is water. The islands and main land form have
been built up from excavations and the whole is a vast concept that extends
visually far beyond its boundaries. The **plan** (**383**) shows the complex of
separated palaces and buildings, each symmetrical, self-contained and
evocative in name. The **painting** (**384**) is of a typical landscape detail of the
Old Summer Palace, now destroyed. Beyond the **Bridge of the Jade Belt**
(**385**) and the Pagoda on Jade mountain hill rise the Western Hills. South
from the main complex are the **Bridge of the Seventeen Arches** (**386**)
and the artificial island that contained the sanctuary of the Dragon King.

385

386

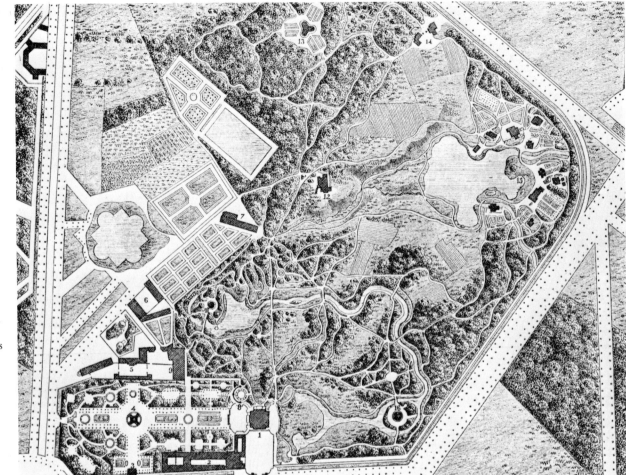

387 Gardens of the
Petit Trianon

388, 389

China in miniature was re-created in the courts of eighteenth-century Europe from travellers' descriptions and sketches. Expression ranged from individual *objets d'art* to large areas that were interwoven with both academic classicism and the new school of the *jardin anglais*. **The gardens of the Petit Trianon at Versailles (387)** identify all three styles in juxtaposition. The plan after Baltar shows, on the left, the 1762–68 château and classical gardens by J. Gabriel for Louis XV and Madame du Barry. Only a few years later, in 1774, Louis XVI made the so-called **Anglo-Chinese park (388)** for Marie Antoinette, recognizable in the centre of the plan by the serpentine river, the idea probably suggested to the architect R. Mique by the Comte de Caraman. Following this (1774–94) came the Anglo-French picturesque **park and hameau** or hamlet **(389)**, designed by Mique in collaboration with the painter Hubert Robert. Here the Queen escaped from the formality of the Court to simulate rural life; the Petit Trianon as a whole is intensely symbolic of the changing attitude of men's minds.

Sweden responded easily to *chinoiserie*, partly because of close trade relations with China; partly because of the eclectic influence of Queen Ulrica, sister of Frederick the Great; and partly because of an inherent Scandinavian elegance that persists today, and which may have grown from a timber tradition. The **plan for the park at Drottningholm (390)** by F. M. Piper (1799), encompassing but not destroying the existing formal gardens, had been preceded by the magnificent Chinese pavilion (*c.* 1766, marked 'China' in the plan). Piper had travelled extensively in Europe and had studied and copied Chinese landscape woodcuts. The plan is a fascinating Anglo-Chinese amalgam, delineated by perhaps the most sensitive topographical draughtsman of the age.

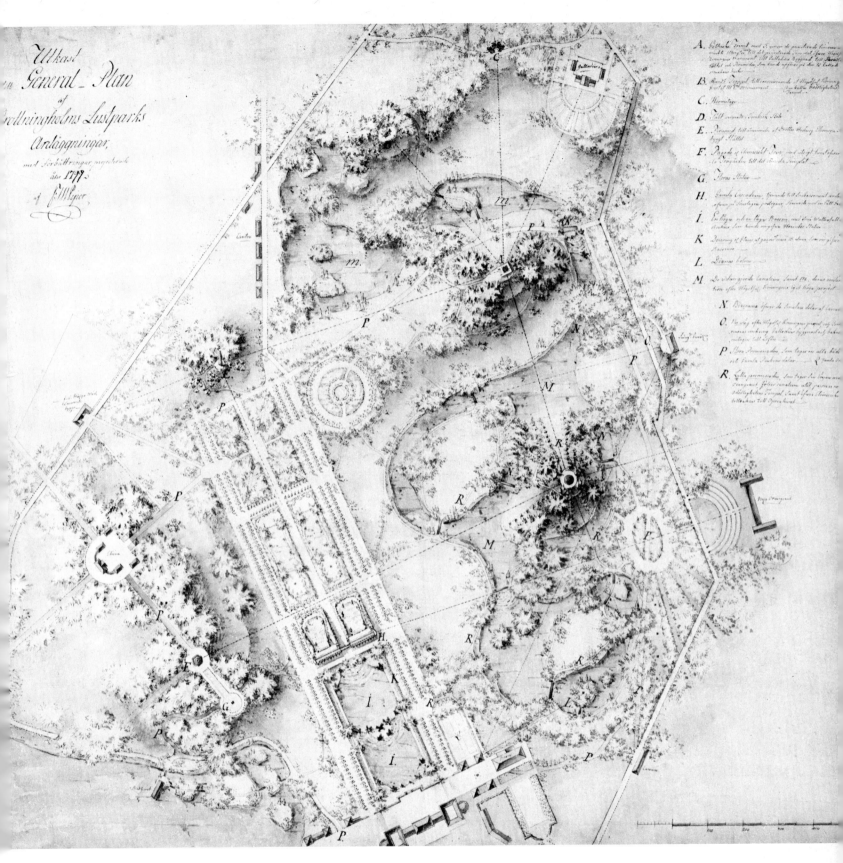

390 DROTTNINGHOLM

A	Gothic tower	I	Pools
B	Round temple	K	Grass bank
C	Hermitage	L	Diana's house
D	Turkish tent	M	Lake
E	Pyramid	N	Arbour
F	Pagoda	O	Outer path
G	Statue of Flora	P	Grand promenade
H	Large cascade	R	Minor walks

391

392

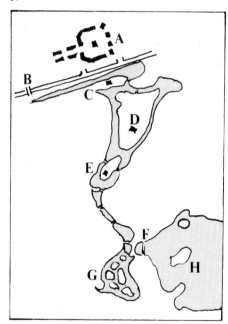

394

393 TSARSKOE SELO (PUSHKIN)

A Chinese hamlet
B 'Bolshoi Kapriz'
C 'Creaking' Pavilion
D Concert Hall (classical)
E Turkish kiosk
F Palladian bridge
G Archipelago
H Great lake

THE park of the palace of TSARSKOE SELO (Pushkin), south of St Petersburg, laid out for Catherine the Great, is characteristically a medley of all the prevailing styles. The palace itself is Italian Baroque; the gardens extending from it are French; a considerable lake based on *jardin anglais* principles includes monumental *objets d'art* ranging from a Turkish bath to a Palladian bridge; finally and unexpectedly comes a **chinoiserie riverscape** (**393**) of particular charm (*c.* 1779). The **water-scenery** (**391**) twists and turns along the river to provide a changing spectacle. The climax is the **creaking pavilion** (**392**) and the **Bolshoi Kapriz** (**395**) designed by Quarenghi. Beyond is the **Chinese village** (**394**) designed by the Scottish architect Cameron (drawing by Quarenghi).

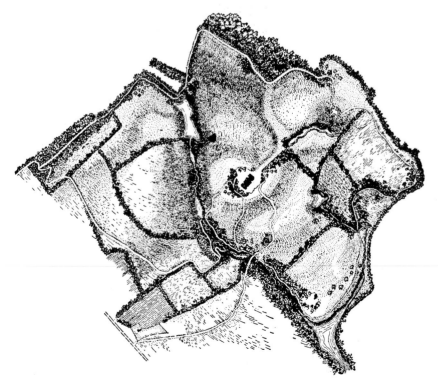

Origin *115.* The School was indigenous to England, springing from a relation to nature that had always been latent but only now emerged from beneath the fashionable Italian and French classical overlays. The movement was literary, spontaneous, and seems first to have been fired to take physical form by Sir William Temple's description of the Chinese School, to which it was clearly sympathetic. Nature was no longer subservient to man, but a friendly and equal partner which could provide inexhaustible interest, refreshment and moral uplift; irregularity rather than regularity was proclaimed as the objective of landscape design. Lord Shaftesbury's *The Moralists* (written 1709) lifted the new art into the sphere of intellectual philosophy, revealing that the laws of nature were as universal and unchanging as the Newtonian laws of the heavens, and therefore that the ecology could harmonize with the mathematics of a Palladian mansion. At first only sinuous Chinese-like curves grafted on to a classical plan indicated the change, but Sir John Vanbrugh (1664–1726), architect and dramatist, spanning the old world and the new, created at Castle Howard (begun 1701) a great canvas whereon the undulating countryside itself seemed to organize the monumental objects of architecture upon it. A new conception of space and of man's relation to environment had appeared.

Development *116.* During the first half of the century the many aspects of the new art were gradually revealed: the nostalgic revival of past ages; the blinding realization of the beauties of wild nature; the intricacies of the new-found sense of space. Stephen Switzer (1682–1745) seems to have been the first to expound the new principle. Alexander Pope (1688–1744) epitomized the common objective: 'He gains all points who pleasingly confounds, surprises, varies, and conceals the bounds.' William Kent (1684–1740), painter and architect, jointly with Charles Bridgeman (d. 1730) invented the ha-ha or sunk ditch, and thus 'leapt the fence and saw that all nature was a garden'. Kent alone achieved a synthesis in design that later disintegrated into separate and rival schools. These were identified in the words of Horace Walpole (1717–97) as follows: (*a*) *The Ornamental Farm* (*ferme ornée*) which lifted the utilitarian scene into the field of art; (*b*) *The Forest or Savage garden*, or more precisely, the Picturesque, the domain of painter, scholar and dilettante; and (*c*) *The Garden Which connects a Park*, concerned with space design, rationalized by Capability Brown (1716–83), and intellectualized by Humphry Repton (1752–1818).

Comment *117.* The theory of the *Ornamental Farm* (page 232) was held in high contemporary esteem, but had no immediate influence. It was the one art that was not entirely escapist. The idea that a farm or a factory can be lifted into a work of art was illustrated in classic poetry by the *Georgics* of Virgil, and is seen in the modern factory at Herning in Denmark (page 362). The art of the *Picturesque* depended on personal taste, took long to mature, and was so vulnerable to decay that only painters could freeze it for posterity. It remains the ideal of the majority of self-designed private gardens. The so-called *Garden Which connects a Park* was concerned more with form than content, was simple to make and maintain, and appealed to the professionals because the art was on a grand scale and, like architecture, could be systematized. The art has survived, flourished and become universal for two apparent reasons: in an overcrowded world it creates added imaginative and nostalgic space, and in an age of mass production it ensures individuality to architecture by the inspiration drawn from the nature of each site. The principal trees to realize these ideas and planted prolifically were oaks, elms, beeches, ash and limes, Scots pines and larches being used sparingly to give variety of tone. New trees, such as the cedar (1670), were being introduced from abroad.

AN ASPECT OF THE ENGLISH SCHOOL that has hardly survived came to be known as the ornamental farm (*ferme ornée*) whose roots may be traced to such splendid seventeenth-century features as **Inigo Jones' architectural windmill (396)** at Chesterton, Warwickshire, built in a hedgeless agricultural environment in 1647. In 1743 William Shenstone, poet and inventor of the term 'landscape gardener', developed the idea on his estate, **The Leasowes (397)**, near Birmingham. Without interfering with the practical and utilitarian, he transformed it into the sublime by romantic walks, views, thought-provoking urns, obelisks and trophies, as well as cataract and grotto, and thirty-nine seats for the contemplation of these things.

233

398 Castle Howard

A Entrance gate   B Castle Howard   C Walled
garden   D Temple of the Four Winds   E Bridge
F Mausoleum

399

400

401

THE TRANSITION FROM CLASSICISM to romanticism in England can be appreciated in a single masterpiece – Sir John Vanbrugh's **Castle Howard** in Yorkshire, begun in 1701. **The plan (398)** shows the revolutionary idea of detaching a classical mansion from the authoritative straight line of its avenue approach. As a stage designer, Vanbrugh must have experienced the art of creating idyllic imaginary space within a small compass. Here, he is practising on a great scale. The mansion stands in the centre of the scenery and its tenuous attachment to the avenue is an early suggestion, developed later in the century, that a house should be entirely cut off from the outside world. The stage all round was vast and the scenery like some Arcadian landscape organized according to the character of the natural landscape. The later **painting by Hendrik de Cort** (1742–1816) **(401)** interprets this new conception of the organization of buildings in space. From the **Temple of the Four Winds (400)** the mausoleum is seen in the distance and the Vanbrugh bridge to the right. Architectural details like the **castellated entrances (399)** to the grand avenue are bizarre and dramatic, suggesting medieval chivalry and reminding us again that Vanbrugh was a man of the theatre. Horace Walpole later wrote: 'Nobody had informed me that at one view I should see a palace, a town, a fortified city, temples on high places, works worthy of being each a metropolis of the Druids, the noblest lawn in the world fenced by half the horizon, and a mausoleum that would tempt one to be buried alive.'

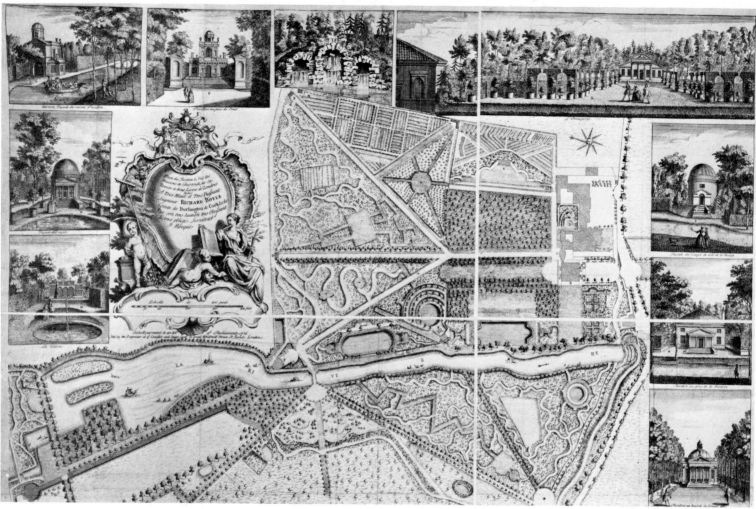

402

WILLIAM KENT (1685–1748), painter, furniture designer, architect, was also described by Horace Walpole as 'the father of modern gardening'. After returning in 1719 from a prolonged stay in Rome he directed his versatility in all three arts towards the creation of a new one: the translation into reality of the contemporary painters' conception of the humanist landscape. Palladian architecture set in wild imaginative landscape might compose on canvas, since it was seen from a single viewpoint, but it required an advanced sense of form to compose the intricacies in three dimensions. Kent's first commission, for his patron the Earl of Burlington c.1731, was **Chiswick House, Middlesex**, shown in the **plan by La Rocque (402)** dated 1736. The gardens were designed in collaboration with the fashionable Charles Bridgeman, and the somewhat confused plan suggests that Kent was responsible for the Palladian mansion (plan: top right) and the highly original river landscape, and Bridgeman for the remainder with its diagonals and undertones of *chinoiserie*.

Horace Walpole considered the designs for **Rousham, Oxfordshire (403, 404)** to be the 'most characteristic and charming' of Kent's gardens. The first plans seem to have been drawn by Bridgeman, but undoubtedly the realization is that of the now matured William Kent. We can detect the same house-riverscape association as at Chiswick, but now the river meanders in its own right and all the sylvan groupings, such as the **cascades (405)**, are linked to it and to the scenery beyond. The 'eye-catcher', a building in silhouette only, can be seen on the skyline in the **view from the house (406)**.

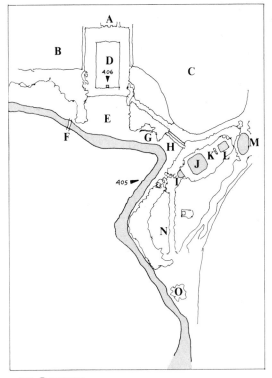

403 ROUSHAM

A Mansion
B Kitchen garden
C Paddock
D Bowling green
E Concave grass slope to river
F Garden bridge
G Theatre
H Waterworks, arcade, and concave slope to river
I Cascade
J The great pond
K Upper cascade
L Upper pond
M The new pond
N The elm walk
O Clump of elms

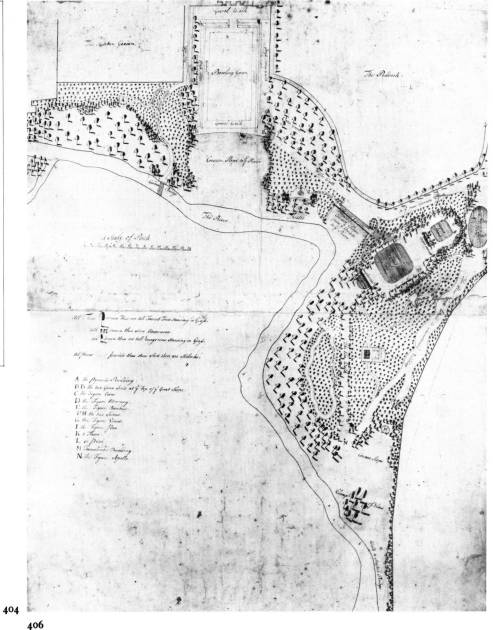

404

405

406

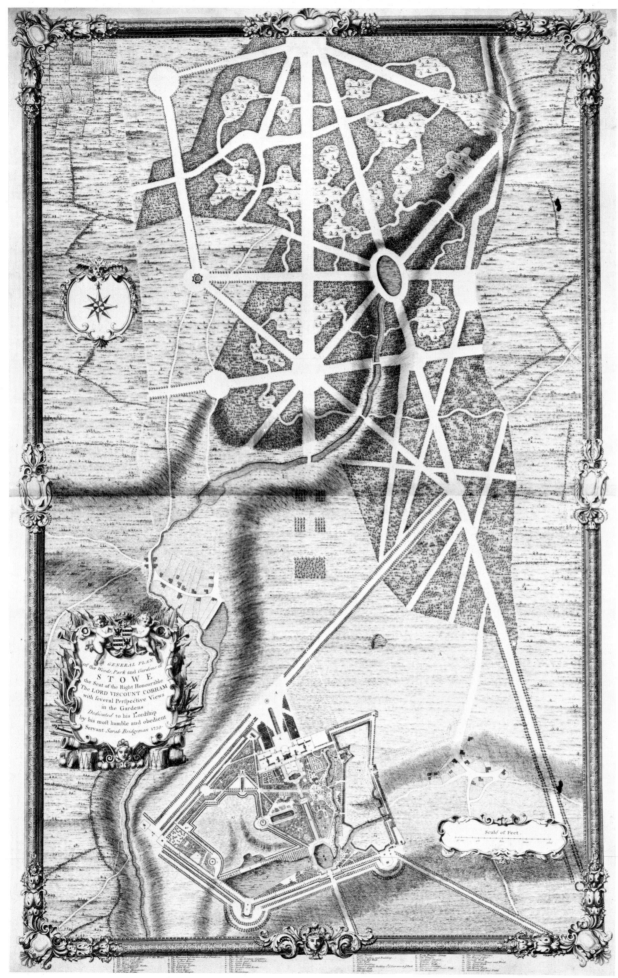

THE GARDENS OF STOWE, Buckinghamshire, were begun in 1715 by Lord Cobham and throughout the century were without rival in richness of variety. Just as Versailles expressed absolute monarchy, so Stowe came to express liberal Whig philosophy. The **original plan of Stowe (407)**, from an engraving in 1739 by Rigaud and Baron, was by Charles Bridgeman in association with Vanbrugh. The distance from north to south is nearly three miles. The inner park is encompassed by a formal frame of trees and the first ha-ha or sunk fence, which allowed unimpeded views of the surrounding landscape. The outer park, attuned to hunting and riding, has a Baroque immensity of scale. The **lithograph (410, 411)** made in 1777 shows the inner gardens as adjusted to English principles by Bridgeman and Kent about 1738. The grouping ingeniously absorbs the formal central avenue and creates **pictorial space when seen from the house (409)** and elsewhere, clearly inspiring Capability Brown, who worked here as a garden boy. It absorbs also the idyllic and literary **Elysian Fields (408)** of William Kent. In the next half-century, the two philosophies of form and content embodied by these peaceful scenes were to tear each other apart by every means known to the pen (p. 245).

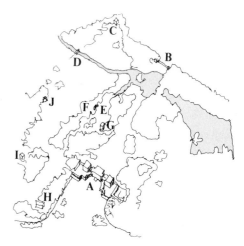

411 STOWE
A Mansion
B 'Entrance' pavilion
C Temple of Friendship
D Palladian bridge
E Elysian Fields
F Temple of British Worthies
G Temple of Ancient Virtue
H Temple of Concord
I   Queen's Temple
J Gothic temple

410

412

414

THE GARDENS OF STOURHEAD, designed (1740–60) for himself by the banker Henry Hoare and possibly inspired by Pliny's description of the source of the Clitumnus, may be unique as a classical allegory in landscape of man's passage through the world, almost certainly based on Virgil's *Aeneid*. The architecture was by Henry Flitcroft (1697–1769). Although an original conception, the influence of the contemporaries Kent and Bridgeman is manifest, and beyond them, the paintings of Claude Lorraine (1600–82). **Claude's poetic re-creation** (412) of classical legends (here, Aeneas on the coast of Delos) appealed strongly to the English gentry on the Grand Tour, who began to see landscape through his eyes. The **park of Stourhead** (414) – the drawing is by the Swedish architect F. M. Piper – was separated from the mansion (F on the diagram), though not so completely as it is today. It consists almost solely of a closed walk round the artificial lake. The allegory begins with birth at the Temple of Flora (A), passes round to the grottoes of the underworld (B), emerges to reach the Pantheon of earthly glories (C) and finally, through the rock arch suggestive of mortality (D), to ascend heavenwards to the **Temple of Apollo** (E) (417). **Looking west** (415) towards the Pantheon, the Temple of Flora is to the right, out of sight, and the Temple of Apollo to the left. The Gothic cottage (just visible) was a later addition. The hillsides were heavily planted to increase the sense of enclosure and remoteness. The lake, seen here through the **rock arch** (416), reflects the sky and is a natural symbolic centre round which the allegory takes place.

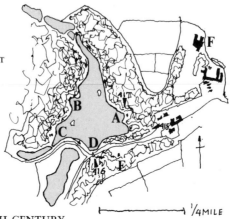

413 STOURHEAD:
  THE ALLEGORICAL CIRCUIT
A Temple of Flora
B Underworld grotto
C Pantheon
D Arch
E Temple of Apollo
F Mansion

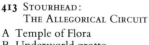
¼ MILE

415

416

417

418

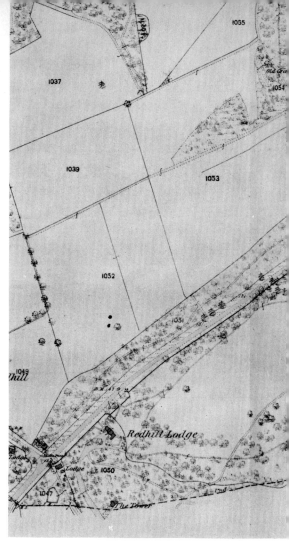

419

421

Painshill in Surrey was the unaided creation of a layman, Charles Hamilton, who worked continuously on the landscape from 1738 to 1771. Like his contemporary Hoare at Stourhead, Hamilton was profoundly influenced by the Italian painters, finding in such paintings as **St John on Patmos (418)** by Nicolas Poussin (1593–1665) the discipline and the meaning that lay behind apparent chaos. His theme seems to have been as poetic as the allegory at Stourhead: out of an unpromising scene to make an artificial landscape that would tell the story of past civilizations and their place in the great wilderness of nature. In contrast to Stourhead, he made it linear – a study in time and movement as in a Chinese scroll. The symbolic objects were to be revealed in progression along a broad, sinuous and island-studded river apparently without beginning or end. **A plan of 1871 (419, 420)** shows the illusory river, whose waters were lifted by wheel some twelve feet above the River Mole. The valley sides were intricately planted with azaleas and rhododendron (among the first in England), hardwoods, and conifers of many species, especially the cedar of Lebanon. **William Gilpin's sketch (421)** of 1772 looks west from the Gothic temple; the **present-day view (422)** looks east towards it.

PAINSHILL PARK

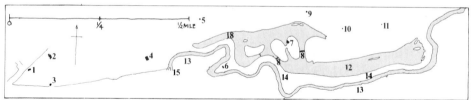

420 PAINSHILL, SURREY

1 Lodge 2 Redhill Lodge 3 Tower
4 Temple of Bacchus 5 Turkish tent
6 Mausoleum 7 Grotto 8 Bridge 9 Bath
house 10 Gothic temple 11 Statue 12 Raised
artificial lake 13 River Mole 14 Dyke
15 Water wheel

422

423

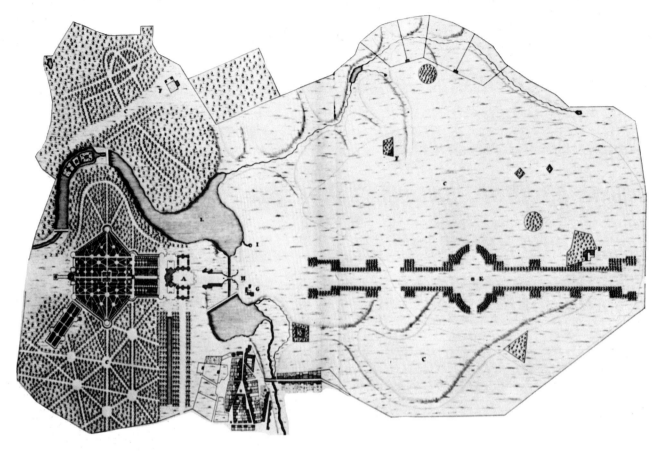

424

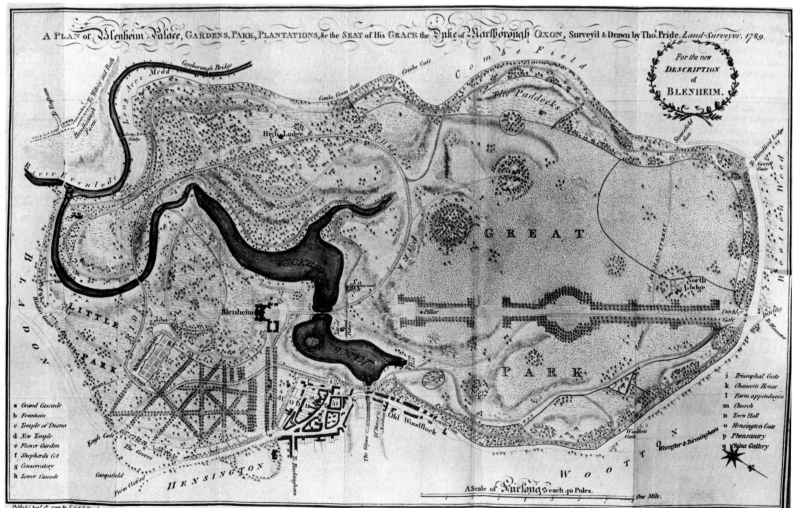

425

The second half of the century was dominated by LANCELOT (CAPABILITY) BROWN, who represented one of the two schools of romanticism that had been united under William Kent but were now in collision. In essence, the issue was one of content versus form. The schools were analysed in *The Landscape* (1794) by Richard Payne Knight, scholar, connoisseur and advocate of the picturesque. The **garden undressed** (**426**) is picturesque, since it is involved in the intricacies of nature, is personal and apparently irrational, and is primarily the concept of the painter. The **garden dressed in the modern style** (**427**) is centred round the architecturally minded Brown and his preoccupation with form. His output was immense and his scale heroic and impersonal. He would adapt a standard system of design to each site, requiring only rolling land and water that could be made to appear an endless river. He planted trees in groups or clumps, originally invented by Kent. The mansion, from which nothing utilitarian must be seen, sat in an idyllic sun-and-cloud landscape of infinite size. Only deer fed in the park, for they were themselves idyllic since fox-hunting had now superseded stag-hunting (making straight forest rides no longer necessary). Nor did he neglect planting for commerce: identity of interest between private aesthetics and national necessity encouraged the whole landscape movement, and it has been calculated that Brown and Repton between them planted twenty million trees.

426, 427

The transformation of **Blenheim Palace**, Oxfordshire, from a noble classical landscape to a romantic one was probably Brown's most accomplished work. The **original layout** (**423**) was made by Henry Wise in collaboration with Sir John Vanbrugh. The drawing appears flat and classical symmetry predominates. The eye is concentrated along the great avenue to the memorial column; the Vanbrugh bridge spans an unwanted ravine; the lakes are static and separated. **Brown's plan** (**424**), made in 1764, retains the geometry but with a subtle change of emphasis that makes natural form predominate. The lakes are joined and the banks bevelled to make a continuous river, giving purpose to the bridge and visual unity between palace and water; the **view is from the Woodstock arch** (**425**). In the Great Park itself the boundary walls are concealed with forest indentations and the spaces are scenically designed.

428, 429

430, 431

HUMPHRY REPTON (1752–1818) continued the principles of Capability Brown, whom he defended in *Sketches and Hints on Landscape Gardening* (1795). He broadened Brown's range of design and humanized it but, in so doing, compromised the purity of the art. His place in history is established by his analytical writings, which were the first seriously to record the optical as well as the psychological sciences upon which the art was based. Repton presented each project to his client in a Red Book that included *before* and (lift the flap) *after* drawings accompanied by a carefully written report. At **Bayham Abbey, Kent (428)**, the Red Book analyses the nature of the countryside before alteration and proposes the siting and architectural style of the mansion: 'the character therefore should be of greatness and durability. The park should be a forest, the estates a domain, the house a palace.' In Repton's **proposed new landscape (429)** the relation of mansion to trees and water is fundamental (the house was finally built detached from the water); the lake, with ends concealed, is a broad river leading round the old abbey ruins (out of the picture to the right); the farmland becomes parkland, whose scattered preserved and new trees give scale and irregularity. **His 'before' (430) and 'after' (431) sketches** made later for **Brighton Pavilion** shows his use of foliage in the urban scene and his ingenious solution to the fashion for flowers that began in the middle of his career.

URBAN LANDSCAPE-PLANNING evolved from the impregnation of the classical principles of town-planning by those of the contemporary country park. The designer of Bath, Somerset, John Wood I (1704–54), already had experience in classical 'green' town-planning through his work in Yorkshire. In conjunction with Ralph Allen, he expanded Bath from a Roman medieval town into a fashionable spa in which the new sense of space landscape came to predominate and set standards for the future. His son, John Wood II (1728–81), continued the practice. The **view over Bath (433)** shows in the foreground the Royal Crescent and Circus (Wood II, 1767–75); in the distance is the serpentine Lansdowne Crescent (end of century, John Palmer, architect). Adjoining and overlooking Bath is **Prior Park (432)**, built for Ralph Allen by John Wood I *c.* 1730, the landscape and Palladian bridge in the view from the terrace probably designed by Capability Brown in 1765. Just as the private park has eliminated the urban middle distance by tree planting, so in the city itself the green landscape creates the illusion of country brought to town.

433

432

THE NINETEENTH CENTURY

Geographical *118.* World energy and power were now centred round France, Germany and England, with a rapidly rising United States of America and a late emergent Japan. The mass production of iron, the invention of steel and of the steam-engine, transformed communications and reduced the globe to a measurable size. After Trafalgar (1805) the English took absolute command of the seas, holding it throughout the century. Because of their island condition they were free of the wars that harassed the Continent, and were able to establish and sustain colonies anywhere in the world and to control the increase in commerce, especially to North America. Among other goods, plants from the remotest parts now flowed into England. At the end of the century, an observer from the air would have seen huge areas of smoke, slums and wastelands round the coal-fields of northern Europe and England; in contrast, romantic landscapes such as the Valley of the Rhine and the English Lake District were still unspoiled and made accessible to increasing numbers of tourists by rail as well as road. On the coasts and inland were seemly spas and seaside resorts, themselves usually set in equally romantic landscapes. In contrast with the rich and civilized landscape in Europe, that of North America was plain and vast, and so far beyond comprehension in size that indiscriminate exploitation of natural resources could for a long time pass unnoticed.

Historical *119.* The American Revolution (1776) established permanently the uniquely liberal constitution of the United States. The French Revolution (1789) created a republic that soon gave way to Napoleon Bonaparte who dominated Europe as a self-imposed monarch (Emperor 1804–14), creating a code of rationalization whose influence still exists. Following Waterloo (1815) Europe returned to a discordant period of autocratic repression of natural national rights and opinions, from which England benefited until after the Franco-Prussian War of 1870. The scramble for land in the newly discovered territories overseas, such as Africa, made the British Empire, including India, the most extensive and wealthy the world had known. At the end of the century Britain had consolidated her position as a naval 'crowned' republic under the stable reign of Queen Victoria, France had settled uncertainly to be a presidential republic, a united Germany had grown into a formidable military empire under the Prussian Hohenzollerns, and the United States had proved the economic value of its liberal constitution. The Latin American states had won independence from Spain and Portugal. China was disrupted by the Western civilizations, but Japan transformed itself in the second half of the century from a medieval to a formidable modern state, challenging the eastward expansion of Russia.

Social *120.* After the upheavals of the French Revolution and Empire, the Continent as a whole returned to social systems much as they were before, with the peasant attached to the land. Although in Prussia, for example, state education was among the most advanced in Europe, the subjects had little political freedom and no share in government. In England power continued to reside with conservative landowners, but under the pressure of the Industrial Revolution (far ahead of that of the Continent) the traditional relationship between the upper and lower classes profoundly changed. Intimacy between landlord and peasant broke down: the peasant, now landless by reason of the Enclosure Acts, which favoured the landlord, barely reached subsistence level; the factory group of 'hands' into which he drifted coalesced into a mass-produced sub-human unit. The rich became richer and more remote, the poor became poorer and overcrowded; in between steadily arose a middle class who in the main sought to emulate the upper class. In 1832 the Reform Bill passed power from country to town, and from that time the alleviation of the conditions of the slum-dwelling lower classes became more and more the responsibility of the public, and was to produce some of the most significant collective landscapes of the age. In the United States of America a new social order was groping its way towards its own form of civilization, not unlike that of England, but without restraint of monarchy, aristocracy, an established Church or traditional culture.

Economic *121.* The years of Revolutionary and Napoleonic France (1793–1815) radically disrupted the existing European economy, but control of the seas for commerce after Trafalgar (1805) and a century of peace after Waterloo enabled England to pass all other countries in the creation of personal and national wealth and prestige. The change from an agricultural economy to one of manufacture meant that it was profitable to export coal and manu-factured goods in return for food and raw materials. The economy being one of free-for-all, huge personal fortunes were amassed by the few and were spent mostly upon their estates. In addition, an increase of 'fund-holders' or small investors from 17,000 in mid-eighteenth century to over 275,000 in 1829 helped to create a middle class intent upon homes and gardens. The Great Exhibition of 1851 proclaimed Britain's might to the world in financial strength, inventiveness in the sciences, and productivity. The more adventurous and dissatisfied artisans emigrated to the colonies. The World's Columbian Exhibition at Chicago of 1893 not only proclaimed the rise to maturity of the United States, but the first truly American appreciation of the economic value of the arts in society.

Philosophy *122.* The intellectual life of the nineteenth century has been briefly sum-marized by Bertrand Russell. It 'was more complex than that of any previous age. This was due to several causes. First: the area concerned was larger than ever before; America and Russia made important contributions, and Europe became more aware than formerly of Indian philosophies, both ancient and modern. Second: science, which had been a chief source of novelty since the seventeenth century, made new conquests especially in geology, biology and organic chemistry. Third: machine production profoundly altered the social structure, and gave men a new conception of their powers in relation to physical environment. Fourth: a profound revolt, both philosophical and political, against traditional systems in thought, in politics, and in economics, gave rise to attacks upon many beliefs and institutions that had hitherto been regarded as unassailable.'

Expression *123.* The phenomenon of the age was an excessive urge for escape into romance, excited by literature and travel. In architecture all countries became littered with styles that were Gothic or Greek, Egyptian or Indian, or Italian High Renaissance. Town-planning was more conservative: the Continent, with notable exceptions, developed from the classicism of Le Nôtre; in England, from a continuation of serene classic architecture and romantic landscape, with frequent Gothic silhouettes. In sympathy both with internationalism generally and with the particular need to absorb foreign plants, the English garden pioneered the way through the 'gardenesque' style to the cosmopolitan nature habitat, in which Japanese influence is marked. But in Europe it is mainly through engineering and painting that the significant direction of landscape art towards a new end can be detected. The century began with Turner (1775–1851), Constable (1776–1837) and watercolourists inspired by the Lake poets. The inspiration then passed to France through Impressionism and Post-Impressionism, prophetic of the revolution that was to take place in man's whole attitude to his environment.

The Classical Landscape

124. The more spectacular urban landscaping was now directed to the glory of the nation rather than the individual monarch. The French disposition to impose classical planning from above, which had reached maturity under Le Nôtre, continued on a grand scale under the Empire. Under Napoleon the country was criss-crossed with tree-lined canals. In Paris the Champs-Elysées and Arc de Triomphe were the expression of an empire at its zenith; architecture was Neo-Greek, elegant and dignified. Mid-century plans by Baron Haussmann (1809–91) became semi-military for the control of mob violence, the regularity of the streets encouraging a romantic park system as an antidote. The French capital remained throughout the century the world centre of classicism and the Ecole des Beaux-Arts the centre of its teaching. In contrast to Haussmann's contemporary Paris, Vienna transformed a medieval military strip of land into the majestic anti-military and romantic-classical Ringstrasse. In 1889 a Viennese, Camillo Sitte (d. 1903), published *The Art of Building Cities* which argued against superhuman urban spaces in favour of an urban environment that was above all of individual human and tree scale. The response was international and immediate, and a new era of democratic planning became foreseeable.

The Romantic Landscape

125. The heart of European romanticism lay in Germany. The poet-scientist Goethe (1749–1832), exploring the human mind and its relation to environment more widely and deeply than any philosopher before or since, responded equally to the romantic and classical. The architect Schinkel expressed likewise these two aspects in his romantic landscape visions and his precise Graeco-Roman revival architecture. In the mid-century the Valhalla of Richard Wagner expressed a national dream-world of which the fantasy of Neuschwanstein was a concrete embodiment. The explanation of this semi-mystical inner world lies in the natural landscape. Just as the English attitude is conditioned to soft undulating land and the French logically to the plains of northern France, so that of south, central and west Germany appears to have sprung from the dark indigenous woodlands, the mountains and the river valleys. Germany was never under Roman occupation. The Rhine is a national shrine of Germanic landscape. East Germany provided the military machine, but (with exceptions such as Pückler-Muskau) it was the remainder that germinated and sheltered culture. The culture was more philosophical, literary and musical than visual, but nevertheless from the combination of East and West was to spring much of the European experimentation into the aesthetic form of the next century.

Comment

126. Neo-classicism and romanticism are coming increasingly to be seen as two sides of the same coin, both looking to an idealized past for inspiration. If not always combined within the same artist (as with Schinkel or David) they almost always co-exist within the same culture. Haussmann and J.C. Alphand in Paris represent a typical partnership of ideas; and it was significant that Munich balanced its classicism with the Englischer Garten in 1789. The London exhibition of 1851 had shown the possible relation between rational engineering and irrational landscape, and the Paris exhibition of 1889 was an even more striking adventure in environment. From the exhibition grounds, which were classically composed and skilfully woven into the fabric of Paris, rose the extraordinary tower (nearly a thousand feet high) of Gustave Eiffel. The tower was proportioned to steel and not to stone; the scale was beyond that of its environment; and the shape functional and unfamiliar. Yet the appeal was immediate and permanent, suggestive of the emotional public urge to break through into that same new world of space that the French painters were themselves endeavouring to probe.

La Roche-sur-Yonne, western France (**434**): a medieval town destroyed by Republican troops in 1794 and rebuilt by Napoleon in 1804. The geometric plan superimposed upon a medieval landscape is symbolic of an imperialism that overrode private interests. This was neither possible nor acceptable in the more liberal countries, where individual property was sacrosanct. Nevertheless, many aspects of the *Code Napoléon* survived Waterloo to contribute to the growth of European civilization.

251

435, 436

437

THE ROMANTIC AND THE PICTURESQUE were two ways of escaping from Napoleonic rationalism. Romanticism led to the exotic and the remote (in time as well as place) and to a grandeur almost impossible of fulfilment. Significantly, it is represented more in painting and the theatre than in architecture and landscape. Among the architects affected by the French occupation of Prussia was K. F. Schinkel, later the leader of the assured Greek revival, whose underemployed imagination before 1815 dwelt weirdly upon the inner meaning of landscape. He could envisage **Milan Cathedral (435)** transported to a hill overlooking Trieste, or the **Palace of the Queen of the Night (436)** in *The Magic Flute* as a grotesque Egyptian temple set in a mighty cave. In complete contrast, Prince von Pückler-Muskau (1785–1873) planned his great **estate in east Germany (437–439)** on the Picturesque principles evolved by Brown, Repton and Loudon, but with the difference that the scene should include all facets and activities of country life and become a living entity rather than an illusion. He thus appears to stand mid-way between the *ferme ornée* (**396, 397**) and modern comprehensive landscape-planning.

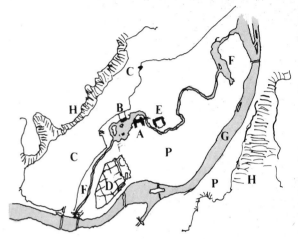

438 ESTATE OF PRINCE VON PÜCKLER-MUSKAU
A Castle B Town hall C Muskau town
D Kitchen gardens, etc E Stable F Artificial stream and lakes G River Neiss H Hill escarpment P Parkland

439

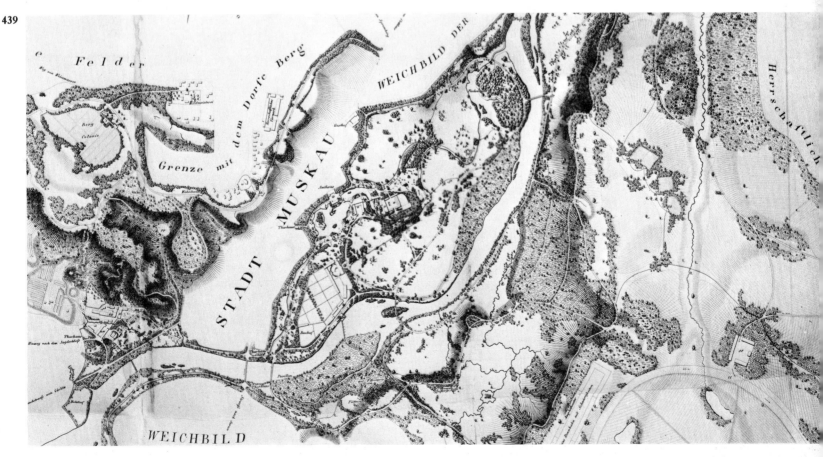

440

441

NINETEENTH-CENTURY ROMANTICISM AND CLASSICISM both reached extremes under the European monarchies in mid-century. **Schloss Neuschwanstein** (**440**), begun 1869 by architect Reidel for the mad Ludwig II of Bavaria and never properly completed, was inspired by the mystic music-dramas of Richard Wagner. Here the King could lead a life of medieval make-believe in a setting that is still powerfully evocative. The desire to escape, temporarily at least, into such a world of romance became more widespread as the industrial age developed and opportunities became general. (The modern equivalent of Neuschwanstein is Disneyland in the USA.)

The removal of the fortifications in medieval cities allowed sudden expansions to take place, and nowhere was the opportunity for the creation of building sites and boulevards (*boulevard* originally meant bulwark) so well seized and realized as in the **Ringstrasse of Vienna**. Promoted by Emperor Franz Josef in 1857, the conditions of a competition called for a boulevard some two miles in length that would comprehend the existing as well as new civic buildings in a planned landscape of green. In comparison with the contemporary rigid classical semi-military plans for Paris by Baron Haussmann, the splendid movement of landscape architecture round the city was classical in form but romantic in spirit.

The nineteenth-century **Panorama of Vienna** (**441**) is taken from a view-point similar to, but higher than, that of Bellotto (**346**). In the foreground from right to left, and in existence before the Ringstrasse, are: the Salesian Nunnery, the lower Belvedere Palace, the Schwarzenberg Palace and Fischer von Erlach's Karlskirche. The Ringstrasse filled the space between these and the medieval city in the mixed style of the period. To the left can be seen the group comprising the Hofburg and the two museums (neo-classical), while on beyond are the Rathaus and the Votivkirche (Gothic revival).

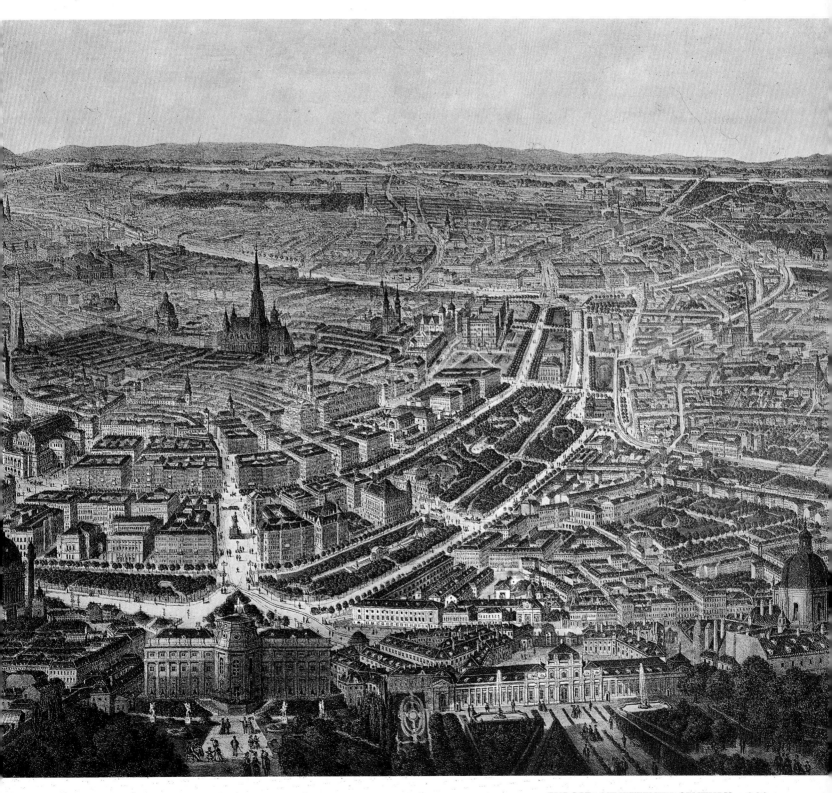

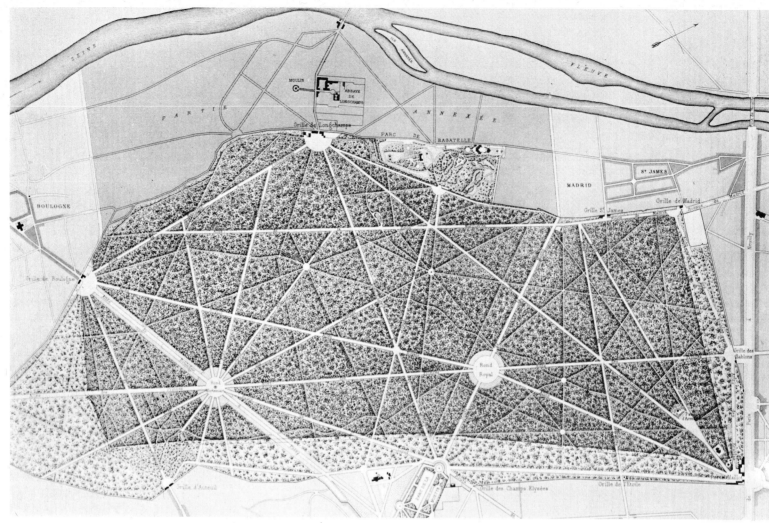

442, 443

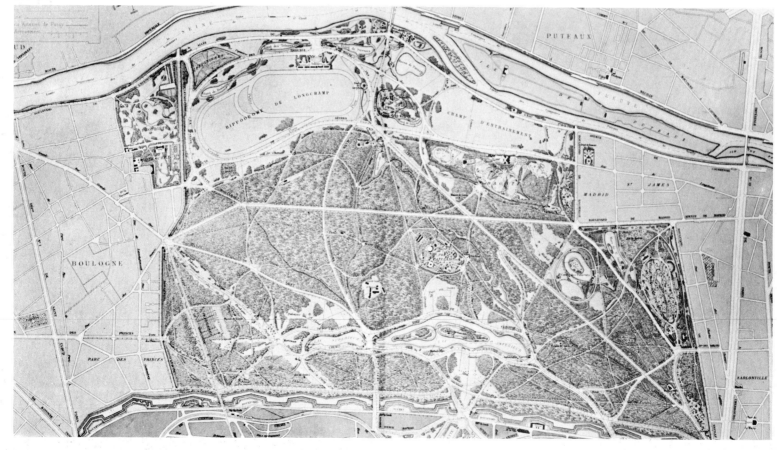

IN MID-CENTURY PARIS a romantic park system was evolved under J. C. A. Alphand to counterbalance the severity of Baron Haussmann's plans for military security. Under these, the city was criss-crossed with avenues that resembled the traditional hunting rides, except that the quarry was man and not beast. The **original Bois de Boulogne (442)**, which had been such a forest, complete with *rond-points*, was transformed in 1852 in the **English Picturesque style (443)** by Hittorf (architect) and Varé (landscape gardener).

The **Parc des Buttes-Chaumont (444–445)** was made *c.* 1863 from limestone quarries later used as a rubbish dump, and is the most dramatic early example of the art of landscape to re-create shape and form from apparent waste. The scene is so violent that it excludes the urban environment and absorbs a railway that pierces it. The detail is as consistent as the whole, being made in cement using the forms of timber or rock. The English gardener William Robinson wrote in 1878:

Old quarries, enormous in size, and surrounded by acres of rubbish, once occupied this spot. It was by cutting away the ground around three sides of these, and leaving the highest and most picturesque side intact, that the present results were brought about . . . enormous stalactite caves, sixty feet in height from plan to ceiling, have been constructed . . . enormous curtains of ivy drape the great rock walls with the most refreshing verdure at all seasons.

444, 445

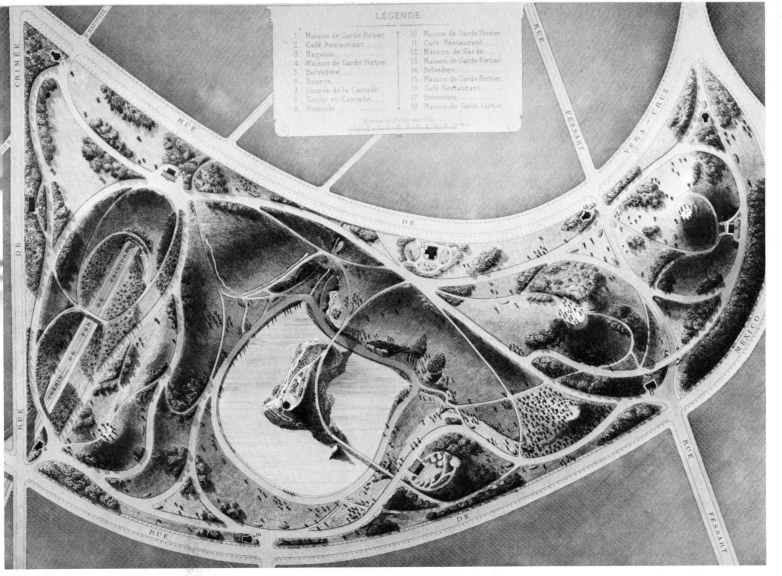

LÉGENDE

446

447

448

THE FRENCH PAINTERS of the second half of the century initiated modern art, foreshadowed constructivist architecture, and may well prove to have been the pioneers of ecological landscape design. Although the Impressionists, as they were styled, were seemingly preoccupied with a newly discovered technique of conveying light and colour to canvas, their true significance lay in their probings and penetrations into the structure of things and, ultimately, of the cosmos itself.

Influenced particularly by Nicolas Poussin (**418**), **Paul Cézanne** (1839–1906) set out to find and express on canvas the inner meaning and order of solid form. His **Aix: paysage rocheux** (**446**) is one of a series of studies of mountain scenery near his home in Provence that led to Cubism: the disintegration of visual form and its re-creation into an art form that was explanatory of its mass and structure. While Cézanne was concerned with solids, **Georges Seurat** (1859–91) was concerned with voids, or rather, with space. Like Piero della Francesca (d. 1492), he was a pioneer in semi-mathematical space; and somewhat like Tintoretto (**292**), he first conceived **Sunday afternoon on the Island of La Grande Jatte** without figures (**447**), which were painted in afterwards (**448**). He composed, therefore, like a landscape designer who must initially create agreeably proportioned space out of emptiness, in order that it may later contain its civilized occupants.

449

Claude Monet (1840–1926) penetrated into matter more significantly than any other Impressionist. He struck at the root principles of classical composition (whether finite or infinite), which are order and stability. His **Lily Pool** (**449**) was only one of many studies made between 1900 and 1909 of the pool he built in his own garden at Giverny. To him, it was a microcosm of nature in restless transformation. He was, in spirit, a Taoist (p. 68), and wrote: 'My only virtue resides in my submission to instinct. Because I have discovered the powers of intuition and allowed them to predominate. I have been able to identify myself with the created world and absorb myself in it.'

127. The principles of the interweaving of the classical and romantic formulated by Repton continued and culminated in Regent's Park. The rise of a middle class created suburbs of villas whose modest gardens sought not only to emulate the traditional park, but to encompass the infinite variety of plants now available. There were new mechanical inventions such as the mowing-machine; glasshouses to allow for bedding out; and a vigorous technical press headed by the 'gardenesque' practitioner J. C. Loudon. The Royal Horticultural Society had been founded in 1804. Parallel with the traditional landscapes there was evolving after 1830 a new concept: the collective environment for the lower classes. The leading pioneer was Robert Owen (1771–1858) in his ideas for New Lanark (1835). It was he, according to G. M. Trevelyan, who first clearly enunciated the modern doctrine that environment makes character and that environment is under human control. Although there had previously been parks with public access, the first built and owned by the public specifically to ameliorate its own industrial conditions was Birkenhead (1843). Not until the present age were Owen's ideas universally recognized.

128. By the half-century the balance of population between town and country was equal, and the earlier sense of civic landscape emanating from the latter had virtually petered out. The green squares that were characteristic of London were continued, but the enclosing architecture was ill-proportioned to the spaces. Architecture varied from Gothic to classic, the villa and garden of the Italian High Renaissance being revived by Sir Charles Barry (1795–1860). Queen Victoria (or rather Prince Albert) built Osborne in the Isle of Wight in Italianate style, Balmoral in Scotland in Scottish Baronial. Development everywhere was left to individuals, the industrial cities with their satanic mills and slum dwellings being allowed to run rampant except for the newly conceived public park. The 1851 Exhibition was a flash of empirical genius in a world of prejudice, even though the male education of the upper, middle and professional classes was such that, in the words of G. M. Trevelyan, 'the world is not likely to see again so fine and broad a culture for many centuries to come'. Despite the absence of a common instinct in architecture, landscape design itself became rich with its ever-increasing international variety of deciduous trees and conifers, its flowering shrubs, plants and rock plants; and the parks and gardens which were created then took on a new use in the twentieth century, when the houses themselves were out of date and had vanished.

129. With a trebled population, with railways and expanded roads criss-crossing the countryside, with towns spreading independently into suburbs, with huge areas ravaged by exploitation, with smoke pollution damaging the life of man and plant and destroying human pride in environment, the end of the century saw Britain in a sorry state of landscape decomposition. The urban society had overwhelmed the old country society, and the new values had not yet found their own equilibrium. When the collective instincts of a civilization are confused, it is private individuals rather than the leaders who stand out like beacon lights in a jungle of issues. Edward Hussey and James Bateman were concerned with the landscape of the mind; Augustus Smith with the potentials of a business partnership with nature; Brunel and Paxton with a new-found aesthetic between engineering and nature; Loudon with the creation of a universal habitat of plants; Robinson with an insular habitat and Jekyll with the transformation of it into art; and above all, Robert Owen with his conception of human ecology, which Titus Salt, Lord Leverhulme and the Cadbury brothers later put into practice.

Turner's study of Fonthill (450), painted in 1799, links eighteenth- and nineteenth-century sensibility: the picturesque seen through the eyes of romanticism. Fonthill Abbey, Wiltshire, was then in process of being built for William Beckford, eccentric millionaire, art-collector, and author of the exotic eastern story, *Vathek*. It was at the same time the most splendid of picturesque follies and the herald of the Neo-Gothic movement. Turner gives it an epic grandeur, setting it in a rocky landscape which is closer to untamed nature than to a country gentleman's park.

451

PICTURESQUE PLANNING, which had been England's main contribution to landscape in the eighteenth century, was now extended from the gentleman's park to the city and from the private to the speculative purse. Nash's plan for West London, in collaboration with Repton, comprised an architectural sequence leading from Carlton House (now destroyed) and St James's Park in the south to **Regent's Park** in the north. **The diagram (452)** is taken from Nash's plan of 1813. **An air view (451)** shows the country scene enclosed within the adjoining eighteenth-century gridiron pattern of private estate-planning. The project today is in principle as planned, although the Zoological Gardens are a later addition, and the north side, intended to remain open with private villas, is now sealed except for Primrose Hill. **Looking east (454)** one sees the monumental stuccoed terraced houses, which in combination appear as a row of palaces, and two of the villas inside the park; six were planned. **A contemporary sketch (453)** shows the idealized setting, in which architecture has been absorbed into landscape.

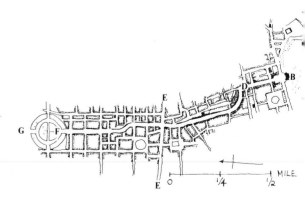

452 NASH'S PLAN FOR WEST LONDON
A St James's Park   B Carlton House
C Horse Guards   D Piccadilly Circus
E Oxford Street   F Park Crescent   G Regent's Park

453, 454

455

THE TRANSFORMATION OF THE ISLES OF SCILLY, off the west coast of Cornwall, from a hostile to a congenial and prosperous habitat began with a Benedictine monastery on Tresco about AD 1000. When Augustus Smith leased the Isles in 1834, the landscape was bare. Round the **abbey ruins** (**456**) where foliage still survived, he observed the narcissus (probably introduced by the monks) growing wild under its protection and flowering early. From this grew the daffodil industry. Smith deduced that in the mild sea climate, the real obstacle to fertility was wind. The Monterey pine (*Pinus radiata*) was adopted for shelter belts and the narcissus itself was cultivated in hedged compartments, seen in the foreground of the **panorama looking north from St Mary's** (**455**). In the middle distance of the panorama is Star Castle (1593), terminating a shelter belt, and in the left background is Tresco Abbey and the plantations under whose protection Smith created the most **exotic open-air gardens** (**457–459**) in the British Isles.

456

457

458, 459

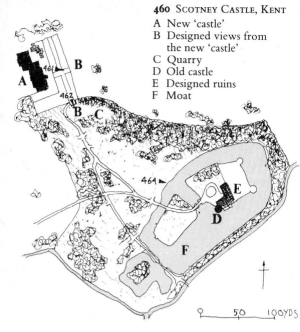

460 SCOTNEY CASTLE, KENT
A New 'castle'
B Designed views from the new 'castle'
C Quarry
D Old castle
E Designed ruins
F Moat

461

462

463, 464

TWO AMATEURS OF GENIUS, Edward Hussey at **Scotney Castle, Kent,** and James Bateman at **Biddulph Grange, Staffordshire,** expressed complementary ways of contemporary thought: the one a continuation of pure English romanticism, and the other cosmopolitan classicism. The old castle at **Scotney** dates from 1378, with classical additions of the sixteenth and seventeenth centuries. The **new castle (460)** (A. Salvin, 1837) was sited by the water-colourist W. S. Gilpin, who also arranged the **views from the house (461, 462)** according to established Picturesque principles. Hussey himself sketched the **view of the house (465)** as seen above the quarry from which came the building stone and, unique in Picturesque history, sketched and planned *in situ* the transformation of the seventeenth-century body of the old castle from a **complete structure (463)** into a **designed ruin (464).**

Biddulph Grange (466, 467) (begun 1842; plan *c.* 1862), on the other hand, proclaims a new era of British internationalism. An overall and ordered composition has welded different landscapes, philosophies and styles into a single whole. The mansion itself is in the style of the high Italian Renaissance, then becoming fashionable. The styles are segregated by miniature mountain ranges composed of soil from the lakes, and heavily treed. The **Chinese garden (468,** plan nineteenth century), for instance, adjoins but is totally separated from the **Egyptian mysteries (469).**

465

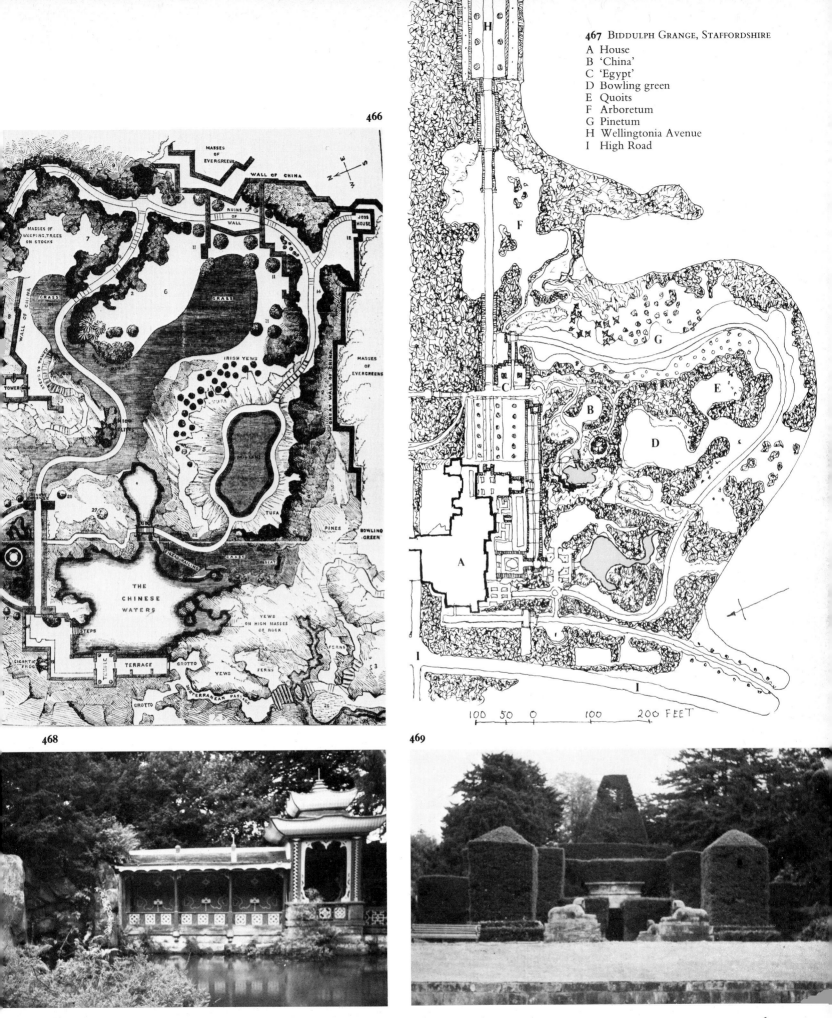

466

467 BIDDULPH GRANGE, STAFFORDSHIRE
A House
B 'China'
C 'Egypt'
D Bowling green
E Quoits
F Arboretum
G Pinetum
H Wellingtonia Avenue
I High Road

100 50 0   100   200 FEET

468

469

THE EMERGING MIDDLE CLASSES, endeavouring to emulate the upper classes, called for a way of life in a single home that was half town, half country. In urban London the Nash–Repton tradition of Regent's Park was continued and adapted to middle-class use in the **plan of the Ladbroke Estate, Holland Park (473, 474)** (1846), a pioneer in combining the small private garden with the private collective garden that was not again to be so fully exploited for nearly a century. The suburbs round the periphery of towns, now accessible by rail, proliferated individual homes. Not only were the gardens miniatures of the aristocratic park, but they were planned to contain as many as possible of the plant species that were now pouring into England. The style known as gardenesque was expounded by J. C. Loudon (1783–1843), a follower of Repton, whose influence through popular publications was universal. The illustrations of **garden details (470, 472)** and a **plan for a suburban villa (471)** are from *The Suburban Gardener and Villa Companion* which he published in 1836. The description and analysis accompanying the plan is given below.

470

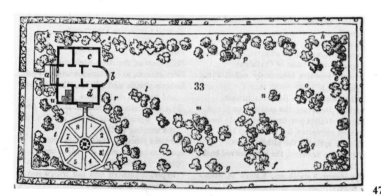

471

472

In limited plots of ground, whatever is their shape, greater variety of view will be produced by placing the house nearer one end, or nearer one side, than in the centre. In the latter case, it is impossible to get depth of view from any side, and thus a great source of beauty is lost. A deep view includes a greater number of objects, and, consequently, admits of a greater variety of effect of light and shade; it increases our ideas of extent, and, by concealing more from the eye than can be done in a confined view, it gives greater exercise to the imagination. Add to this, that in a small place, depth of view is not expected; and, consequently, when it does occur, its effect is the more striking, by the surprise it occasions, as well as by its contrast with the other views, which must necessarily be very limited. In [the figure] *a* is the house, placed at one side of a plot; *b*, the drawing-room, having a view the whole length of the garden: *c* is the dining-room, having a very confined view, and, in short, looking across some bushes, to a screen of evergreens (say hollies or evergreen oaks); *d* is the breakfast-room, or common sitting-room of the family, looking on a flower-garden, to which there is a descent from a balcony by three steps. . . . If the garden were larger, or even of its present size, if circumstances were favourable, a small piece of water, supplied from a dripping rock, at *e*, would have a good effect; and there might be a statue on a pedestal, surrounded with tazza vases of flowers, in the centre of the flower-garden. . . . The rest of the garden, with the exception of the surrounding border between the walk and the boundary wall, is entirely of turf, varied by choice ornamental trees and shrubs, including some fruit trees and fruit shrubs. The standard roses, and the fruit shrubs, such as gooseberries, currants, raspberries, vacciniums, etc., of which there cannot be more than two or three plants of each kind, stand in small circles, kept dug and manured . . . but the mulberry, the quince, the medlar, and the few apples, pears, plums, etc., for which space can be afforded, may stand on the grass. Against the walls are planted one or two peaches, nectarines, and apricots; and against the house, a fig tree and a vine. The remainder of the walls and of the house may be varied by roses and flowering creepers; except the more shady parts of the surrounding wall, which may be covered with the common, the giant, and the variegated ivy. The surrounding border between the walk and the boundary wall is wholly devoted to bulbs, in spring and the beginning of summer; with a row of Russian violets inside the box, for producing fragrance in winter; and patches of mignonette at regular distances, to scent the air during summer. Among the groups of trees, and close by their roots, common cowslips, snowdrops, wild violets, and wood anemones may be planted, to come up among the grass; and, being only planted in a few places, and these near the roots of the trees, they may be easily avoided by the mower. In such a garden as this, small though it be, a very great variety of trees and shrubs might be grown; and the flower-garden is sufficiently large to produce a very good display of the finer kinds of hardy flowers.

473, 474

475

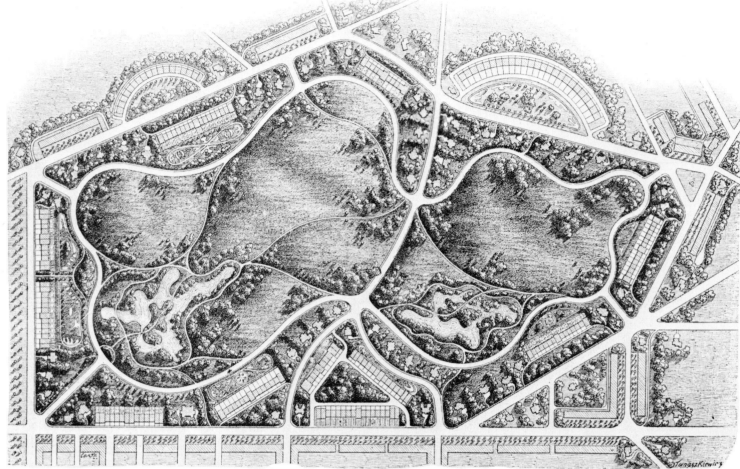

476

477

A NEW AGE is personified in Joseph Paxton (1803–65) – horticulturalist, engineer, land planner, economist and editor. Appointed head gardener to the Duke of Devonshire in 1826, he found in the Duke's historic Derbyshire seat of Chatsworth a congenial outlet for his imaginative, adventurous and gay spirit. The **Great Conservatory** (**477**) of 1836 was the predecessor of the Crystal Palace; the **Cyclopean Aqueduct** (**479**) was made before 1840. In 1843, in response to the call for parks in industrial towns, Paxton laid out **Birkenhead Park** (**476**) as a combined project of suburb and open space, the first to be created from public funds and to be owned by the public itself. Having no mansion and, therefore, no centrifugal point, the perspectives were random and the drive peripheral. The landscape open space design was basically traditional, but the **waterscapes** (**475**) suggest new influences from Japan. The **Crystal Palace** (**478**), set in Hyde Park for the Great Exhibition of 1851, foreshadowed an era when engineering devoid of stylistic architecture would fuse with English romantic landscape to become an art. When the palace was re-erected in Sydenham, **the grounds** (**480**) were laid out as an essay in Paxtonesque classical monumentality.

478

479   480

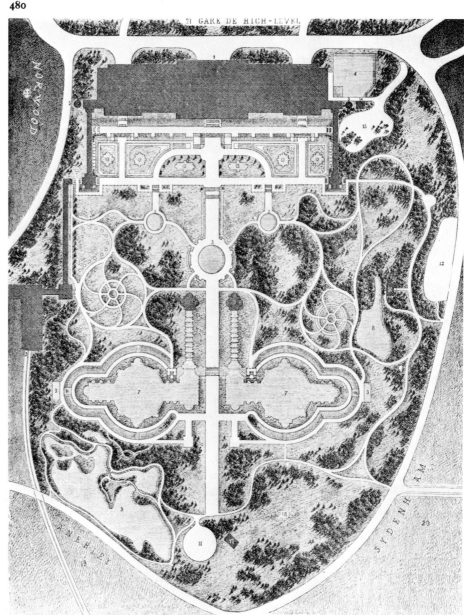

THE PRACTICAL AND THE ROMANTIC were the twin poles of nineteenth-century England. Although these two conflicting ideas were often ingeniously interwoven, as in the case of the railways, they were more convincing when kept apart. The piers of Isambard Brunel's splendid **bridge across the Avon** at Clifton (**481**) (1832–64) were originally designed to be Egyptian, and only afterwards took their present de-stylized form. In contrast with this expression of function, **Arundel Castle, Sussex (482)**, was transformed by the Dukes of Norfolk throughout the century from a genuine Norman stronghold into the idealization of a medieval fortress. The architecture is poor but the comprehensive landscape composition (which includes the late-nineteenth-century chapel) is among the most assured and grand of the Victorian world of make-believe. The **view from St James's Park, London (483)**, is an essentially nineteenth-century lyrical scene that evolved gradually and by chance after the transformation by John Nash of a long canal into the present informal lake. To the left is seen the Horse Guards (completed 1752; architect: William Kent); to the right, a tower of the Foreign Office (1868–73; architects: Sir George Gilbert Scott and Matthew Digby Wyatt); and in the distance, behind the Horse Guards, the fairyland turrets of Whitehall Court (1884; architects: Archer and Green).

481

482, 483

484, 485

THE VICTORIAN GRAND MANNER reached its zenith at the turn of the century in two landscapes that symbolized the end of one era and the beginning of another. **Bodnant, Denbighshire (485, 486)**, in remote Wales, was created by the first Lord Aberconway. The view is towards Snowdonia. As a great habitat of plant species from all over the world, it is suggestive of the sophistication, world-wide culture and individual wealth of the leaders of contemporary society. In contrast, **Hampstead Heath overlooking London (484)**, acquired for public recreation in 1871, is apparently indigenous and wild, affording the common citizen a brief experience of nature that may be either **active (487, 488)** or **contemplative (489)**, or both.

487, 488

486

489

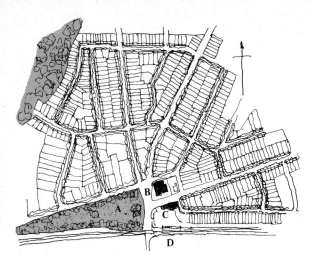

490 Bedford Park, Chiswick
A Acton Green
B Church
C Tabard Inn
D Railway station

THE RETURN TO NATURE as a retreat from Victorian sophistication was initiated by the middle classes and expressed itself in the search for the English rural scene. William Morris (1834–96) led the Arts and Crafts movement. In town-planning it first appeared in the **Bedford Park Estate, Chiswick (490)**, laid out in the 1870s as a village community, with Norman Shaw as principal architect, a predecessor of the garden city. Parallel with the ruralization of the middle classes, Cadbury Brothers upgraded industrial slum housing into a village community adjacent to their chocolate factory at **Bournville, Birmingham (491)** (plan dated 1898). In landscape, a revolt against foreign importations of plants and architectural styles was led by William Robinson (1838–1935), who advocated in *The English Flower Garden* (1873) an indigenous landscape, such as the **Lawn Garden at Golders Hill (492)**, that would seem to have emerged from the English countryside. A painter turned gardener, Gertrude Jekyll (1843–1932), accepted the ecological return to nature of Robinson, but transformed the relationship of plant to plant into a work of art. Her home at **Munstead Wood, Surrey (493)** (begun 1876), was designed by Edwin Lutyens, the garden by herself. In *Colour Schemes for the Flower Garden* (1914), Jekyll showed her particular preoccupation with colour, planning a special garden with a sequence of orange, grey, gold, blue and green sections. The **planting plan (494)** and description (below right) is for the blue garden:

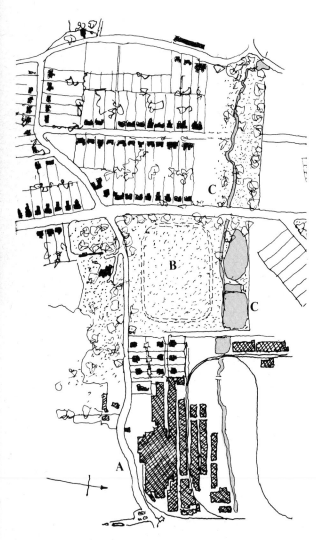

491 Bournville, Birmingham
A Factory
B Playing fields
C River landscape and lakes

492

493

494

After the grey plants, the Gold garden looks extremely bright and sunny. A few minutes suffice to fill the eye with the yellow influence, and then we pass to the Blue garden, where there is another delightful shock of eye pleasure. The brilliancy and purity of colour are almost incredible. Surely no blue flowers were ever so blue before! That is the impression received. For one thing, all the blue flowers used, with the exception of Eryngium and *Clematis davidiana*, are quite pure blues; these two are grey-blues. There are no purple-blues, such as the bluest of the Campanulas and the perennial Lupins; they would not be admissible. With the blues are a few white and palest yellow flowers; the foam-white *Clematis recta*, a delightful foil to *Delphinium Belladonna*; white perennial Lupine with an almond-like softness of white; *Spiraea Aruncus*, another foam-coloured flower. Then milk-white Tree Lupine, in its carefully decreed place near the bluish foliage of Rue and Yucca.

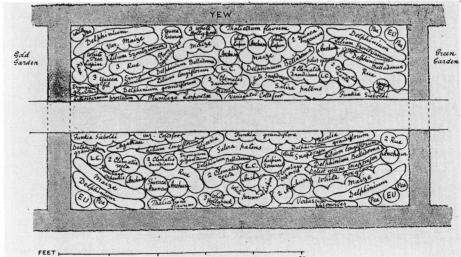

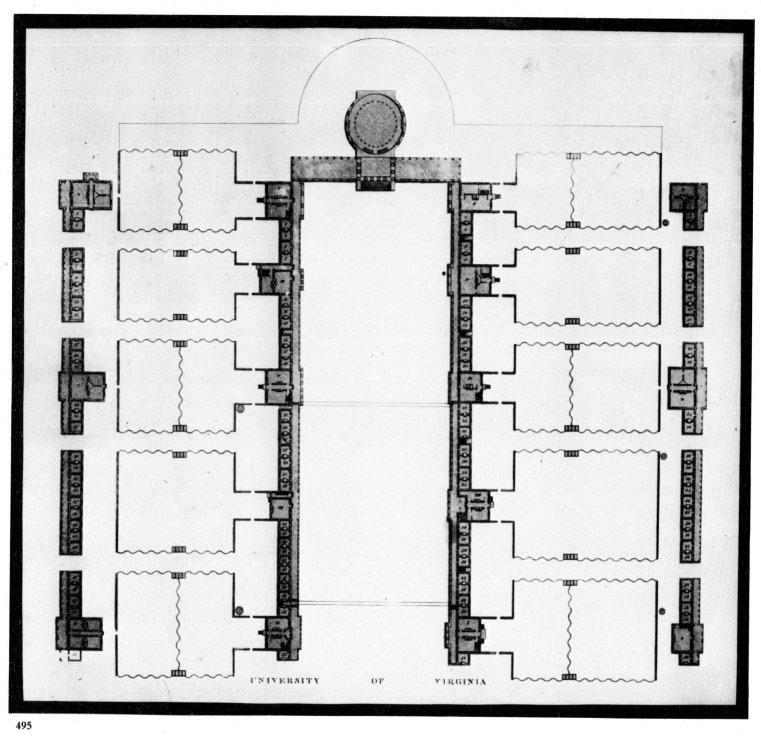

UNIVERSITY OF VIRGINIA

495

496

497

Growth *130.* In 1800 the population scarcely exceeded five million persons, occupying 868,000 square miles; in 1900 the population was seventy-five million, occupying nearly three million square miles. Throughout the period there were more than fifteen million immigrants from all parts of Europe. Expanding westwards from the original colonial eastern seaboard, the Americas reached and acquired California in 1848 (Washington to San Francisco: 2,500 miles). Settlers followed the adventurers, dispossessing the indigenous Indians. The land divisions and property plots were divided by T-square and drawing-board rather than topographically, as in the Old World. The apparently inexhaustible natural resources of this rich and varied continent were exploited with tremendous energy, the extractive industries relying upon the Great Lakes for transportation, the agricultural on a railway system whose mileage by 1865 exceeded that of all Europe. Society itself was bedevilled and divided by slavery until the Civil War (1861–65). In the rush for the creation of material wealth there was little time for the arts, which for prestige reasons were imported wholesale from Europe. By 1900 the wastefulness of uncontrolled exploitation of natural resources was at last apparent to government.

Landscape Design *131.* The colonial heritage came from Renaissance Holland and England, and the architecture of the agrarian South continued elegantly in the eighteenth-century tradition. Thomas Jefferson (President 1801–9), well travelled, cultured and fascinated by the implications of landscape design, endeavoured to lay the foundations of a national landscape art that wavered between French and English influence. Admiration for Versailles and the desire for monumental grandeur caused the choice of L'Enfant for the plan of the new capital on the Potomac, Washington. The English influence of Repton emerged under the landscape architect A.J. Downing (1815–52); but it was left to Frederick Law Olmsted (1822–1903) to initiate the sequence of public parks, of which Central Park, New York (1857) was an early example, that were to capture the imagination of the urban cities of the north. The pseudo-classical architecture of the Chicago Exhibition of 1893 showed the influence of the Ecole des Beaux-Arts in Paris, which governed the geometrical and architectural layouts of the new universities and of the great exhibitions that followed. Domestically America made little contribution comparable to Europe. The front gardens of the wealthy remained open and unfenced, symbolic of the nation's essential sense of liberality. In 1899 Olmsted founded with others the American Society of Landscape Architects, thus securing the future of professionalism.

Comment *132.* The two great personalities who stand out for their influence on landscape design are Thomas Jefferson and F.L. Olmsted. Jefferson, one of the last humanists in the Renaissance tradition, attempted to create an expression of modern liberalism through the media of French neo-classicism, Palladianism and finally classical Rome. The campus of the University of Virginia, a masterpiece of landscape geometry and his last work, combines the collective dignity of learning with the individual sensitivity of the person. The domestic is united to the monumental. Jefferson, who also wrote the university curriculum, was a man of universal understanding and vision far transcending the limits of a specialized professional. Olmsted on the other hand was a specialist, travelling extensively in Europe solely for the study of public parks. Jefferson the scholar provided an environment for security and contemplation; Olmsted the landscape-designer one of temporary escape from urban conditions. Aided only by a few colleagues and pupils such as Charles Eliot (1859–97), Olmsted's vision almost alone led the American nation from the concept of the isolated urban park to that of city and country as being a single design.

University of Virginia, designed by Thomas Jefferson and built 1817–26. **A contemporary plan (495)** shows the open-ended campus (now enclosed) and gardens contained within serpentine walls, and a **drawing (496)** suggests how individuality can be retained within a collective monumentality, symbolic of a democratic state. The relation to landscape is made clear in the modern sketch **(497)**.

498, 499

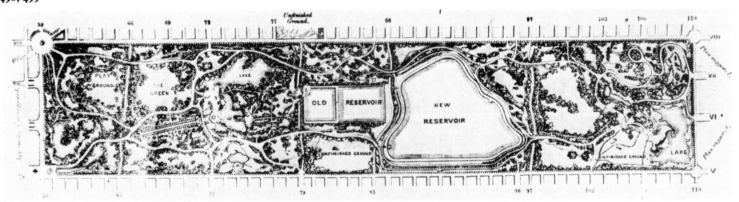

500

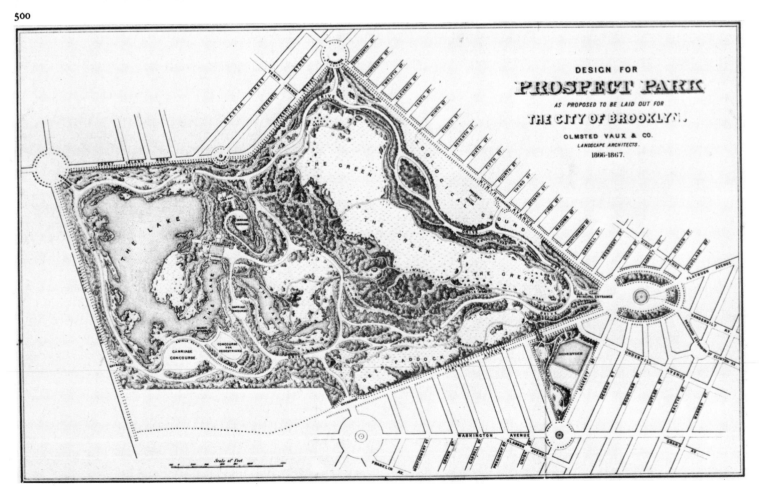

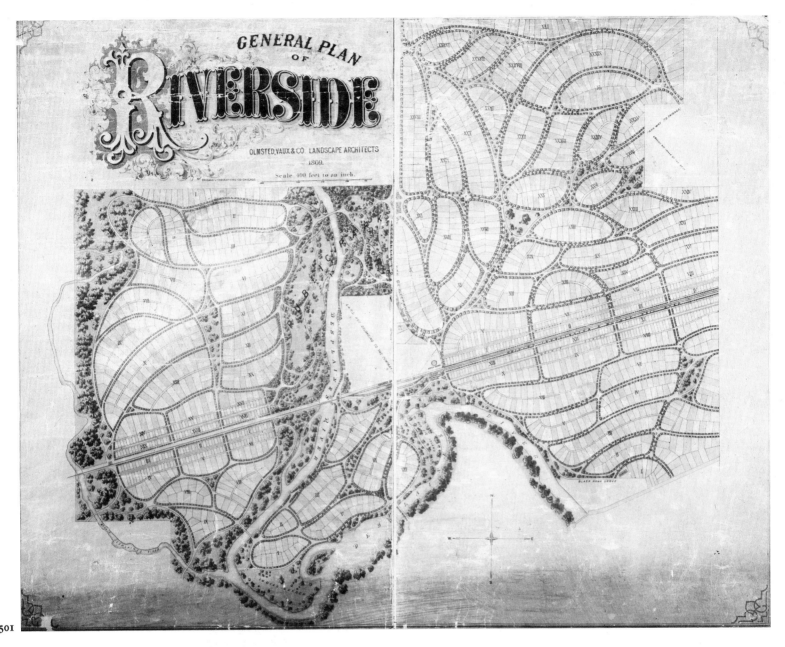

GENERAL PLAN OF RIVERSIDE

OLMSTED, VAUX & CO. LANDSCAPE ARCHITECTS
1869.

Scale 400 feet to an inch.

501

LANDSCAPE SPACE DESIGN was pioneered by F.L. Olmsted (in partnership with the English architect Calvert Vaux), whose progress can be charted in five stages: Central Park, New York (1857); Prospect Park, Brooklyn (1866); Riverside Estate, Chicago (1869); The Parkway, Boston (1880); and the World's Columbian Exposition, Chicago (1893). His indirect influence outside his executed works is beyond assessment. **Central Park (498, 499)** introduced a new concept of landscape urban space that was inward-looking, large in size but deliberately small in its many rich and varied elements. New planning techniques included underpasses for four essential crossroads. Partly because of the site encumbrances, such as the reservoir, the design is technically not so mature as **Prospect Park (500)**, which is unified in a single idea and is academically a classic. **Riverside Estate (501)** is an extension of the theory of park design to include domestic life, one of the earliest attempts to break the rigid gridiron of all American town-planning. An extract from the landscape architect's Report is given (right):

In the highways, celerity will be of less importance than comfort and convenience of movement, and as the ordinary directness of line in town-streets, with its resultant regularity of plan, would suggest eagerness to press forward, without looking to the right or the left, we should recommend the general adoption, in the design of your roads, of gracefully-curved lines, generous spaces, and the absence of sharp corners, the idea being to suggest and imply leisure, contemplativeness, and happy tranquillity.

502

503

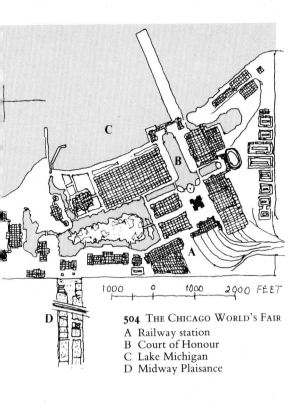

504 The Chicago World's Fair
A Railway station
B Court of Honour
C Lake Michigan
D Midway Plaisance

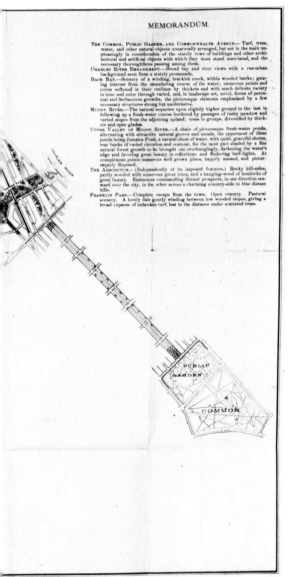

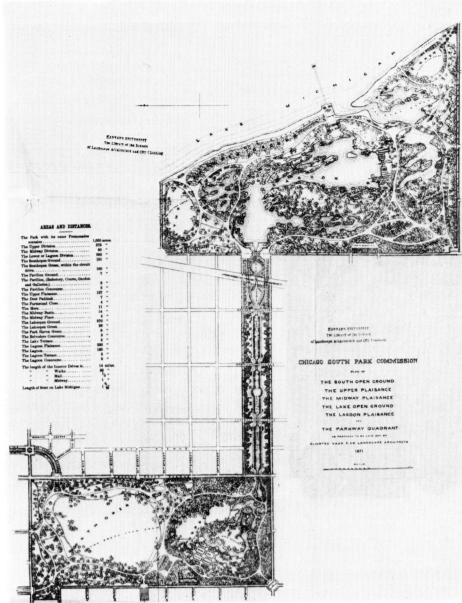

505

Boston and Chicago, both in 1893, saw the first attempts to organize into a single concept the complete recreation areas of a major city. The Metropolitan Park System of Boston grew from Olmsted's proposal to convert the marshlands of **Back Bay** (502) into a public park. Franklin Park followed in 1884 and there evolved the idea of a continuous string of green spaces and corridors linking this with Boston Common. The plan, known as **Olmsted's Parkway** (503), was published in 1886. Thereafter, the expansion of thought and imagination continued under Olmsted's new partner, Charles Eliot, the Parkway itself becoming only a fragment, however crucial, within a greater Boston complex.

The environmental team of all the arts was first tried on any scale at the World's Fair, Chicago, 1893, with Olmsted as general supervisor. In 1871 Olmsted and Vaux had made a **plan for the South Park** (505), of which only part had been executed. In 1890 Olmsted chose an undeveloped lakeside site for the exhibition, laying out the grounds in collaboration with the architects, Burnham and Root. The **World's Fair** (504) captured the public imagination, but the disposition seems a compromise between uncertain classic and romantic, while the architecture was retrograde. The same team later created the great Washington Mall concept of 1905 (562).

THE TWENTIETH CENTURY: 1900–1945

Environment *133.* The human species had roughly doubled in number during the nineteenth century, and was now pressing to make its patterns upon all but the most remote and self-protecting parts of the globe, such as the South American hinterland and the Polar regions. Wild life, especially that which was larger than man, was threatened with extinction. With notable exceptions like the Great Wall and Grand Canal of China, and the Roman roads, all major patterns previous to the industrial age had in general been conditioned by agrarian systems of local land tenure related to geography, and by the capacity of human and animal labour. The materials that made this pattern were likewise local. But now the scientific innovations that had begun two centuries previously were making themselves manifest: the patterns were becoming larger and cruder; there were scars of denuded land surfaces, such as the dust-bowls, that were added to those of denuded forests; the cities had expanded beyond the size that could be regionally supported, and the air about them was permanently polluted. Industrialized man had now begun to alter the agrarian balance and timing of nature upon a global scale, and in doing so to bring upon himself problems which he alone must now solve.

History *134.* Although the death of Queen Victoria marked the end of an era in the progress of civilization, imperialism as a motive continued vigorously. In 1911 Britain, at the height of her Empire, announced the foundation of a classically planned Indian capital at New Delhi. The First World War eliminated the Austrian and German empires and the Russian monarchy, creating the Union of Soviet Socialist Republics (1917). The war exhausted Europe, but nonparticipants (such as the Scandinavian and Swiss democracies) prospered, and real wealth from the participants flowed into the Americas. The economic depression of 1929 led to the New Deal of Franklin D. Roosevelt (president 1933–45) which recognized on a national scale that the use of force by man on nature was ultimately less advantageous than co-operation with it. In Europe the democracies were irretrievably involved in a clash of ideologies between Communism and Fascism. In the East a militant Japan erupted on to the mainland of a China weakly groping its way after the fall of the Manchu dynasty in 1912. The Second World War still further weakened Europe, and world power passed equally to the United States and Russia. Civilization itself was now global and inextricably interlocked.

Social *135.* The historic agrarian structure of society had been the tightly knit and personal unit of peasant, tenant farmer and resident landlord. All took pride in an environment in which they lived and worked. In the newly developed and heavily populated industrial countries this structure was now mainly superseded by impersonal organized labour complemented by the public company with its anonymous shareholders, and by a rapidly expanding and counter-balancing middle class. The industrialists had no interest in environment other than that of production. The traditional and now heavily taxed resident landlord was preoccupied with the preservation of historic values and it was almost wholly from the middle classes that there emerged creative ideas towards the progress of civilization. In England the Garden Cities movement began as a middle-class private venture based on moral values. In the USA endowments by wealthy patrons furthered research and this made possible many of the innovations of the New Deal. Throughout the Western world it was from the middle classes that individuals arose to express new ways of living in a servantless society.

Economic *136.* The capitalist system continued as the basis of Western economy, and now most countries had changed from agriculture to manufacture. The impacts of the change were felt most acutely in densely populated England. Agriculture had declined and foreign trade had created a prosperous island population whose numbers were far in excess of what the land by itself could have supported. This was manifest soon after the First World War. Both quantitatively and qualitatively the countryside became overcrowded: land was sold indiscriminately for building; materials were manufactured and synthetic, rather than local and real; mechanical methods of farming called for larger fields and fewer hedgerows; the mass-planted conifer with its quick returns began to oust the hardwood; and over all appeared the beginnings of a network of wires. Landscape-planning had been conceived by the environmental societies, but now it was accepted as an economic necessity. The two wars had shown the tremendous productive power that could only be generated by the state; by 1950 most countries not only operated planning control but could and did provide funds and initiative for material projects far beyond the resources of private enterprise, which filled the interstices.

Philosophy *137.* The beginning of the century marked a further and critical attack upon fundamental beliefs. In 1907 Albert Einstein's theory of relativity opened up a revolutionary conception of time and space. Science was now advancing beyond normal comprehension, tapping sources of power that could equally create prosperity for the human race, or cause its destruction. The place of religion in the advanced countries was basically taken by a moral code of conduct. Philosophy itself could give little guidance as to the nature and meaning of the new universe, but the struggle between intuition and intellect was recognized. The Frenchman Henri Bergson (1859–1941) was the philosopher of intuition, wishing to make intellect 'turn inwards upon itself and awaken the potentialities of intuition which still slumber within it'. The main intellectual opposition sprang from the dialectical materialism of Karl Marx (1818–83), a philosophy seemingly appropriate to a modern industrial state. The supreme architect of intuitive philosophy was Antoní Gaudí; that of intellectual materialism, Le Corbusier (at least until late in his life). But everywhere the emerging modern arts were united in their dedication to revealing through the subconscious what lay behind appearance.

Expression *138.* Almost alone the Scandinavian countries, unharassed by a nineteenth-century type of industrial revolution and by war, had achieved an elegant synthesis between environment and mode of living. In the industrialized countries, where confusion and chaos ruled the environment, two different creative forces were germinating independently one from another: one the science of land use in the interests of the community as a whole, the other a new art form. The former was concerned with urban design, land and landscape-planning, and the conservation and proper exploitation of natural and historic resources. The latter arose from the Constructivist movement in art before the First World War: the so-called 'functional' and 'international' architecture based on machine production and truth to factual purpose, but containing within it a profound search by individuals for a new liberalization of space and the consequent study of machine proportions. By the end of the period the science of planning and the new architecture, which had often been in conflict, had begun to coalesce; the role of landscape design as synthesizer between universal and particular was recognized; and the concept of comprehensive landscape-planning had been finally accepted.

285

Land Design

139. Although Scandinavia led in delight, Germany in planning efficiency, France in sophistication and Britain in the retention of tradition, the most significant single factor in land design was the birth of the modern science of town- and country-planning. This had long been germinating, but the distinct co-ordinator and parent was Patrick Geddes (1854–1932) and the place, the Outlook Tower, Edinburgh, described by him as 'observatory and laboratory'. In *Cities in Evolution*, published in 1915, Geddes penetrated far into an ecology that comprehended the arts of civilized life as well as the sciences. He maintained that his views were a development of the synoptic vision of Aristotle, that saw the city as a whole, and that this had expanded to become global. His thoughts paralleled the Garden Cities movement initiated by Ebenezer Howard (1850–1928), and were later to inform the writings between the wars of Lewis Mumford (*Culture of Cities*, 1938) and inspire the 'biological' analysis of the County of London Plan of 1943. Associated with these movements, but not of them, were gifted individual architects working in isolation, who each to his own satisfaction resolved the relation of architecture to landscape. By the end of the period, a collective conception of landscape began to crystallize, and the profession of landscape architecture was established, long after that of America.

Building Design

140. The purist Constructivist movement, that was eventually to become dominant in the world of building, originated almost simultaneously in Russia, Holland, Germany and France. Its every step was contested by authority and layman, and in education it was not until after the First World War that its ideas began to supersede those of the Ecole des Beaux-Arts in Paris. In architecture there were two main sources of turbulence: the individualist Le Corbusier, unacceptable to the French people, and the Bauhaus at Weimar in Germany, created in 1919 by Walter Gropius (1883–1963) and closed by the Nazis in 1933. At the Bauhaus, the arts of all kinds were synthesized and mathematicalized, those arising from nature being excluded. The contemporary way of thought of Constructivism is admirably symbolized by the Dutch painter Mondrian (1874–1944) in a series of abstractions in which a realistic tree loses its identity to become geometrical. Architecturally, the preoccupation was primarily with the creation of fresh mathematical proportions and the elimination of traditional confined space, now made possible by new building techniques such as steel and reinforced concrete, glass and central heating. The early impact upon the environment of these ideas was revolutionary, buildings seeming to become strangers from another world.

Comment

141. Throughout the whole period, the twin forces of ecology and Constructivism were in opposition. The ecologists instinctively turned away from modern architecture in the new garden cities and elsewhere, for primarily they were concerned with the human element to be found in the familiarity and gentleness of traditional homes, gardens and trees. The Constructivists, on the other hand, were inspired with the discovery of a staggering new art form which, in the hands of designers of genius, was truthful to knowledge and noble in aspiration, but exclusively for intellectuals. When directed promiscuously towards society, the movement led logically to mass-produced architecture and concrete jungles removed from nature and devoid of human feeling. Seen in perspective, the separateness of these two fundamentals of environment has been a disaster, not merely to Europe, but to the whole world. Possibly the only landscape-designer of the period to amalgamate these legacies (deriving respectively from Aristotle and Plato) into a single and balanced work of art was the Swedish architect Gunnar Asplund (1885–1940). Today it is recognized beyond doubt that amalgamation is necessary in an ecosystem, not only to realize the vision of Patrick Geddes but to lift it beyond this into the realm of great art.

BRITISH IMPERIALISM reached its zenith before the First World War and, as with the Roman Empire, projects overseas gave opportunities of space design not possible in the home country. The visionary Cecil Rhodes (1853–1902), in developing the continent of Africa, created great landscapes from Cape Town to the Victoria Falls. His tomb, which he planned himself, is a plain double-square rectangular slab surrounded by boulders and let into the rock floor of the **World's View** (**506**) in the Matoppos Hills, Rhodesia.

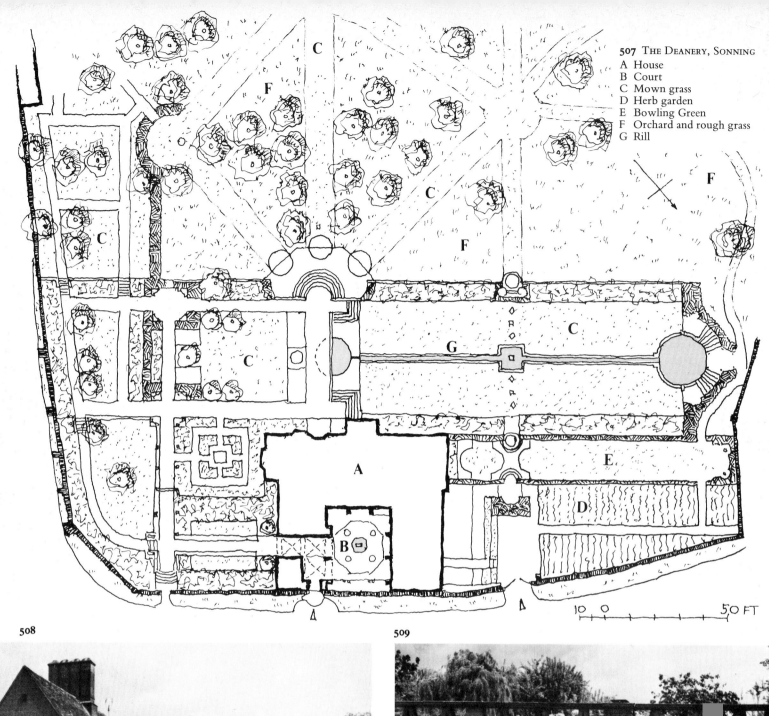

507 The Deanery, Sonning
A House
B Court
C Mown grass
D Herb garden
E Bowling Green
F Orchard and rough grass
G Rill

10 0   50 FT

508

509

510

THE BRITISH ARTS AND CRAFTS MOVEMENT found in Edwin Lutyens (1869–1944) its leading architectural exponent. His art and influence lay basically in the design of upper-class houses and gardens, in which he collaborated with Gertrude Jekyll (**493**), and later, in the English garden cities. He was unmoved by European rumblings of a new art expressive of the age and turned to the past for inspiration. Through his versatility, inventiveness, dexterity in composition and technical mastery of natural materials, his work delighted the senses without sentimentality. **The Deanery, Sonning, Berkshire** (**507**) (1900), grew from the pastoral scene of orchards and red brick walls. Medieval in conception, house and garden together are in fact a more sophisticated design than would have been realizable in the English Middle Ages. The idea of the **rill garden** (**508**), if not its **detail** (**509**), recalls the thirteenth-century Generalife at Granada (**45–49**). Even more than the Deanery, **Marshcourt, Hampshire** (**511**), is an experiment in time and structure, for the style is basically Tudor with Italian overlay, the materials are chalk with flint, and the extension of the house into the landscape overlooking the River Test a deep study of open and closed form, and of relation to site. The view is along the **west walk** (**510**), parallel with the valley.

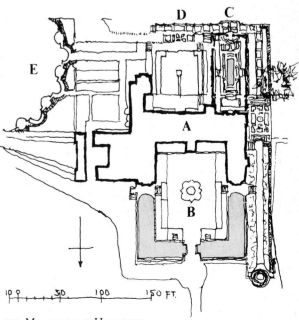

511 MARSHCOURT, HAMPSHIRE
A House B Forecourt C Enclosed sunk garden D Pergola walk E Grass

512, 513

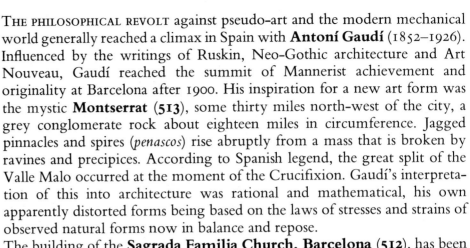

THE PHILOSOPHICAL REVOLT against pseudo-art and the modern mechanical world generally reached a climax in Spain with **Antoní Gaudí** (1852–1926). Influenced by the writings of Ruskin, Neo-Gothic architecture and Art Nouveau, Gaudí reached the summit of Mannerist achievement and originality at Barcelona after 1900. His inspiration for a new art form was the mystic **Montserrat (513)**, some thirty miles north-west of the city, a grey conglomerate rock about eighteen miles in circumference. Jagged pinnacles and spires (*penascos*) rise abruptly from a mass that is broken by ravines and precipices. According to Spanish legend, the great split of the Valle Malo occurred at the moment of the Crucifixion. Gaudí's interpretation of this into architecture was rational and mathematical, his own apparently distorted forms being based on the laws of stresses and strains of observed natural forms now in balance and repose.

The building of the **Sagrada Familia Church, Barcelona (512)**, has been continuous from 1884 to the present day. In it, Gaudí re-created the spirit of Montserrat, regarded by him as sacred, and this still incomplete fragment is perhaps the most thought-provoking metaphysical structure in the modern world. His **plan for the Park Güell (514)** (1900) was intended to be the centre of a garden city, with an open-air theatre above a columnar market. The **upper terrace and fantasy chimney (516)** indicate the sense of movement and instability that is now known to exist behind all natural form. The surface detail echoes the rock structure at Montserrat. The **great stairway (515)** leads up to the market beneath the upper terrace.

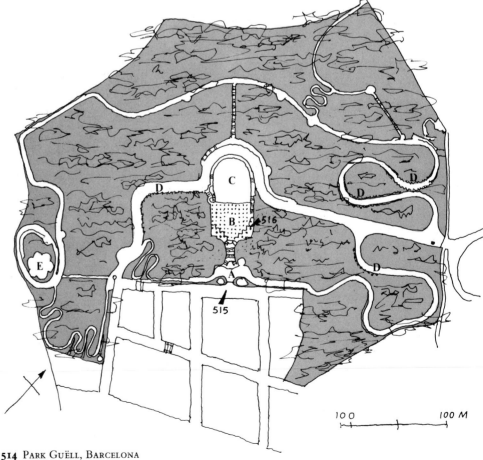

514 PARK GUËLL, BARCELONA
A Stairway B Hypostyle hall with terrace above C Greek theatre D Columnar viaduct or terrace E Chapel

515, 516

CLASSICAL VALUES that had become obscured under pseudo-classicism were revived by the Swedish architect **Gunnar Asplund** (1885–1940). A pure classicist rather than a Mannerist, Asplund's objective was twofold: to discard superficial style and re-create the essence of classicism in a modern language; and to harmonize geometric values with those of landscape. The **Woodland Cemetery, Stockholm (518)** (the plan as existing in 1940), was designed with S. Lewerentz. The view is **from the entrance (521)**. Although the structure of the layout is geometric and proportioned, the whole is subordinate to the artificial hill. The hill, concealing an adjoining suburb, is a universal and timeless symbol complementing the Christian cross, which is particular. The **plan of the City Library and Observatory Gardens, Stockholm (517)** (1920–28) shows the subtle manner in which the massive classical volumes of circle within square are orientated to respond eccentrically to the axis of the adjoining hill, as though pulled by gravity. **The hillside (519)** impinges on the library, which is surrounded by **the public gardens (520, 522, 523)**.

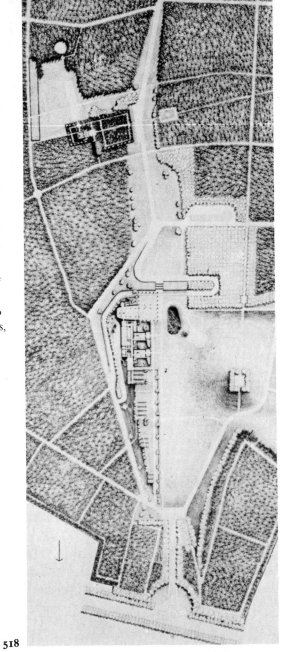

518

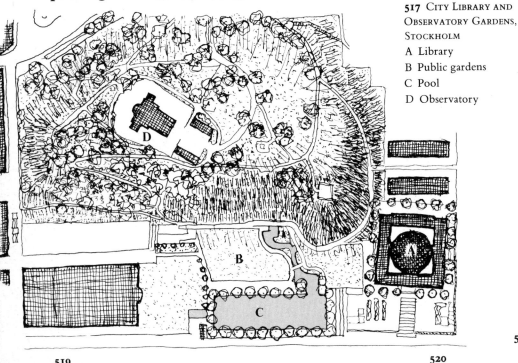

517 City Library and Observatory Gardens, Stockholm
A Library
B Public gardens
C Pool
D Observatory

521▷

519

520

522 523

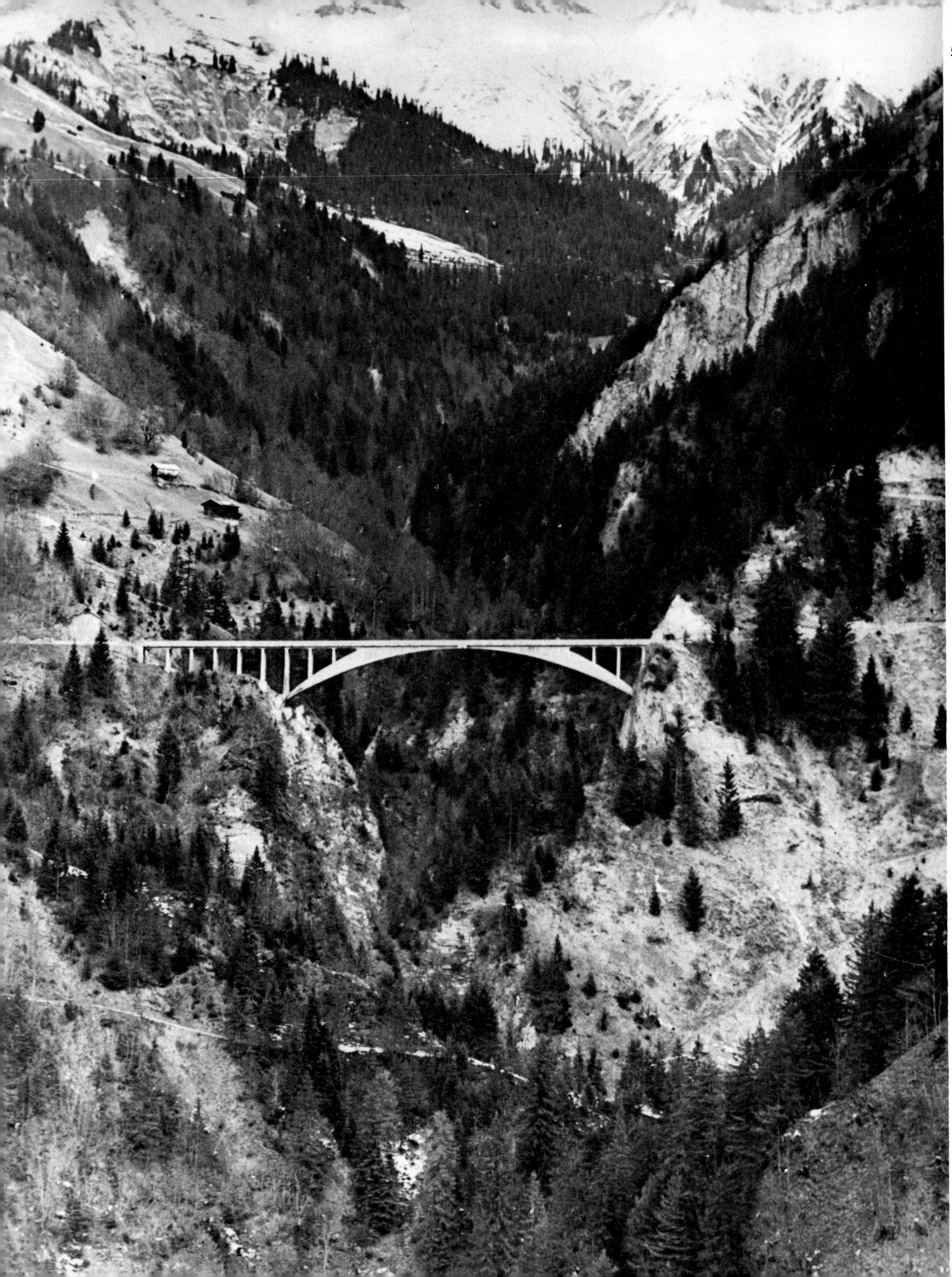

THE MECHANICAL SCIENCES opened up an enticing vision of a new way of life and a new art form. The **Salginatobel Bridge, near Schiers, Switzerland (524)**, by Robert Maillart, opened in 1929, suggested in modern idiom the beauty of pure structure independent of art. In the same year the sculptor Jean Arp created **Fragments encadrés (526)**, a recognition through art of the relation of biology to an otherwise mathematical cosmos. The outstanding exponent of the new machine age was the architect and artist, Le Corbusier, who held that the house should be a machine to live in; not repressive, but well proportioned mathematically and uninhibited spatially. The theoretical vision of the **Ville Radieuse (525, 527)** in 1935 proposed equality and light and air for all. The principles were to apply also to industry: the **Usine Verte (528)** (1944) had glass walls through which was seen the green landscape that Le Corbusier recognized as essential, but only in the abstract. The concept of art was universal and international. The purity and single-mindedness of this approach to life appealed to the intellectuals, but was rejected by laymen on guard instinctively against dehumanization. In later life this great artist inquired more deeply into human nature.

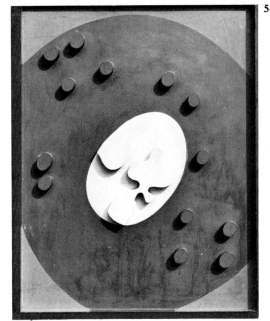

526

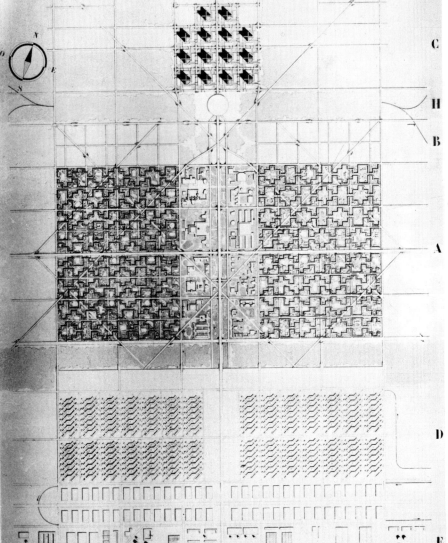

525

527

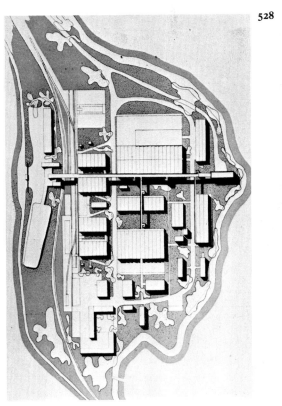

528

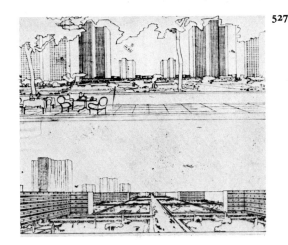

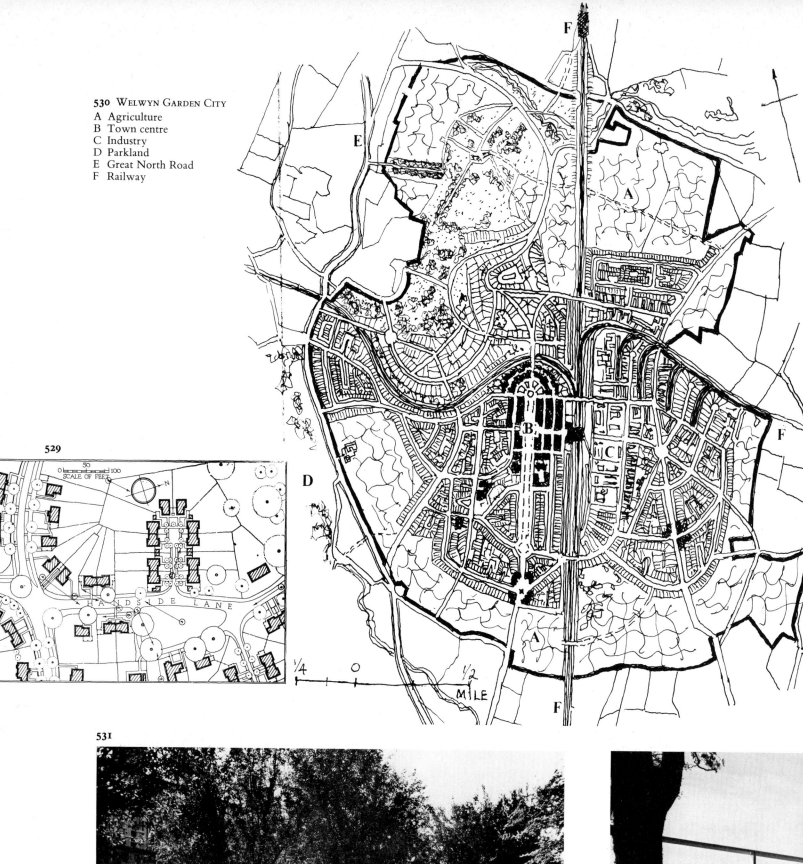

530 Welwyn Garden City
A Agriculture
B Town centre
C Industry
D Parkland
E Great North Road
F Railway

529

SCALE OF FEET
0   50   100

HANDSIDE LANE

¼   0   ½
MILE

531

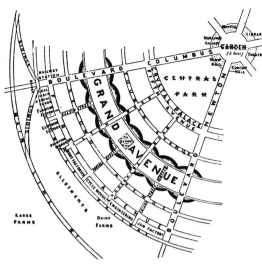

HOMES AND GARDENS throughout England were aesthetically unmoved by the technocratic revolution, but planning itself progressed. The concept of a balanced ecological town, commercially viable, had been formulated in 1898 by Ebenezer Howard in his **Diagram for a Garden City** (**532**) for about thirty thousand persons. This was initially realized in 1905 in Letchworth, Hertfordshire, and the next decisive step, in 1920, was a **plan for Welwyn Garden City** (**530**) by the classical architect Louis de Soissons. The town was friendly and familiar in appearance, but was socially split by the railway: the town centre and middle-class homes to the west, industry and industrial housing to the east. The **detail plan** (**529**) and **photograph** (**531**) show a typical 'close' of semi-detached houses of brick and tiled roofs opposite a village green, all submerged in trees that govern the skyline. **Halland, Sussex** (**535**), was an exception to the general traditional trend, for the **plan** (**534**) by architect Serge Chermayeff, with landscape architect Christopher Tunnard, harmonized the unfamiliar new international architecture and way of thought with the traditional English countryside; the **end of the terrace** (**533**), with sculpture by Henry Moore, shows the integration with the landscape. Because of central heating and large panels of glass, it was now possible visually to integrate the interior of the house itself with its surroundings.

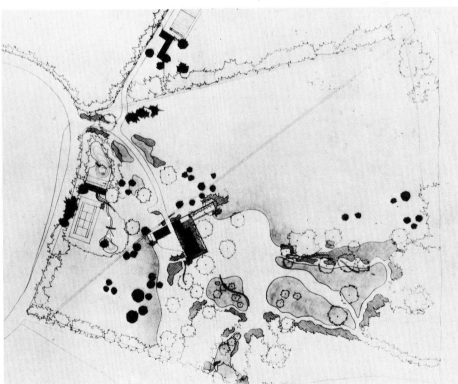

533

534, 535

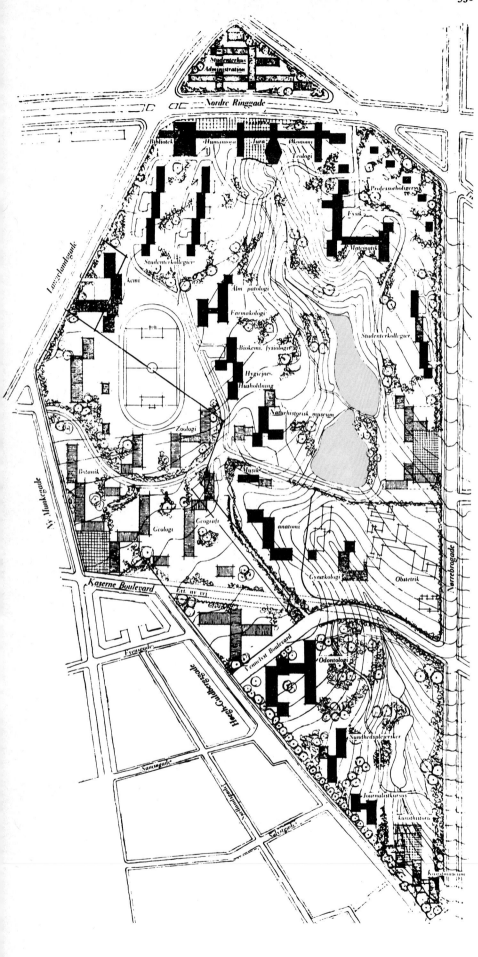

536

537

538

539

540

PARTICIPATION IN ECOLOGY was recognized as an integral part of adult education in the design of **Aarhus University**, **Denmark**, in 1932. In contradiction to the classical view, the university was conceived as a romantic biological group in relation to site, growth and domesticity. It was designed by Kay Fisker, C.F. Møller and P. Steegmann, architects, and C.Th. Sørensen, landscape architect, who appears to have been the presiding genius. Growth has been continuous, the form adapting itself to circumstances but never departing from original principles. The **plan of 1965 (536)** shows the university as then existing (black) and as envisaged. The buildings are grouped round a glacial ravine and interplanted mainly with oak, thorn, maple and beech. The architectural unity is based on parallelism, simplicity of block form and standard brick facing with low-pitched tile roofs. There is no difference in character between teaching and residential units. The **general view (538)** and the detail of the **open-air theatre and assembly hall (537)** were photographed in 1950, that of the **assembly hall and library (540)** and **theatre (539)** in 1972. The library completes the composition, which is now partly obscured by matured trees. The walls throughout are slowly being transformed from mellowed brick to textured green by Virginia creepers and ivies, as shown in the **Department of Pharmacology (541)** and by comparison of **(537)** with **(540)**.

541

542

543 544

545

546 547

548

THE CITY AS A TOTAL LANDSCAPE became an objective and began first to be realized in **Stockholm, Sweden.** There had been no nineteenth-century industrial revolution in Scandinavia to blight planning and depress public standards; the summers were short, but with brilliant sunshine and long daylight assured; and the formidable natural landscape of Stockholm was such as to enforce its character upon the urban form. **Planning** (549) included: (*a*) the idea of 'green fingers', aided by natural topography, penetrating into the city; (*b*) the acceptance and close study of unfamiliar architectural forms within the ancient centre, such as the first **high-rise flats** (542) in Europe, seen across the Riddarfjorden; and (*c*) the introduction of green landscape into the streets themselves, only made possible by clean air, public sensitivity and absence of vandalism. The inventiveness and elegance of this urban furniture was due to the Director of Parks, Holger Blom. Typical scenes were: **a garden shelter** (545), the **movable flower containers** (544) which came to be adopted throughout Europe; a **bandstand** (543) adjoining a restaurant in Berzelli Gardens; **children's climbing sculpture** (548), a prototype of its kind; **wild flowers** (547) along the Malarstrand; and **park seats** (546) set within flowers.

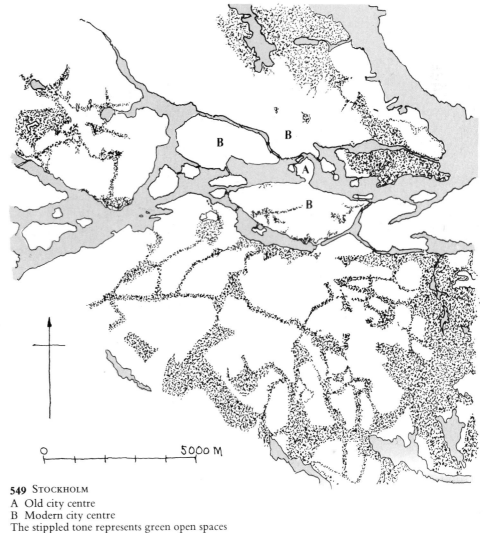

5000 M

549 STOCKHOLM
A Old city centre
B Modern city centre
The stippled tone represents green open spaces

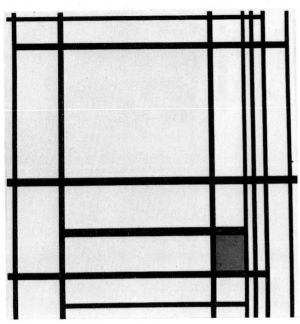

THE MODERN PARK for active rather than passive recreation was pioneered in Europe by the **plan for Bos Park, Amsterdam** (552), conceived in 1928 and begun in 1934. The essence of Dutch landscape was an austere flat geometry that is reflected in the work of the native artist Piet Mondrian, whose painting of abstract form, as in **Manhattan** (550) (1937), was a basis of the Constructivist movement in thought and art. Bos Park was an escape from this, and the plan the outcome of a balanced team of professors, botanists, biologists, engineers, architects, sociologists and town planners. The site was below sea level and swampy; from traditional drainage techniques there evolved a forest out of which seemingly were carved the appropriate shapes for collective sports. It is these shapes that give the park dynamism, for there is little variety in tree groupings and species, which are mainly oak and alder. Nature trails abound. The **section** (553) shows how the flat land was remodelled, cut being balanced by fill which included the making of a ski hill. The **air view** (551) looks north-east across the open-air theatre to the rowing canal, seen in the top left corner.

551

552 Bos Park, Amsterdam

1 Swimming pool site
2 Nature reserves
3 Sunbathing
4 Regatta canal
5 Children's football
6 Tennis, hockey, cricket, riding school
7 Hippodrome
8 Toboggan slopes
9 Artificial hill
10 Hockey
11 Children's play
12 Open-air theatre
13 Deer park
14 Games
15 Camping
16 Experimental farm

553 Bos Park, Amsterdam

A Sea level
B Regatta canal (4·50 m below sea level)
C Roads (2 m below sea level)
D Park-canal system (5·50 m below sea level)
E Artificial hill (12 m above sea level)
F Roadway (0·25 m above sea level)
G External lake (1·60 m below sea level)

THE TRANSFORMATION OF NATURAL GEOGRAPHY for man's use began before recorded history, but modern resources now enable him to act on such a scale and with such speed that there would appear to be no ultimate limit. Two such achievements are the kibbutz landscape claimed from the desert in Israel and the polders claimed from the Zuider Zee in Holland.

A **kibbutz** is a self-governing democratic community, theoretically supporting itself entirely on agriculture. The first kibbutz was founded in 1909; today there are 235, with a population varying between 200 and 700. These independent intimate groups of **homes, gardens and trees (556)** with **communal dining-hall (554)** stand isolated in their machine-scale agricultural environment. The view of the **Jezreel Valley from Nazareth (555)**, with a kibbutz in the middle distance, is a fragment only of a pattern of rural planning that has successfully resolved the modern problem of human and inhuman scale in juxtaposition.

554, 555

556

In Holland, the battle was against the sea. The evolution of the present Dutch landscape began in the sixth century BC with the making of mounds (estimated in all at one hundred million cubic yards) to lift farms from inundation. The building of clay walls or dikes began in the ninth century AD and there followed the reclamation of land behind the dikes. The first proposal to close the Zuider Zee was made in 1667 and finally accomplished in 1932. Thereafter began the draining of five polders in succession, adding 550,000 acres to the land surface and a fresh-water lake of 296,520 acres. The process began with the building of perimeter dikes, seen in the construction of the **Oosterpolder dike (557)** south of Schokkerhaven. The sea water was pumped out, the floor desalinated and levelled, and roads constructed. The land was then sown with colza and wheat, followed by barley, lucerne and flax, and finally came the farms, villages and towns. The **final landscape (558)**, undisturbed by romanticism, was inevitably one in which human habitation was part of pure geometry.

557

558

1900 to the First World War

142. Mainly developing from the Columbian Exhibition of 1893, the period was dominated architecturally by European classicism. The American Academy in Rome had been founded in 1894, recognized by the state in 1905, and a Fellowship in Landscape Architecture established in 1915. Charles Platt had written on Italian gardens in 1894 and afterwards created sensitive neo-Renaissance gardens. The Macmillan Commission plan for Washington in 1901 was an architect's classical conception of space with the Lincoln and Jefferson Memorials later to be noble termini to the axes in place of water. Elsewhere city plans were based on the teachings of the Ecole des Beaux-Arts in Paris, culminating in the monumental project by Daniel Burnham for Chicago in 1909. In contrast, and in advance of anywhere in Europe, was the growth of the profession of landscape architecture, the American society (ASLA) being founded in 1899. The largest single employer of landscape-architects was the National Park Service, with problems without historic precedent. Although, as an art, landscape design was less historically stylized than architecture, it remained totally detached from the deep movements stirring in Europe. Its own particular seed was germinating, to flower after the First World War.

The First World War to 1945

143. While the cities continued to grow between the First and Second World Wars as urban jungles, the landscape scene on the American continent was quietly but determinedly transforming itself from a traditional to a new way of thought. In Brazil, where climate and lack of tradition were favourable to a new art, and where Le Corbusier was more welcome than in his native France, landscape design was raised by Roberto Burle Marx to a status that paralleled the modern art movements in Europe. In the USA another individualist, Frank Lloyd Wright, emerged from the arts and crafts movement to be the natural opponent of Le Corbusier in evolving a modern domestic art springing from the soil rather than the machine. Behind all fresh thought on the proper use of land in the USA was now the formidable collective movement of landscape architects and allied professions. The New Deal of 1933 was a fulcrum between past and future. Not only was the Tennessee Valley Authority created, but the National Park Service (already far more important than any equivalent in Europe) was widened to incorporate more national parks, national parkways and national seashores, and above all given special powers to undertake far-reaching research into the place of nature in the modern world.

Comment

144. The century began in the USA with a continuing desire for bigness for its own sake, the Washington Mall being an outstanding exception where bigness has attained classical grandeur despite loss of scale to the individual. Culture at first continued to be imported at second and even third hand from Europe, but the period was one of transition and between the wars landscape design had sufficiently advanced in public appreciation to be able to create the Westchester Parkways as a contrast to Manhattan, and urban planning and architecture to create the Rockefeller Center, the first serious attempt to rationalize the jungle skyline of cities. The estate planning initiated by Clarence Stein and others was revolutionary. Frank Lloyd Wright certainly stands out during the period as the champion of ecological man, but in his later years the brilliant endeavour to cloak constructivism with romanticism was not as convincing as their actual synthesis in his earlier domestic work. Nevertheless, this pseudo-romanticism has been the inspiration for much modern architecture in its struggle to identify and humanize itself in a mass-produced world.

SYMBOLS OF THE AGE OF TECHNOCRACY are the **Golden Gate Bridge, San Franscisco (559)**, and **Yellowtail Dam, Montana (560)**. Their structure, like that of the spider's web or the sea-shell, is based on laws of nature that already exist in the universe. They are therefore a natural rather than an art form.

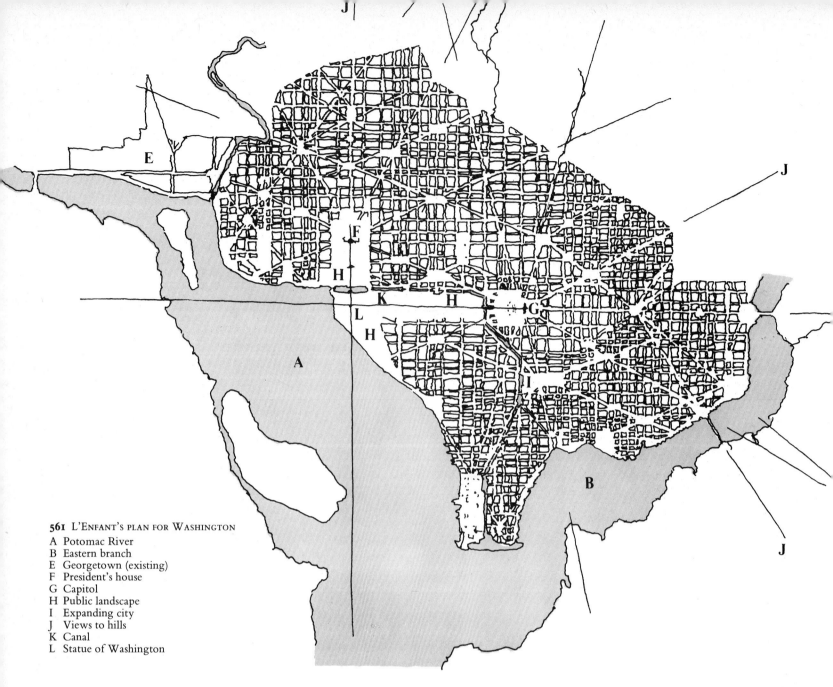

561 L'ENFANT'S PLAN FOR WASHINGTON

A Potomac River
B Eastern branch
E Georgetown (existing)
F President's house
G Capitol
H Public landscape
I Expanding city
J Views to hills
K Canal
L Statue of Washington

THE REPLANNING OF THE MALL, WASHINGTON, was chief among the terms of reference of the Macmillan Commission, appointed in 1901 to study the city afresh. After 1830, strict adherence to the L'Enfant plan had been abandoned. The memorial obelisk (555 feet; designed 1836 by Robert Mills, built off centre and completed 1884) and the reconstructed Capitol (dome 1850) rose majestically above a mall that had become cluttered and incoherent; the Potomac itself had been reduced by filling-in to become an engineer's river and now lay remote from the Mall; the city diagonals were intractable in relation to traffic and the shape of building plots. The members of the Commission, all associated with the Columbian Exhibition of 1893, were: D. Burnham, architect; F.L. Olmsted junior, landscape architect; C.F. McKim, architect; A. Saint-Gaudens, sculptor. The **perspective (563)** is of their proposals. The **L'Enfant (561)** and the **Macmillan plans (562)** are shown for comparison. In the former, two qualities are apparent: the dynamism of the radials and the open water terminals of the Mall. It was impossible to revivify the original Baroque conception, and in converting the Mall from an infinite landscape composition to a closed architectural composition, the Commission established firmness, an intentionally supra-human scale and a new grandeur.

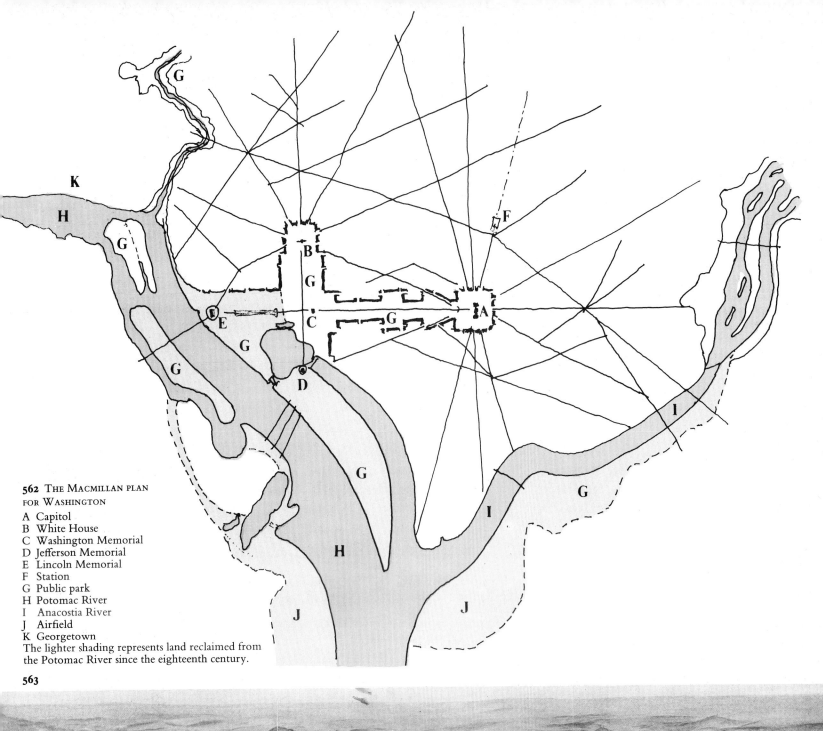

562 THE MACMILLAN PLAN
FOR WASHINGTON

A Capitol
B White House
C Washington Memorial
D Jefferson Memorial
E Lincoln Memorial
F Station
G Public park
H Potomac River
I Anacostia River
J Airfield
K Georgetown
The lighter shading represents land reclaimed from
the Potomac River since the eighteenth century.

563

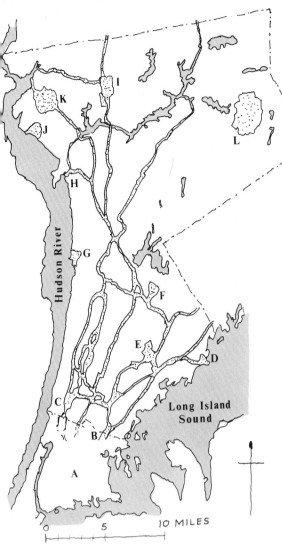

THE PLANNING REACTION in the USA against the gridiron, the car and sheer bigness, begun by F.L. Olmsted, continued only spasmodically after the First World War. It was in recoil from **Manhattan (564)** (seen here from the air) that the **Westchester Park System (565)** was begun in 1922, spreading northwards from New York (Jay Downer, chief engineer; Gilmore D. Clarke, landscape architect) and linking all recreational areas in Westchester county. The concept of a parkway was new, since, unlike the classical boulevard, it was a road *within* a park. In 1927, to combat the car, private enterprise created in **Radburn, New Jersey (568)** (Clarence Stein and Henry Wright, architects), the first estate to segregate cars from humans by car 'closes' and a collective garden. In 1935, as part of the New Deal, **Greenbelt near Washington (567)** was laid out as a complete new town incorporating both Radburn and English Garden City principles. In 1941, private enterprise created **Baldwin Hills Village, Los Angeles (566)** (R.D. Johnson, with Wilson, Mirrell and Alexander, architects), built round an elongated village green and segregated from cars, but contained within a standard gridiron. These experiments were like beacon lights to future planners.

565 THE WESTCHESTER PARK
SYSTEM
A City of New York
B Glen Island Park
C Tibbetts Brook Park
D Playland Eye Beach
E Saxon Woods Park
F Silver Lake Park
G Kingsland Point Park
H Croton Point Park
I Mohansic Park
J Crugers Park
K Blue Mountain Reservation
L Foundridge Reservation
The stippled areas are parks and parkways; the dotted line is the county boundary

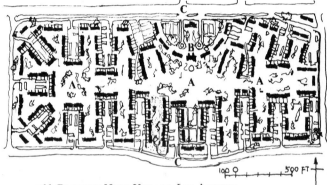

566 BALDWIN HILLS VILLAGE, LOS ANGELES
A Village green
B Club house
C Car entrances and close

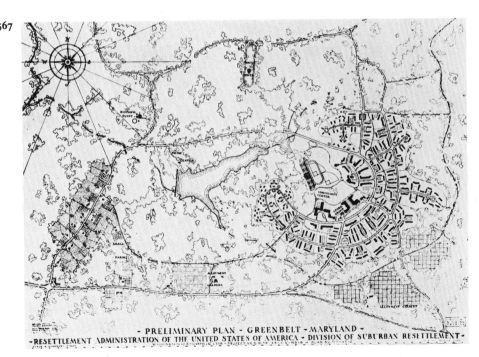

567

568

DOMESTIC LANDSCAPE ARCHITECTURE owed much to a single client, Edgar J. Kaufmann. In 1936 he commissioned Frank Lloyd Wright to build **Falling Water, Bear Run, Pennsylvania (569)**. Later, Wright wrote in *Architectural Forum*: 'There in a beautiful forest was a solid high rock-edge beside a waterfall and the natural thing seemed to be to cantilever the house from that rock bank over the falling water. . . . I think you can hear the waterfall when you look at the design.' The liberation of space by glass walls enabled **three distinct space designs** (plans **570, 571, 572**; section **573**) to be superimposed one upon another, each associated with the outer landscape.

Kaufmann's next adventure, **Desert House, Palm Springs, California (574)**, was different as to both site and architect. The site was desert with outcrops of rock interspersed with cedar, citrus, yucca and oleander. The architects, Richard Neutra with his son Dion, planned an **integration of free geometry (575)** with natural form. Such freedom was possible only through new technology, including refrigerated water circulation and the first use of desert-wind louvres.

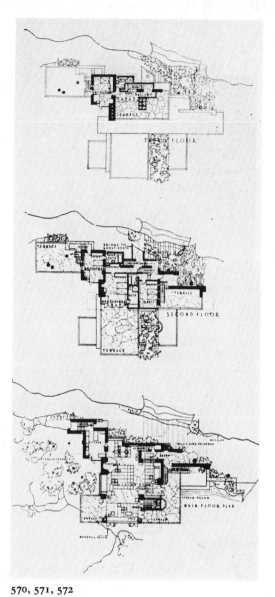

570, 571, 572

573

569

574, 575

576

THE TRANSLATION OF ABSTRACT ART into landscape originated in Brazil through Roberto Burle Marx (b. 1909). Painter, designer of fabrics and jewellery, stage designer and animator of fêtes and festivals, biologist and gardener, Burle Marx channelled these qualities into the single art of landscape design. Though he had visited European gardens and responded to the English School, his own education and inspiration really lay in the Brazilian forests with their **luxuriant plants (578)** and sinuous rivers such as the **Amazon (576)**. The sketch for his first public garden in the **square at Recife, Pernambuco State (577)**, is revealing for two reasons: the nature of the drawing itself is tender and figurative, and the tropical plants are contained within geometry. The **plan for the Kronforth Garden, Theresiopolis, Rio de Janeiro (580)**, was made two years later. The drawing is now that of a painter determined to record powerfully the spirit rather than the reality of his design. The spirit is his personal vision and interpretation of the Brazilian forests and their rivers, and only considerable practical skill and gardening experience can translate the drawing into reality. This having been done, one experiences much the same sensation as through participation in an abstract painting whose purpose it is to convey a great idea beyond the power of nature itself to do. Technically, Burle Marx uses plants either for their individuality or repetitively for their texture, much as a painter uses pigment. Both uses are seen in the **Kronforth Garden (579)**. The later matured work of Burle Marx is shown below **(593–596)**.

577

578   579

580

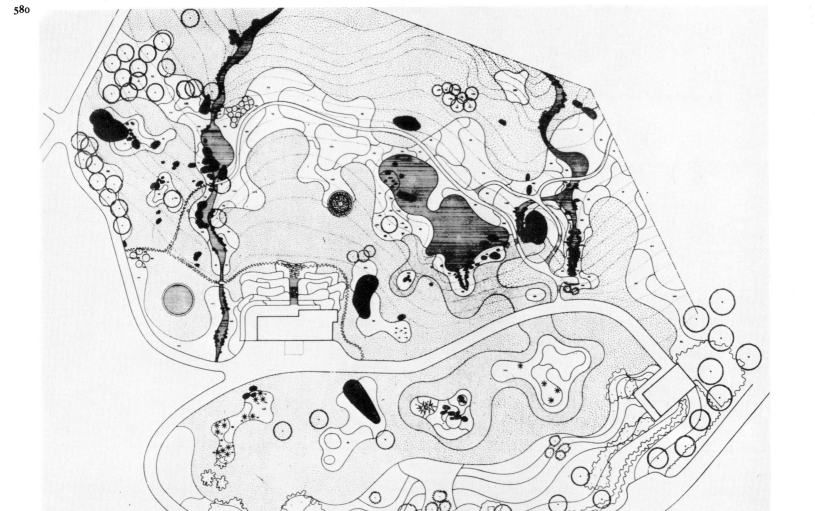

581

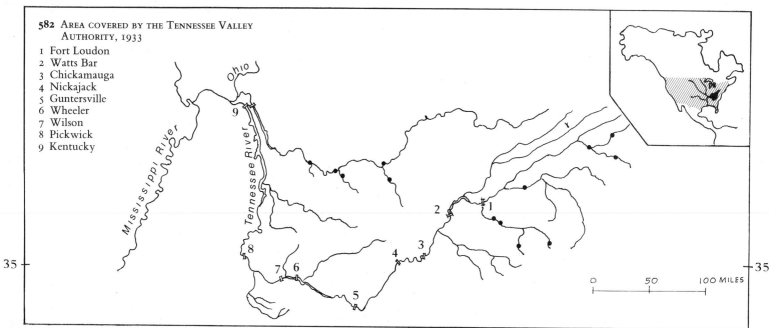

582 Area covered by the Tennessee Valley
        Authority, 1933

1 Fort Loudon
2 Watts Bar
3 Chickamauga
4 Nickajack
5 Guntersville
6 Wheeler
7 Wilson
8 Pickwick
9 Kentucky

THE USE OF RECURRING RESOURCES to produce energy was fundamental to the philosophy of the Tennessee Valley Authority. Established by Congress in 1933, the **area of comprehensive planning (582)** extended 650 miles along the Tennessee River and included an existing population of four and a half million. The objectives were to provide (*a*) twenty-one dams for hydro-electric power, flood control and navigation; (*b*) research and encouragement of afforestation, agriculture and mixed industries; and (*c*) facilities for public recreation. **Norris Dam (581)**, the first, was completed in 1936. The **general plan of Norris (583)**, the adjoining township, to house workers and become a permanent settlement, was made in 1933–34. In its integration with forest landscape, its nature trails, paths and underpasses, and the individuality of the homes, it reflected in microcosm the ideology of the Authority. **Douglas Dam (584)** was completed in 1943. (Note: the TVA's maximum hydro-electric power was reached in 1950, and naturally recurring resources exactly balanced the demand. But this very success attracted more industry than the region could support. Coal-mining had to be developed to cope with the new requirements. By 1973, strip-mined fossil fuel accounted for nearly four times the power output of hydro-electricity. By 1982 it is predicted that fossil fuel and nuclear energy between them will account for seven times the 1950 capacity. The Tennessee Valley, from being a uniquely balanced ecology, is now 'normalized' and on a level with other industrial areas.)

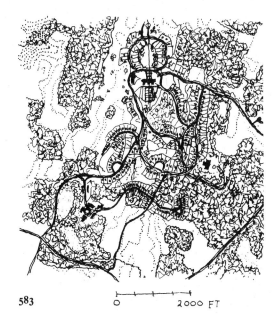

583

0   2000 FT

584

The State and National Park movements in the USA originated in the second half of the nineteenth century, mainly through the influence of F. L. Olmsted. National Parks were devised to preserve tracts of natural landscape completely unspoiled. The first was Yellowstone, opened in 1872. Since then, the most pressing problem has been to protect the landscape from the visitors, who must be kept under restraint without being too conscious of it. In the water-based ecological **Everglades (587)** (conceived 1935, commenced 1947), **overhead walkways (585)** that can be lifted when necessary bring the visitor at all times close to the plants. State Parks have in some ways the opposite function. Highly concentrated, gregarious, artificial, they provide open-air recreation for a modern, highly mobile public and attract them away from the wild and solitary places. **Jones Beach, New York (586)**, laid out in 1929 for the Long Island State Commission, can accommodate countless thousands of people and cars, which are its natural furnishings.

586

THE TWENTIETH CENTURY: 1945–1975

Environment   *145.* There had been little change in the geography and climate of the earth during the short period of recorded history, but there had been total change in man's attitude towards it. No longer did he fear his environment; the local spirits were chased away; the frontiers of knowledge were deep inside the earth's crust and in outer space. Through radio-astronomy he could look in outer space upon the happenings of five hundred million years ago. Not until European Conservation Year in 1970 did he become acutely aware that development of the human species on the historic principle of multiplication could not continue indefinitely. The capacity of the earth to sustain life was not unlimited; natural resources must be conserved and not wasted; population must be related to food available; natural disasters such as earthquakes, inundations and famines were predictable and ultimately might be prevented. This meant a reversal of idea: for survival, all human activities must be part of the biosphere or framework of nature rather than antagonistic to it. Yet the science of ecology, wherein all biological things are linked one to another to sustain a balance, was now recognized, as Barbara Ward and René Dubos expressed it, to be part only of the 'total unity, continuity and interdependence of the entire cosmos'.

History   *146.* By 1950 world power lay with the USA and the USSR. By 1970 the emergence of two further world powers was foreseen: Asia with a dominant China, and Europe united through the Common Market. The four civilizations were ethnically different. The Asian was a consistent resurgence of the Mongol Eastern civilizations, Europe was a continuation of the multiple Aryan Western civilization, the USSR was a more or less modern amalgam of East and West, and the USA was a modern complex of Aryan stock with negroid infusion. By the end of 1973 the Arab states of the retarded central civilization erupted as suddenly as Mohammed, to become overnight a potential fifth world power based on oil economy. Since there was no further land to occupy, the national boundaries were now established and primitive instinct demanded a relation between sovereign state and geographic environment; and land divided unnaturally was a source of irritation and friction. All countries in theory sought to contribute to the common will for peace in the United Nations, dedicated to the protection of the rights of man and to the universal spread of knowledge, technique and means that would ensure the wisest use of land everywhere and the consequential highest arts of civilization. The first world conference on environment was held at Stockholm in 1972.

Social   *147.* The Russian and Chinese Peoples' Republics were preoccupied with the development of the state as an entity and although the preservation of historic landscapes was deeply respected, the true purpose of landscape design remained unrecognized. The creative initiative continued to be with the Western civilizations, which had themselves virtually completed the change from absolute monarchy to democracy. The social change was reflected in landscape: the era of the great private garden had passed and its place taken by countless individual gardens and collective parks. The more even distribution of wealth and leisure had created among all classes, firstly, an appreciation of the true value of the natural environment; secondly, an instinctive desire to participate in it as part of the ecological system and as a release from modern stress; thirdly, the emergence of a common will to resolve the incompatibility of modern living and fundamental biology.

Economics *148.* Only when the primary needs of subsistence and shelter were provisionally satisfied would the advanced democratic countries seriously consider the major expenditure of surplus wealth and energy on landscape design as a necessity rather than a luxury. In England, good national landscape was not universally accepted as good national business until 1970, some twenty-five years after its acceptance by the more forward-looking industrialists. Expert psychiatry and lay common sense both agreed that confused environment might be the cause of mental illness in a nation and not merely in an individual; that unconscious therapeutic prevention was more agreeable and less expensive than medical care. The dilemma lay in the economic balance of needs: those that were pressing and obvious and those that were indirect. In rejecting expert economic advice on the choice of Cublington in the agricultural Buckinghamshire countryside for a new international airport, and adopting instead the waste areas of Foulness on the Thames Estuary, the British government placed the quality of living before all other considerations. Whether or not it was practicable, the decision, made in 1971, and revoked in 1974, revealed a deep concept of the values of landscape design.

Philosophy *149.* 'What we are doing, in basing a larger and larger part of our energy supplies upon atomic energy,' wrote Barbara Ward and René Dubos in 1972, 'is to bring down to earth the powers which would never have permitted any kind of organic life to develop on this planet, had not billions of years been spent in building up protection mechanisms – the oceans, the first creations of oxygen and ozone, the breaking out of the all-encompassing atmosphere by the earth's growing cover of green plants.' While intellectual philosophy renounced its traditional task of providing a theoretical framework for beliefs and values and scientific man was seemingly bent on self-destruction, intuitive man was building up counter-protective mechanisms through the mind. He was creating a common will spiritually as well as materialistically, to protect the biosphere, himself within it, and the fulfilment of his own unknown destiny. The philosopher-priest Teilhard de Chardin formulated the metaphysical idea that all life was moving towards a common unity; the abstract artists of the ages had now established beyond doubt that while the individual consciousness in man was as varied as the surface of the planet itself, the subconscious was homogeneous and universal. The manifestation of the counter-mechanism was the scientific 'green revolution' and *the art of the revolution that of landscape design.*

Expression *150.* The natural world consists of a combination of two forces: the life force, in which for survival no two objects can exactly repeat, and the inanimate, uniform forces of physics. Into this scene the human species projected a third element: the expression of its complex self, its needs and its aspirations. Its ideas were abstract and could only be fulfilled through existing materials and laws which were changeless. This element was already powerful enough to have largely reshaped the surface of the earth, but when it ignored those laws, it did so at its peril. Violation manifested itself in ugliness. Violation meant absolute waste, waste as the antithesis of nature was ugly, and ugliness begat ugliness elsewhere. The fundamental human criterion from which all else stemmed was the preservation of the identity of the individual as a life force within a vast inanimate machine upon which it had come to depend. The means towards this end, the core of landscape design, was first the creation of his own personal environment, the home; and expanding from this the adaptation of the habitat, the region, the country, the ethnic groupings and regroupings, and finally and hopefully, the planet as a whole. His mind responded gratefully to the tranquillity of geometrical proportion, but it was inevitable and indeed necessary that in landscape design his feeling should be drawn towards the mysticism of romanticism, the art of the biosphere.

The home *151.* While the renewed creative force of the Old World, the European, was active mainly in a cold climate between latitude 60° and 35° north, that of the New World was spread out across the Equator from latitude 45° north to 40° south. Uninhibited by history, with unlimited space, nomadic instincts and a congenial climate except in the north, the new inhabitants had virtually shaken free of European influence before the Second World War, to begin to create their own landscape art. This, at first, was at its most virile in Mexico and South America, where the impact of Le Corbusier on town-planning was far greater than in his native Europe. From the Ville Radieuse of 1935 sprang Brasilia, the world's supreme example of the homogeneous collective city. In direct contrast to such an ordered existence, the holiday areas of Florida and the West Indies evolved collective seaweed-like patterns of land and water excavated from marshlands, which were themselves new to landscape. Between these extremes were many varieties and species of both the collective and the individual habitat, aimed at escape from the sense of mechanical production.

Landscape *152.* Latin America continued the creation of a virtually new biologically orientated art, pioneered by Roberto Burle Marx. Only in Mexico was there a sense of history. In the USA generally orthodox principles had already been established; now, parallel with modern American art, which was itself for the first time influencing Europe, original townscapes inspired by modern conditions of traffic and verticality began to transform and re-create city centres. In land-use planning the USA had already reached a climax in the sudden forward movement of the New Deal in the early thirties and by 1950 TVA had vindicated itself both politically and practically. Thereafter, except for the continued development of the national and state parks, any forward movement in the field of ecology came from the fundamental research within the universities. The theory of the artificial ecosystem was fully established in 1960, but not until 1970 was it really accepted as comprehending man and not nature alone. Yet it had already been intuitively recognized and interpreted by the painter Jackson Pollock (1912–56).

Comment *153.* It is not enough for man to be part of an ecosystem. He is in search of an abstract idea which in history was expressed in the silhouette of domes, towers and spires, and which he seems at a loss to replace at the present day. He sees all round him commercial buildings confusing the skylines and in appalling juxtaposition with the old. The New World is less entangled than the Old with historic values and it is possible to detect in the USA the beginnings of a new expression of *Homo sapiens*. The historic conception of the values of landscape is reversed. The visual scene of a typical city such as Atlanta, capital of Georgia, is of an abrupt and dramatic high-rise commercial centre, from which decentralized low-rise multiple shops intersperse with suburban housing, the more prosperous of which are set individually in continuous wooded parkland. A church spire may rise above the treescape. It is probable that, whereas the generation of metaphysical ideas emanated in history from central church or temple, today it is primarily generated, or lies open to be generated, within the precincts of the home, the person and the self.

PUBLIC REGARD for landscape after the destructiveness of the Second World War is witnessed by the spacious if academic design for the environment of the **United Nations Headquarters**, New York (**588**), and the expansive **Palisades Interstate Parkway**, New Jersey section (**589**) (1950). The landscape architects for both were Clarke and Rapuano, designers of the Westchester Park parkway system (**565**).

323

THE TWO CAPITALS OF BRAZIL represent the two extremes of man's relation to landscape. The **old capital, Rio de Janeiro (590)**, is dominated by mountains and its shape determined by them. The new inland capital, **Brasilia**, 584 miles north-north-west, is designed to make its mark in a flat luxuriant jungle landscape (*c.* 16° south) that extends indefinitely. Although under consideration for over a century, the new capital was fundamentally established within the five-year presidency of Juscelino Kubitschek, beginning in 1956. A competition was inaugurated, won by Lúcio Costa in 1957; by 1961 the future of the capital was assured. It was, therefore, the product of virtually a moment in time. The **design (592)**, showing the influence of Le Corbusier, is the world's supreme example of the unified city plan; like an aeroplane, whose shape it resembles, it cannot be left unfinished, added to or altered. The collective rather than the individual is uncompromisingly dominant. Beautifully poised beside its lake, it is as much a noble monument to architecture (rather than to society) as were the great works of antiquity. The **Government buildings (591)** were designed by Oscar Niemeyer; the cathedral to the right is shown unfinished.

590

591

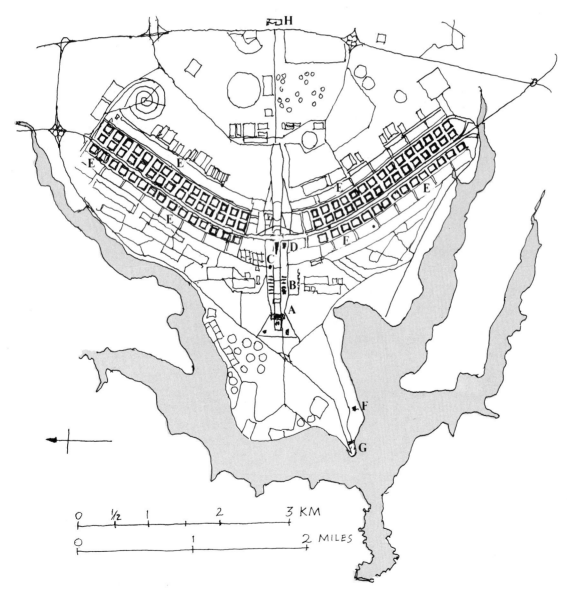

592 BRASILIA
A Legislature and
  Secretariat
B Ministries
C Cathedral
D National Theatre
E Residential
  superblocks
F Hotel
G President's palace
H Railway station

0   ½   1   2   3 KM

0   1   2 MILES

593

LANDSCAPE AS AN ORDERED COMPLEMENT TO ARCHITECTURE continued to characterize the work of Roberto Burle Marx (pp. 314–15), elegantly illustrated by the garden of the **Larrogoiti Hospital, Rio de Janeiro (593)**. The scope of the artist now includes the co-ordination of multiple uses within a single landscape plan. One of the most recent projects is the systematization of the **São Paulo Botanical Gardens (594–596)**, covering a forest reserve of over two square miles. The proposals comprise the Botanical Garden, a zoological garden, an astronomical observatory, an experimental animal farm, a psychiatric hospital and a school for backward children. Itineraries on foot have been designed as an educational cycle.

594: drawing for the new systematization of the Botanical and Zoological Garden of São Paulo: the entrance. (Project in collaboration with J.C. Pessolani, J. Stoddart and Fernando Tabora.) **595:** the science museum, pavilion for flower exhibitions and theatre. **596:** plant houses on the lake.

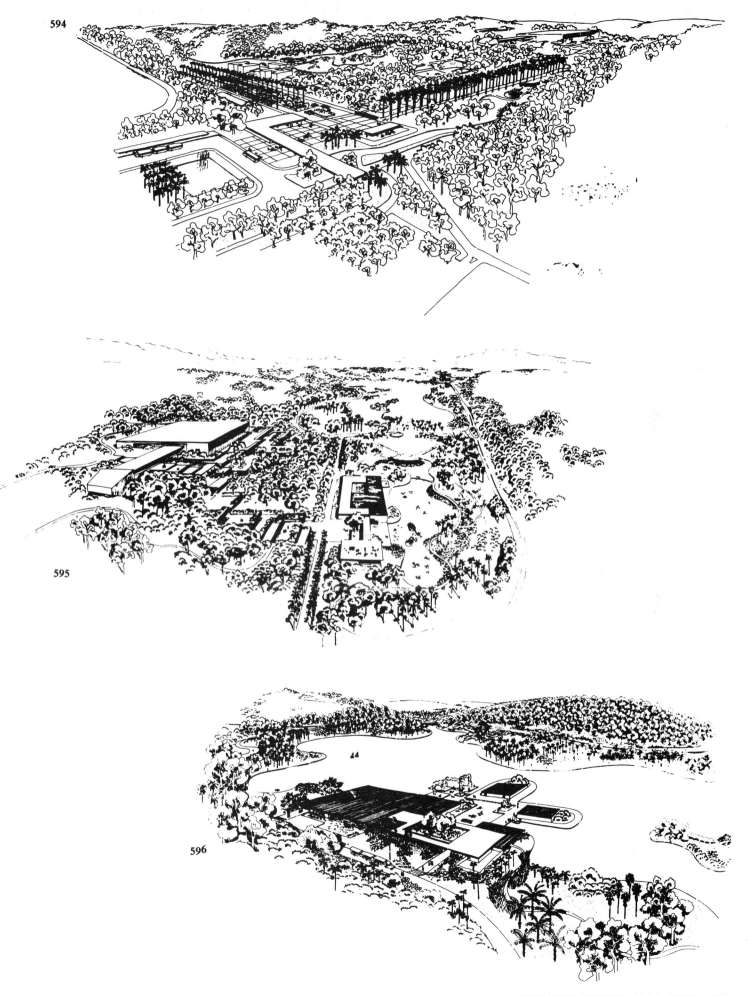

594

595

596

597

THE PRESENCE OF HISTORY, giving an added dimension to modern art and architecture, permeates Mexico City (**148**) more forcefully than anywhere else in the Western Hemisphere. The spirit of the Aztecs, unlike that of other Pre-Columbian civilizations, was not entirely eradicated by the Spaniards. While modern planning and space design originate from the principles of Le Corbusier and are without tradition, they have been insufficient to satisfy the rich emotional vein inherited from the past. The landscape contents are as formidable, violent and colourful as any in the Americas. Mexico City, on the site of the old Aztec capital, lies at twelve thousand feet on latitude 19° north. The **internal court of the Museum of Anthropology (597)** (1964) shows a spectacular curtain of water that is acceptable only in a warm, dry climate. The giant has always been part of the myths of history and the **water god of the New Chapultepec Park (599)**, lying with arms outstretched, his jaguar-like mask shaded by a banana tree, evokes the primitive and the unknown. The **water curtains and fountains (598)** revive the luxuriance and abundance known to have existed in the ancient city.

598, 599

600

SCALE IN LANDSCAPE, both horizontal and vertical, has increased beyond historical precedent. Three horizontal scales, for example, are manifest in an airport, where the ratio of movement (and consequently of space) of man:car:aeroplane is about 1:20:400. The exaggerated drama and poetry of the **Terminal Buildings of Dulles Airport**, south of Washington, D.C. (**602**) (architect: Eero Saarinen), seems justified; the **approach** (**601**) (landscape architect: Dan Kiley) has been brought to apprehendable middle- or car-scale almost solely by the multiple use of trees, relieved by massed colour planting.

On the other hand, the effect upon the retina of an exaggeration of the *vertical* scale can be either stimulating or devastating. **Peach Tree Center, Atlanta, Georgia** (**600**) (architect: John Portman), rises abruptly as a unified design from a low urban environment fringed with a domestic landscape of trees. In the foreground is one of many ground-level sculptures, *Renaissance of the city* (fibreglass, thirty-three feet high; sculptor Robert Helmsoortal, inspired by Fernand Léger's *Le jardin d'enfants*, Biot, France). The sculpture is gigantic and primeval, the summits of the buildings are linked like trees in a forest, and the whole spectacular scene inevitably raises the questions: whither man now? is he returning to where he began?

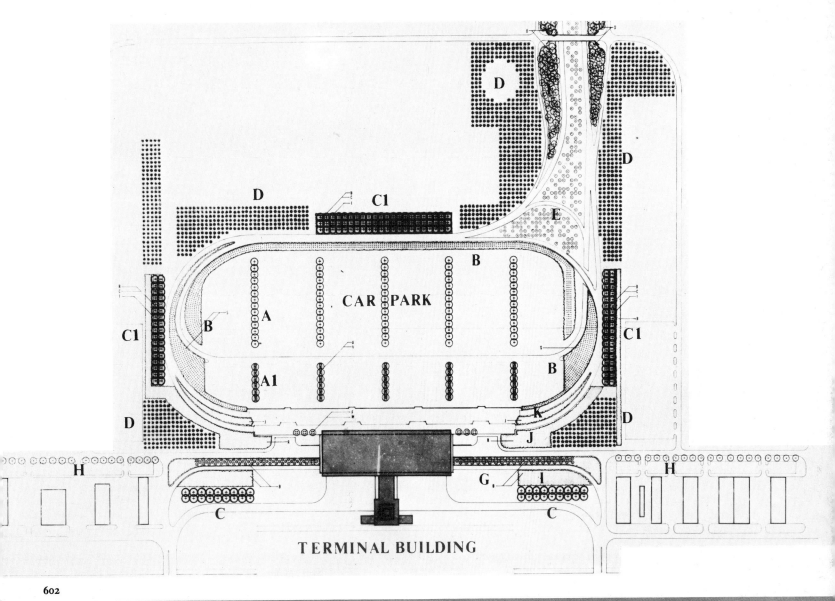

D

D

D

C1

B

CAR PARK

A

C1

B

A1

B

K

D

J

D

C1

C1

E

H

C

G

I

C

H

TERMINAL BUILDING

602

603

604

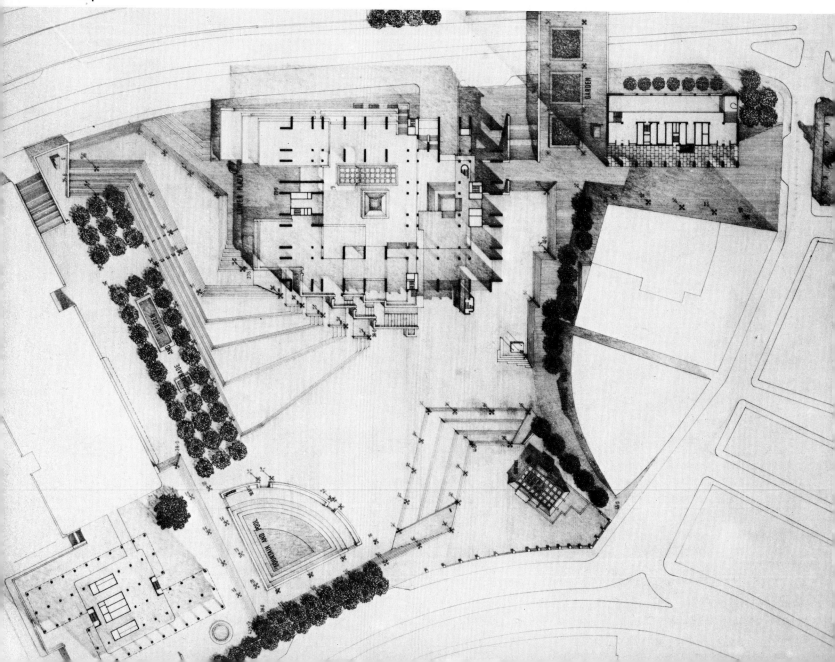

605

606

To bring nature into the centre of cities and thus to be associated with it, has been an objective of all advanced civilizations. The pool in **Boston City Hall Plaza, Massachusetts** (**603**), is only a fragment of an urban plan for the **City Hall and Plaza** (**604**) (*c.* 1971; architects: Kallman and McKinnell) which seems to give cohesion to an otherwise chaotic environment, even to the silhouette. **Lovejoy Plaza, Portland, Oregon** (**605**) (1966), is an abstract inspired by the High Sierra of California. The landscape architect, Lawrence Halprin, has written: 'I believe not only does form equal process in nature, but I also think that we derive our sense of aesthetic from nature. . . . I view the earth and its life processes as a model for the creative processes.' In this dry climate, the **water forms** (**606**) are incomplete without people to participate, wet or fine.

THE CONCEPT OF THE SKY GARDEN is as old as Babylon and the basic requirements have changed only in one respect: clean, unpolluted circulating air must now be added to (*a*) a minimum depth of soil, (*b*) protection from wind and (*c*) abundance of water, with good drainage, to offset evaporation. With modern technique there is no imaginative limit to the revival of this ancient art. The **plan of the roof garden of the Place Bonaventure Hotel, Montreal (608)** (1967; landscape architects: Sasaki, Dawson, Demay Associates), is a continuum whose water-scenery has no beginning and no end. The **air view (607)** shows the height above the city; the **internal view of birches (609)** and the **night scene (610)** show how far the illusion of country within town can be maintained. It is the art of the theatre.

607

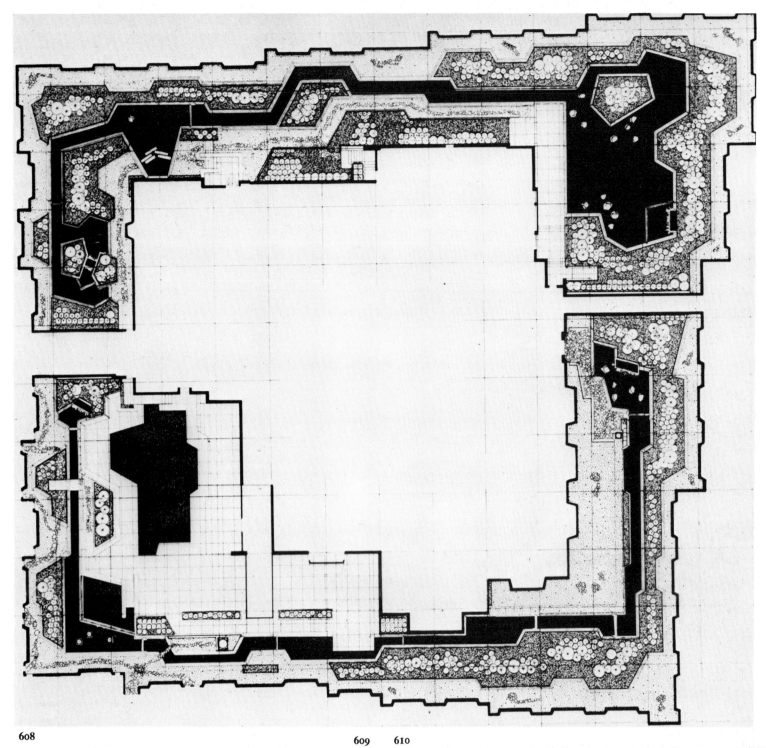

608

609   610

THE PRIVATE GARDEN REMAINS CONSTANT as the peculiar expression of the individual. While the **swimming pool at Sonoma, California (611, 612)**, designed by Thomas Church in 1948, is a study in the relationship of biological form, geometry and natural landscape, it is as capricious as the **garden in Los Angeles, California (613, 614)** by Eckbo, Dean Austin and Williams. In *The Landscape We See*, Eckbo wrote in 1969:

Private gardens make up a large part of the total area of humanized landscape and are greatly variable in the detailed relations between house and site, the broad and intricate individualized creativity, personal expression by choice and whimsy, family life, and the range of visual pleasure. . . . Residential design is the most intricate, specialized, demanding, responsible, and frustrating field for designers . . .

By *quality* I mean a relationship between an individual or a group of people and a landscape. This relationship involves human perception, comprehension and reaction as a process which measures quality. The essence of landscape quality is neither in the landscape itself nor in people, but rather in the nature of the relationships which are established between them. Thus quality may vary with time and place, with human nature, and with the nature of the landscape in which it lies.

611, 612

613, 614

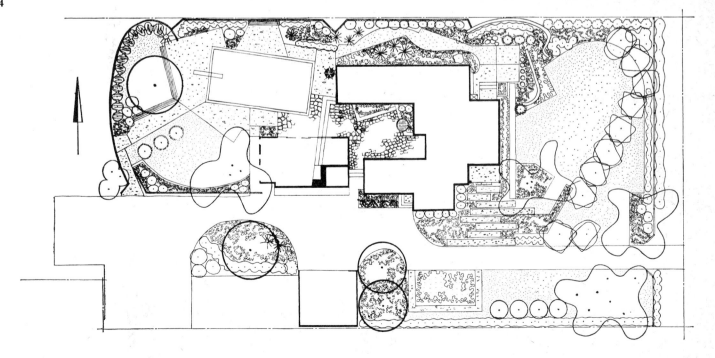

615, 616

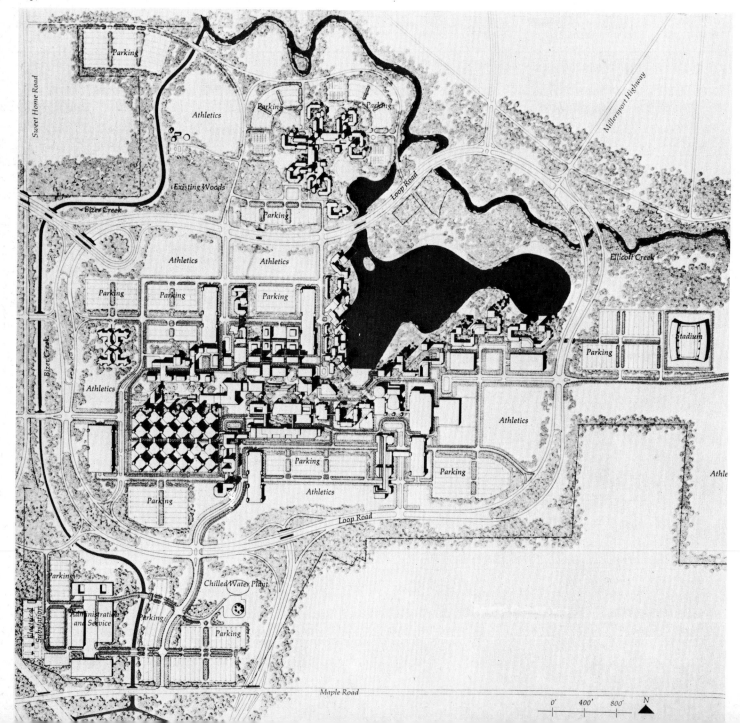

617

A UNIVERSITY IS THE INCUBATOR OF *Homo Sapiens* at his most formative stage. The larger the number of students, the more comprehensive the teaching organization, but the greater the danger of loss of personal identity. The campus, therefore, needs to equate numbers with the single individual and a mass environment with a human habitat. The shaping of the landscape should encourage reflection as well as the acquisition of knowledge. The student can be either reassured or disorientated by these considerations. **Amherst Campus**, **Buffalo**, is part of the State University of New York. The **comprehensive plan** (**616**) was prepared in association with thirty architectural and consulting firms by landscape architects Sasaki, Dawson, Demay Associates. The planned student and staff population is fifty thousand and the key to the breakdown of numbers is the system of colleges or home bases, each with a maximum of one thousand students, of whom only 40 per cent are residential. Sub-groups are, thereafter, expected to form themselves; to encourage this, the **residential habitat** (**615**) (Davis, Brody Associates) is romanticized. The **model** (**617**) shows, top left, the mechanized teaching centre, with the residential landscape in the foreground.
Statistics Area, 1,250 acres; students, 35,367; faculties, 7; car parking, 23,573 parking lots.

618

A MAN-MADE ECOSYSTEM derives from the scientific study of every facet of the natural terrain and, thereafter, from the evolution of a new, ecologically balanced landscape to absorb the human and his various activities. The studies here are taken from *Design with Nature* by Ian L. McHarg, 1971. Above is a **summary survey map (618)** of existing water and land features in part of the metropolitan area of Philadelphia, showing the basic random nature of the earth's patterns. The dark foreground indicates river floodplains; steep lands are shown in black. **Two theoretical studies (619, 620)** show how a humanized landscape is evolved from deductions drawn from surveys.

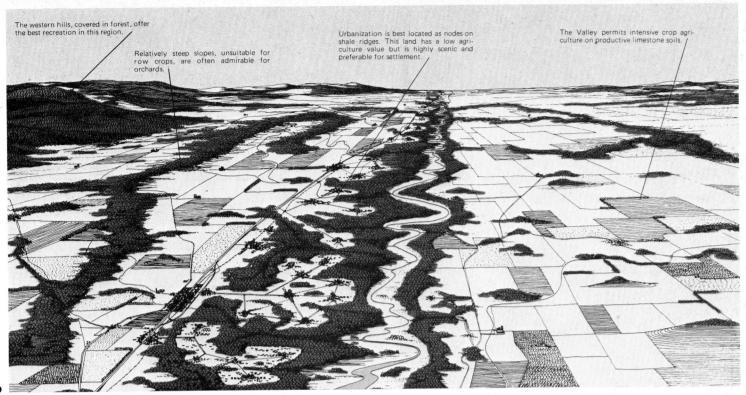

The western hills, covered in forest, offer the best recreation in this region.

Relatively steep slopes, unsuitable for row crops, are often admirable for orchards.

Urbanization is best located as nodes on shale ridges. This land has a low agriculture value but is highly scenic and preferable for settlement.

The Valley permits intensive crop agriculture on productive limestone soils.

THE GREAT VALLEY

The Great Valley is one great agricultural region east of the Rockies—a broad, generally flat valley with predominantly rich limestone soils. There are, however, three subdivisions—the western hills on sandstone, shale, limestone and quartzite, the wide belt of Martinsburg shale and the valley proper of limestone and dolomite. In brief the hills provide the maximum recreational potential, the limestone the agricultural resource, and the shale the best locations for urbanization. This last is important as it ensures that urbanization does not occur over the aquifer.

The resources and their distribution are most felicitous—wooded hills, a fertile valley, a swath of shale suited for urbanization, the latter bordered by a fine river and exhibiting considerable scenic quality.

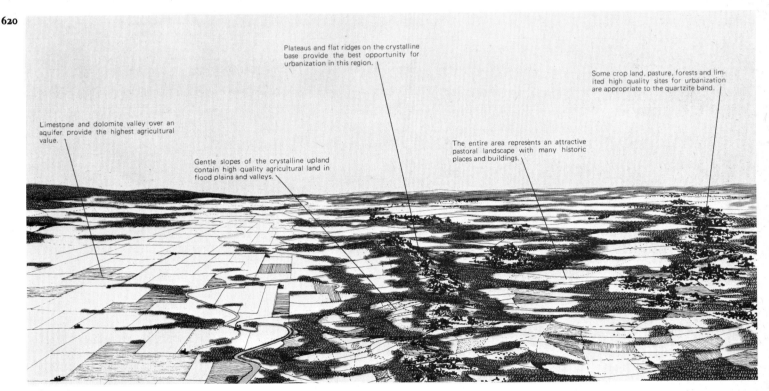

Plateaus and flat ridges on the crystalline base provide the best opportunity for urbanization in this region.

Some crop land, pasture, forests and limited high quality sites for urbanization are appropriate to the quartzite band.

Limestone and dolomite valley over an aquifer provide the highest agricultural value.

Gentle slopes of the crystalline upland contain high quality agricultural land in flood plains and valleys.

The entire area represents an attractive pastoral landscape with many historic places and buildings.

THE PIEDMONT

The section of the Piedmont illustrated reveals a great complexity—a limestone and dolomite valley, a preCambrian upland of crystalline rocks fissured with intrusions, a broad band of quartzite, yet another of shales. Intrinsic suitabilities respond to geology and the consequential physiography, hydrology and soils. The limestone and dolomite valley is most suited for agriculture, the shales for pasture and non-commercial forests, some crops, pasture and forests are appropriate to valleys and flood plains in the crystalline area. The most suitable urban sites fall in the crystalline region on flat plateaus and ridges. They are absent on limestone, rare on the shales. This is an area on the edge of urbanization. Opportunities abound but planning must respond to the specific opportunities and constraints afforded by the region.

THE MAN-MADE ECOSYSTEM IS THE MEANS TO AN END, but not the end in itself. Its extent and limitations are difficult to comprehend. It obeys the laws of nature, just as does the Golden Gate Bridge (**559**). It must absorb the peculiarities and idiosyncrasies of man, such as the semi-natural patterns on the surface of the earth of **Habitat, Montreal Exposition 1967 (621)** (architects: Moshe Safdie with the Harper Lantzius consortium), or **Cocoa Isles, Florida (622)** (1957; landscape architects: Eugene R. Martini and Associates). If it is in due time to give rise to a fresh landscape art, the first subconscious interpretation of its meaning will be recorded through the artist. Already Jackson Pollock, in **Number 28 (623)** and other works, seems to have been preoccupied with this restless, swirling and inspiring world of which we now know how inextricably we are a part.

621, 622

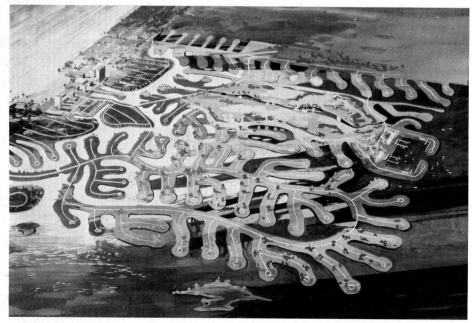

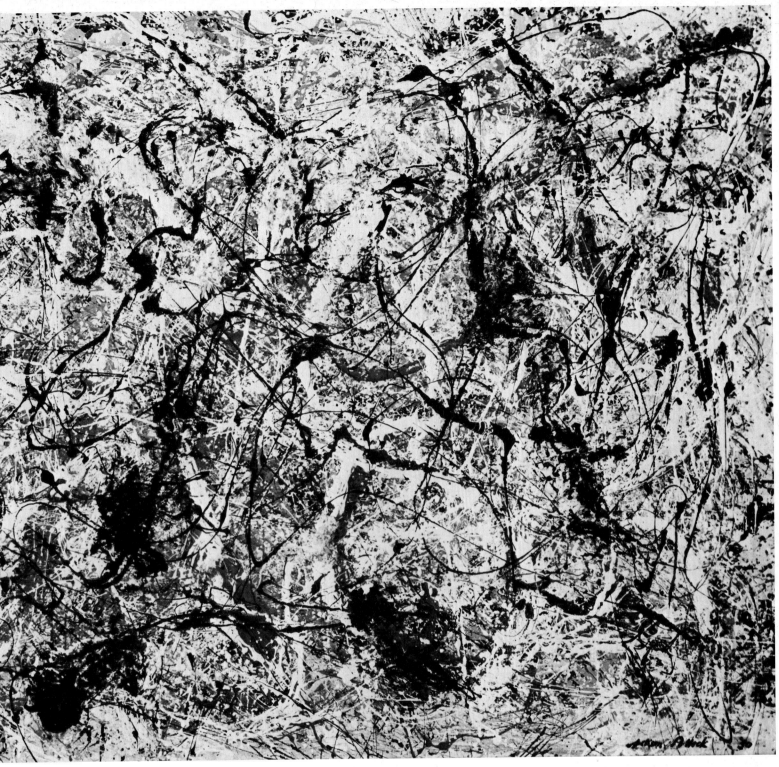

623

His painting confronts us with a visual concept organically evolved from a belief in the unity that underlies the phenomena among which we live. Void and solid, human action and inertia, are metamorphosed and refined into the energy that sustains them and is their common denominator. An ocean's tides and a personal nightmare, the bursting of a bubble, and the communal clamour for a victim are as inextricably meshed in the coruscation and darkness of his work as they are in actuality. His forms and textures germinate, climax and decline, coalesce and dissolve across the canvas. The picture surface, with no depth of recognizable space or sequence of known time, gives us the never-ending present. We are presented with a visualization of that remorseless consolation – in the end is the beginning.

Alfonso Ossorio, in an introduction to the exhibition catalogue, *Jackson Pollock 1951.*

LONGON

SOCIAL & FUNCTIONAL ANALYSIS

A SIMPLIFICATION OF THE COMMUNITIES & OPEN SPACE SURVEY SHOWING THE EXISTING MAIN ELEMENTS OF LONDON. AROUND THE CENTRE CONSISTING OF THE PORT CITY & WEST END ARE GROUPED THE RESIDENTIAL COMMUNITIES WHICH ARE DIVIDED INTO A. THE CENTRAL COMMUNITIES AROUND THE WEST END B. THE EAST END & SOUTH BANK COMMUNITIES WHICH HAVE A HIGH PROPORTION OF OBSOLESCENT PROPERTY & IN THE MAIN ARE ADJACENT TO OR MIXED WITH INDUSTRY C. THE SUBURBAN COMMUNITIES. THE MAJOR OPEN SPACES & INDUSTRIAL CONCENTRATIONS ARE ALSO SHOWN.

- CENTRAL COMMUNITIES AROUND WEST END
- CENTRAL COMMUNITIES WITH HIGH PROPORTION OF OBSOLESCENT PROPERTY
- SUBURBAN COMMUNITIES
- TOWN HALLS
- MAIN INDUSTRIES WHARVES WAREHOUSES & RAILWAYS
- OPEN SPACES & LARGE INSTITUTIONS WITH SUBSTANTIAL OPEN SPACE
- WATER WAYS RESERVOIRS ETC.
- MAIN SHOPPING CENTRES

The home 154. Britain continued to be the pioneer of organic as opposed to static town-planning. In 1945 the Greater London Plan presented a comprehensive analysis indicating that the metropolis was in principle an organism of amoeba-like townships clustering round a centre. The essence of the small town was the compact individual house and garden. Together with the experience of the Garden Cities movement, this analysis formed the basis of the first post-war New Towns, whose design cycle was as follows: *c.* 1950, neighbourhood units of houses and gardens in open green spaces round the centre, the size determined by the walking distance to school and shopping (Harlow); *c.* 1960, movement to compactness and recognition of the car as fundamental to design (Cumbernauld): *c.* 1970, final disappearance of the neighbourhood unit, generous space planning based on a car-motivated gridiron of roads adapted to an undulating countryside with traffic-free interstices large enough to contain individual homes within a romantic landscape (Milton Keynes). This recent about-turn to nature was exceptional, for in most countries the urge to conserve space in towns created concrete jungles, often well planned intellectually, but with loss of tree-house-garden and neighbour relationship.

The landscape 155. The emergence of a modern materialistic landscape out of an historic landscape was now apparent throughout the advanced countries – a phenomenon, new to this world, that was causing disruption in the cities and discord in the country. By reason of density of population and distribution of wealth, the growing pains were most acute in England. The visual manifestations were (*a*) the conflict between the material and spiritual values of history (example: the urban silhouette); (*b*) the conflict of scale between machine and human energy (example: the power-house in the agricultural countryside); (*c*) confusion in the juxtaposition of works (example: the motorways) and pressures for multiple use of land (example: the National Parks); (*d*) the inheritance of waste, pollution and the sordid from the previous age; and, basic to all, (*e*) the man-made and machine-based ecosystem that was beginning to supersede the slow processes of nature (examples: redisposition of trees and hedgerows). To re-create order out of apparent chaos there arose what may be described as a sequence of master gardeners: the comprehensive landscape-planner, the urban-planner, the landscape-designer and the garden-architect.

Comment 156. A change in the visual world about us is inevitable and distinction or disaster rests entirely with ourselves. The change process is more complex than at any time in history, not so much because of the universal scale of operations as because of the unknown factor at the end of the chain reaction to *any* single disturbance of nature; a chain that took over a billion years to forge is not lightly reconstituted. In history, the constructive changes of landscape were strictly planned within the known and experienced natural laws, while those in command had a safeguard against human error in the predominance of intuition and instinct in the making of decisions. But although the planner today relies on the intellect, his colleague the artist is exploring and revealing here and there the emotions that are common from Scandinavia to Australia and Japan, irrespective of race, creed and political belief. Art and instinct reveal the truth, but with the intellect this is not always so. How else can we explain the Sydney Opera House, a phenomenon contrary to all rational thought?

A NEW APPROACH TO PLANNING was envisaged in the **social and functional analysis of London (624)** by A. Ling and D. K. Johnson, prepared as part of a study for the County of London Plan published in 1943 (J. H. Forshaw and Patrick Abercrombie). It disclosed that the 'Great Wen' was not a meaningless sprawl, but one whose communities had grown biologically and naturally around a heart. Within the communities were countless small houses with their backyards. The backyards were an inner sanctum, often transformed into individual romantic gardens. Two views of **a garden in north London (625, 626)** show a typical backyard when first planted and sixteen years later.

345

627

628

A RETURN TO THE RURAL as the planners' objective received particular impetus in England after the Second World War. The first wave of New Towns were based on a system of self-contained communities or neighbourhoods grouped round a centre (similar in principle to London itself, of which they were satellites, each with a population of about sixty thousand). Their size and disposition were governed by pedestrianism within each neighbourhood, with public transport to the central area. The neighbourhoods were separated by green landscape; the scale was that of the tree. Although the plans grew from the previous garden cities, the conception of the relationship between town and country was changing. In **Mousehole 1947 (627)** Ben Nicholson revealed an affinity between geometry and agricultural landscape that went deeper than the Arts and Crafts movement. In 1948 Frederick Gibberd published his **first plan for Harlow New Town, Essex (629, 630)**. The form grew from the complex of agricultural field patterns, but had been rationalized into an art form that might be a landscape-designer's interpretation of *Mousehole*. In the country, the additions to the villages of the Loddon Rural District Council, Norfolk, by architects Tayler and Green, such as **Woodton (628)**, established a standard of public housing in rural areas.

629

630 Harlow, Essex
A Central area
B Green landscape
C Neighbourhood
D Industry
E Agriculture

Simultaneously with the English new towns, **Tapiola, near Helsingfors, Finland (631)**, was planned with the similar objective of relating individual to environment. Whereas the English towns were conditioned by an agricultural landscape, hardwood trees and a climate of latitude *c.* 52° north, Tapiola was designed for virgin conifer forests and rock- and water-scenery in a latitude of 60°.

631

HOMES FOR THE MIDDLE-INCOME GROUP, initiated by private enterprise, were now required to be owner-maintained and to provide an escape from a noisy world. Nevertheless, the requirement that a home be half town, half country, remained unchanged. Many combinations were devised, but designers returned to the Radburn and Baldwin Hills principles (566, 568): separated vehicle access, small enclosed gardens and collective landscape. The **Span Estate at Blackheath, London** (632) (Eric Lyons and Partners, architects; Ivor Cunningham, landscape architect), developed an extra sensitivity between architectural and plant form. The **estate plan at Fredensborg, Denmark** (636) (J. Utzon, architect), shows how the chain housing separates the outer world (white) from the inner (contoured). The **outer façades** (633) are fortress-like. Within, private **courtyard gardens** (634) overlook but are physically separated from a **grass landscape** (635) that passes out of the picture into imaginative space. Denmark also developed the individuality of the detached home within an estate. The **plan of a house at Bagsvaerd** (637) (A. Bruun, landscape architect) shows the same exclusiveness in its **exterior** (638), with its pavement car-port. The plan itself is original, classical and tranquil. There are many rooms or garden spaces, within its small area, from the **beech walk** (639) to the **flower garden** (640).

632

636

633

634, 635

637 HOUSE AT BAGSVAERD, DENMARK

A Stone wall   B Grass   C Beech hedge   D Play garden   E Outhouse
F Kitchen yard   G Eating place   H Flower garden   I Car park
J Turning place

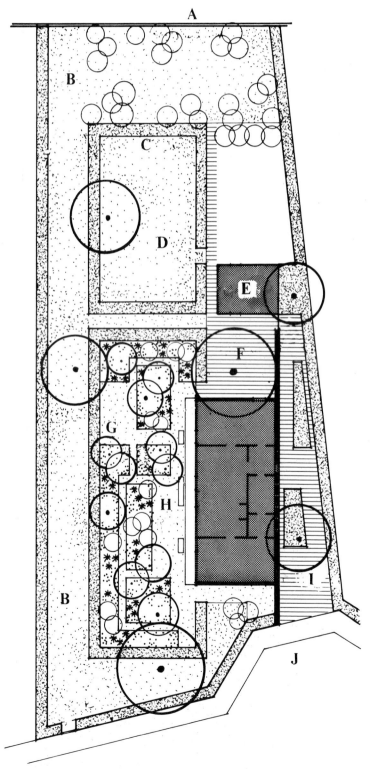

638

639, 640

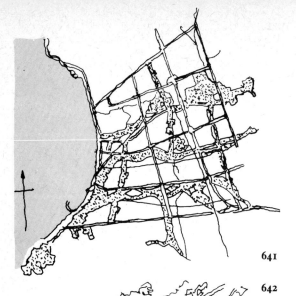

641

642

LE CORBUSIER'S VISION OF LANDSCAPE approached realization after the Second World War. The **outline plan for Marseilles–South (641)** was a ᵗheoretical study (published 1951), showing green fingers of landscape stretching northwards from the sea through a gridiron of roads. The **detail plan (642)** shows his intentions for a group of self-contained communities, or internal townships, within one of the green fingers. One of the communities, known as **L'Unité d'Habitation**, was begun in 1947 and completed 1951. The **section (643)** and **photo (646)** show the rock-like nature of the unit, poised on *pilotis* above a green environment that never fully materialized. The section breaks into a roof terrace of **abstract shapes (644, 645, 647)**, becoming associated with the surrounding mountains.

Following the experience of ground and aerial landscape, particularly at Marseilles, Le Corbusier was free to realize both together in his **plan for Chandigarh (649, 650)**, the new capital of the Punjab, commissioned in 1950. The plan shows the typical interpenetration of green landscape and gridiron pattern of roads, softened to a curve on the instigation of his English collaborators, Maxwell Fry and Jane Drew. The dark centre 'river' is a natural water-eroded valley known as the Valley of Leisure. The **first sketch for the Capitol (648)**, dated 3 May 1951, shows the vision of the city in its relation to the Himalayas.

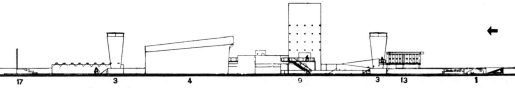

644, 645 L'UNITE D'HABITATION, PLAN OF ROOF-TERRACE

1 Artificial hills   2 Tubs of flowers   3 Ventilation chimneys   4 Gymnasium   5 East solarium 6 Cloakrooms and upper terrace   7 West solarium   8 Concrete tables   9 Lift tower, with terrace entrance and bar   10 Exterior stairs   11 Running track (300 metres)   12 Ramp linking the welfare service (17th floor) with the terrace and nursery   13 Nursery   14 Children's garden 15 Swimming pool   16 Balcony   17 Wind-break (open-air theatre)

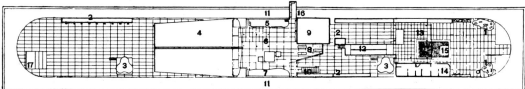

643

646

647

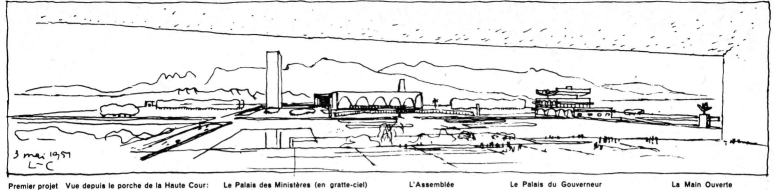

Premier projet Vue depuis le porche de la Haute Cour: Le Palais des Ministères (en gratte-ciel) L'Assemblée Le Palais du Gouverneur La Main Ouverte

648

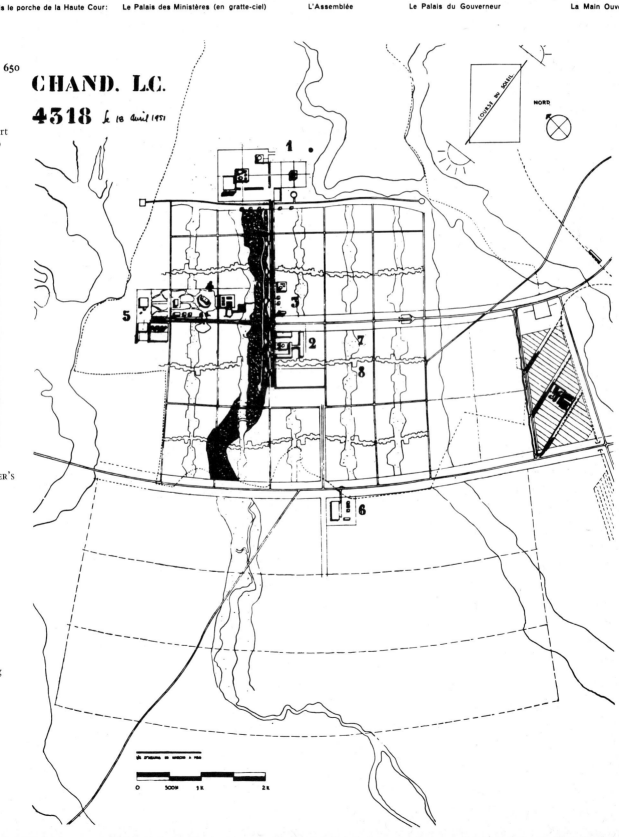

650

CHAND. LC.
4318 le 18 avril 1951

649 A plan of part of Paris drawn to the same scale

650 LE CORBUSIER'S PLAN FOR CHANDIGARH
1 Capitol
2 Commercial centre
3 Hotels, restaurants, etc
4 Museum and stadium
5 University
6 Market
7 Green belt (schools, clubs, sports grounds, etc)
8 Main shopping street

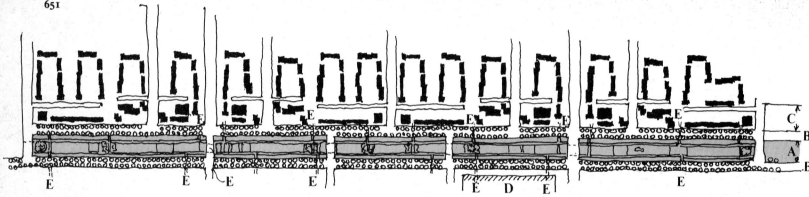

651

652 BRONDSBY STRAND, DENMARK
A Sunk park (shaded)
B Road and ground level
C Pedestrian platforms above car park and garages
D Central shopping
E Subways

653   **654**

A TIGHTENING OF DOMESTIC DENSITIES generally took place between 1950 and 1970, and with it the creation of high-rise flats. By 1970 the social defects of height had become manifest. The tenant was disassociated from his neighbours; his family was cut off from a ground in any case probably sterilized for plant life by wind turbulence and car parking; the texture of his surroundings was hard and hostile; and the family home, the flat, was devoid of personality. **Brondsby Strand, Denmark** (Svend Høgsbro, architect), is an intellectual exercise and model of this period. It is compact and set cleanly in an agricultural environment. It segregates cars from pedestrians, as seen in the **view of the central spine (653)**. There are **safe play areas (654)** within the complex and easily accessible parallel **sunk gardens (652)** for all ages. The silhouette **(651)** has been studied as a single composition, suggestive of such potentially dramatic variations as the pyramids of **La Grande Motte (655)** on the French Mediterranean coast. In opposition to this way of thought, and planned hopefully for an affluent car society, is the new English town of **Milton Keynes, Buckinghamshire** (c. 1970, population 250,000; architects: Llewellyn-Davies, Weeks, Forestier-Walker and Bor; landscape architect: G.P. Youngman). The **tree plan (656)** outlines a romantic rather than a classical grid-iron pattern of roads, within which the early building (1975) is low-rise but high-density.

655

656

A CENTRE OF LEARNING FOR THE HUMANITIES is concerned not only with the intellectual acquisition of knowledge, but with the feeling for it. A quality of time in the environment and a sense of participation in it are part of the educational process. The **University of Urbino**, founded in 1506, grew from an environment that was the birthplace of Raphael and host to such artists and architects as Piero della Francesca, Alberti and Bramante. The natural landscape is small in scale and tumultuously hilly; buildings have always been compelled to fit the site, as is seen in the **view of the city (657)** from the north-east. The **aerial view (659)** shows the firmness and serenity of the Ducal Palace within the city and the richly turbulent landscape to the south. Until the present day, the unifying planner was the natural environment itself, and if the forms of the hills and valleys were disturbed by cross patterning, this was more of a stimulus than an irritant. A **modern residential college (658)** of the magnitude required might well have upset this balance of man and nature, but in siting and in architecture, the buildings, designed in 1970 by Giancarlo de Carlo, have become part of the landscape and the continuity of history.

658

657

659

Ducal Palace ▷
University

Site of
residential college ▷

661

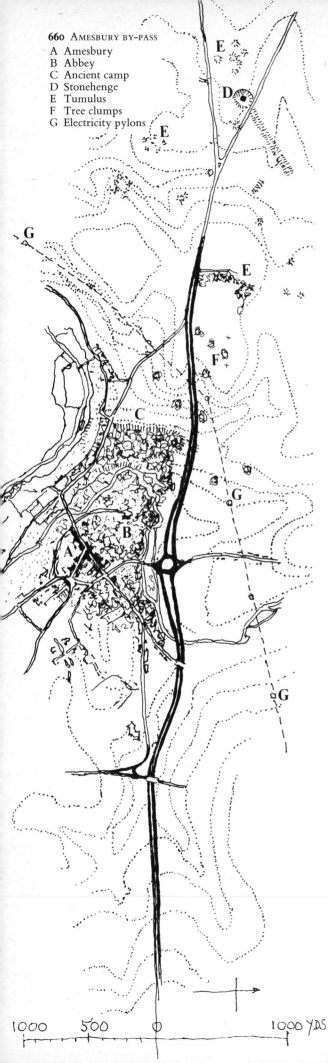

660 AMESBURY BY-PASS

A Amesbury
B Abbey
C Ancient camp
D Stonehenge
E Tumulus
F Tree clumps
G Electricity pylons

1000   500   0   1000 YDS

662, 663

THE CONSERVATION OF HISTORIC VALUES has now become a major objective in planning. Ill-considered motor roads may disrupt a whole countryside and tall buildings confuse and destroy famous silhouettes. The **Amesbury by-pass, Wiltshire (660)** (double track shown in black), not only does not detract from the mystique of history, but adds to the experience and appreciation of it. The motorist from London to the west first sees from the old road the suggestion of **a medieval town (663)** clustered among its trees within Salisbury Plain. The by-pass itself skirts the town gracefully on the north, passing through a landscape of **eighteenth-century tree clumps (662)** to enter prehistoric England. Before him lies Stonehenge **(661)**, solitary except for the tumuli dotted around. A time distance of four thousand years has been traversed in about four minutes. Similarly, the **Heights Plan for Gloucester (664)**, presented in 1966 and still in operation, is intended to defend spiritual values. The plan covers both local and long distance views of the Cathedral and attendant towers and spires. Four **'shafts of vision' (665, 666, 667)** protect specific middle-distance views that have survived.

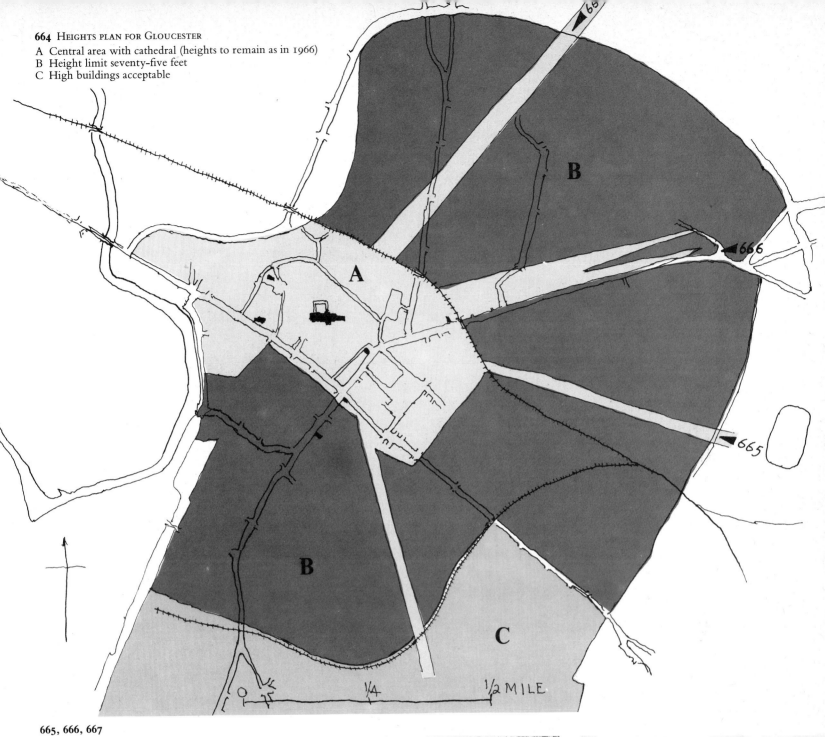

664 HEIGHTS PLAN FOR GLOUCESTER
A Central area with cathedral (heights to remain as in 1966)
B Height limit seventy-five feet
C High buildings acceptable

¼   ½ MILE

665, 666, 667

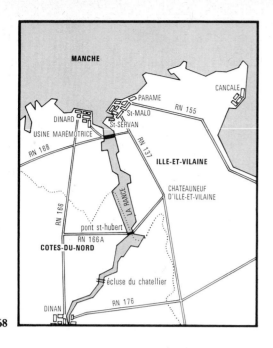

HUMAN AND GIANT SCALE can be reconciled in the civilized landscape if the different values of each and their relationship to each other are recognized. The view looking north of **L'Usine Marémotrice de la Rance, Brittany (669)**, shows how a huge structure can not only be fitted into an historic landscape, but by modesty and restraint can enhance it. The **block plan (668)** shows the region in which it is set. In the foreground of the view, the road crosses the underwater station which generates power from a two-way tidal rise of up to forty-four feet. In the far right is the historic fortress town of St Malo; in the far left, the holiday resort of Dinard. Transmission lines emerge out of sight to the left. While La Rance barrage is agreeably negative in the landscape, **Middelfart Bridge (670)** between Jutland and Fyn, Denmark (1970; engineers: Chr. Ostenfeld and W. Jonson), can afford to be positive. Modelled on the Golden Gate (**559**), the bridge rises even more poetically into the sky to be seen at great distance in the flat Danish landscape.

Afforestation raises a further question of scale and the viability of weaving commercial forests into the countryside, as at **Glentress, Scotland (671)**. Forests are now valued not only for their timber, but for wild life, amelioration of climate, purification of air, stabilization of soil and water régime and, finally, their incalculable value for individual recreation. Sylvia Crowe, landscape consultant to the British Forestry Commission, has written: 'If we accept that forests should form a nature-dominated contrast to the rest of the humanized landscape, then, in designing them, we must enter into the mind of nature with Zen-like humility.'

669

670, 671

675

INDUSTRIAL WASTE, whether of solids or invisible energy, can be destructive to landscape and demoralizing to society. There is in fact no such thing as absolute waste, only that man has been unable to find an alternative creative use. The **model of Hope Cement Works (672)** (1946) in the Peak District National Park, Derbyshire, inaugurated long-term industrial landscape-planning. The worked-out clay quarries have been re-used creatively for recreational woodlands and lakes, while the mouth of the limestone quarry is kept to the minimum to preserve the hillside. Arrangements for the disposal of pulverized fly ash from the Central Electricity Board's **power station at Gale Common**, Eggborough, Yorkshire (1968; landscape architect: Brenda Colvin), are shown **as existing (673)** and **as proposed (674)**. The hill would add to agriculture as well as to the character of an otherwise flat scene. The plan was for thirty years and is under consideration. The cooling towers of **Didcot Power Station, Berkshire (675)** (1965; architect and landscape architect: Frederick Gibberd), are symbolic of energy waste, destructive to the human scale and an intrusion into a famous rural vale that was almost universally resented. The cooling towers were re-composed from the purely **functional (676)** into the **picturesque (677)** so agreeably that horror at their presence is mitigated by an appreciation of their grandeur – gigantic follies composed like gods in converse.

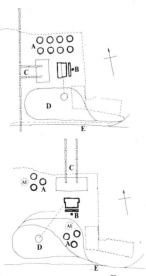

676, 677 DIDCOT POWER STATION, BERKSHIRE, AS PLANNED FUNCTIONALLY (*above*) AND AS RECOMPOSED PICTURESQUELY (*below*)

A Cooling towers (A1, if needed) B Stack
C Transmission lines D Coal store E Existing railway

678, 679

LANDSCAPE FOR THE MIND was summarized by Alexander Pope in his *Prologue* to Addison's *Cato*:

> *To wake the soul by tender strokes of art,*
> *To raise the genius, and to mend the heart . . .*

that is to say, to stimulate or to tranquillize. Two examples, both from Denmark, illustrate these twin facets of landscape art.

The air view of the **Angli shirt factory, Herning (680)** (1965; architect: C. F. Møller; landscape architect: C. Th. Sørensen), shows a complete work of abstract art within which 175 persons are profitably employed. In the foreground, the factory itself encompasses an **empty grass circle (678, 679)** with a continuous ceramic wall by Carl-Henning Petersen. In the rear is a larger grass circle grazed by cattle and separated by a ha-ha from a circumference of works of art. While the Herning landscape is unfamiliar, thought-provoking and intensely creative, that of the **County Hospital, Glostrup (681)** (architects: Ragnar and Martha Yppya; landscape architect: Sven Hansen), is intended to soothe, repair and reassure. The patient is returned first to the familiar and thence to origins. The buildings are geometrical and beyond human scale; the landscape is ecological and humane. The **detail plan (682)** shows the rings of landscape. The **inner ring (683)** contains personal and tactile gardens in which patients and visitors mingle and picnic; the **middle ring (684)** is grass; the third ring will in time become a forest of mystery and imagination.

680

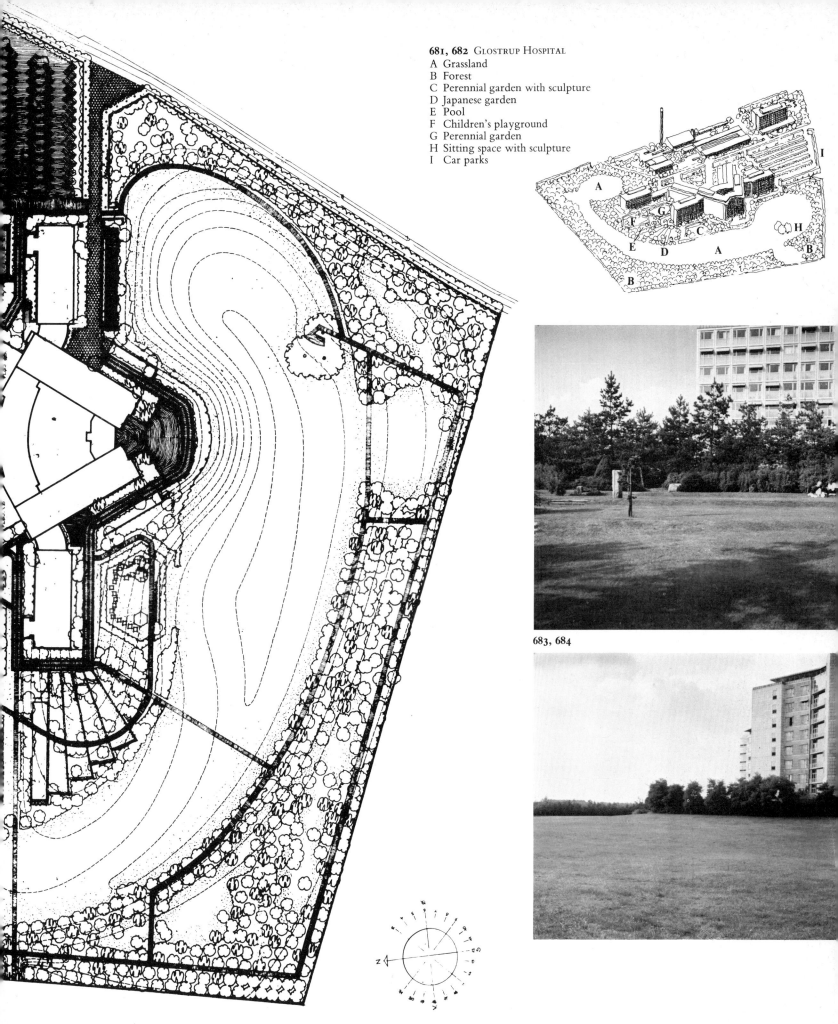

681, 682 Glostrup Hospital
A Grassland
B Forest
C Perennial garden with sculpture
D Japanese garden
E Pool
F Children's playground
G Perennial garden
H Sitting space with sculpture
I Car parks

683, 684

THE MODERN URBAN PARK has grown from the private eighteenth-century landscape park, containing the principle of escape from reality. The **Schlossgarten, Stuttgart (685, 686)** (1960, fountain by Peter Faller), originated from the West German policy of creating permanent city parks from national exhibitions. The site was the formal park and avenues of the Schloss or palace, the geometry disappearing without trace, but also without apparent loss of trees. In totally new parks on virgin sites, modern machinery can quickly reshape flat land into hills and dales, thus creating unlimited illusory space. The proposed **public park at La Courneuve, Paris (687)** (1972, landscape architects: Derek Lovejoy and Partners; developed by Alain Provost and Gilbert Samel), is such a study in transformation and illusion. An extension of an existing park, the natural form will change from flatness to hilliness.

685, 686

The designers describe the purpose of the earth modelling as follows: 'First, eliminate visually from within the park the mediocre surrounding development; second, modify the empty monotony of the existing plain; third, provide economic benefit and source of income from controlled dumping (1,200,000 cubic metres each year over a number of years); fourth, absorb the A16 motorway, associated interchange and main railway line.'

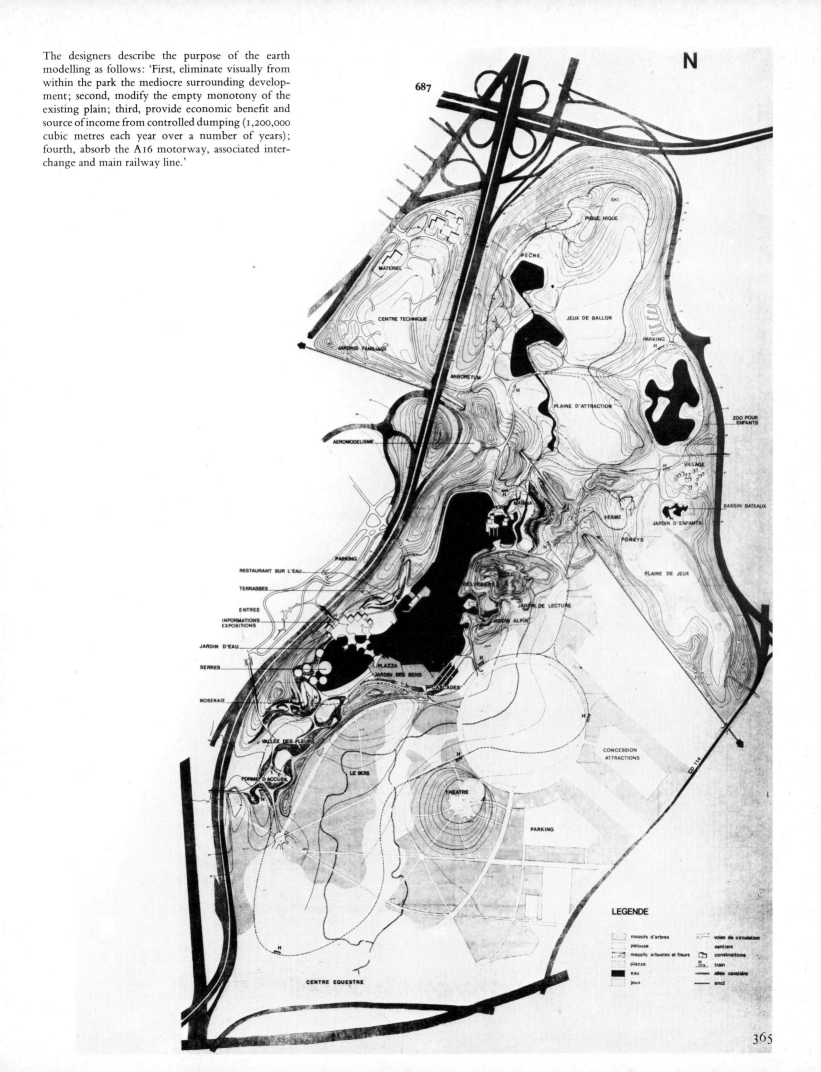

N

687

SKI

PIQUE NIQUE

PÊCHE

JEUX DE BALLON

PARKING

MATÉRIEL

CENTRE TECHNIQUE

JARDINS FAMILIAUX

ARBORETUM

PLAINE D'ATTRACTION

ZOO POUR ENFANTS

AEROMODELISME

VILLAGE

PORT MARINA

BASSIN BATEAUX

FERME

JARDIN D'ENFANTS

PONEYS

PARKING

PLAINE DE JEUX

RESTAURANT SUR L'EAU

TERRASSES

BELVÉDÈRE

ENTRÉE

JARDIN DE LECTURE

INFORMATIONS EXPOSITIONS

JARDIN ALPIN

JARDIN D'EAU

SERRES

PLAZZA

JARDIN DES SENS

CASCADES

ROSERAIE

CONCESSION ATTRACTIONS

VALLÉE DES FLEURS

FORME D'ACCUEIL

LE BOIS

THEATRE

PARKING

CENTRE EQUESTRE

CD 114

LEGENDE

massifs d'arbres	voies de circulation
pelouse	sentiers
massifs arbustes et fleurs	constructions
plazza	train
eau	allée cavalière
jeux	sncf

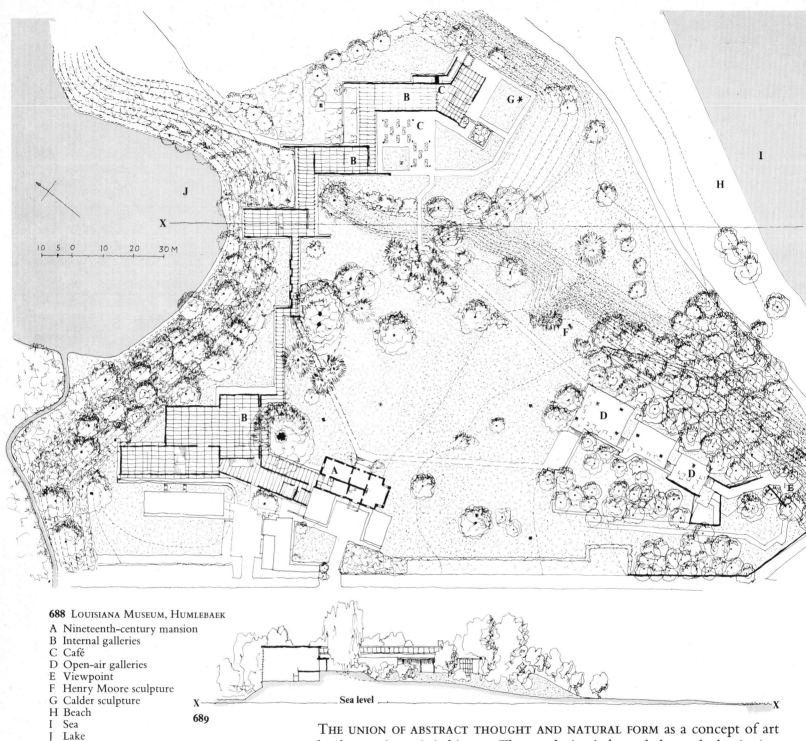

688 Louisiana Museum, Humlebaek

A Nineteenth-century mansion
B Internal galleries
C Café
D Open-air galleries
E Viewpoint
F Henry Moore sculpture
G Calder sculpture
H Beach
I Sea
J Lake

689

THE UNION OF ABSTRACT THOUGHT AND NATURAL FORM as a concept of art has been axiomatic in history. The revolution in knowledge at the beginning of the twentieth century abruptly separated the two, but with the growth of the ecological sciences the concept is returning as the fundamental basis of landscape design. The new galleries of the **Louisiana Museum, Humlebaek (688, 689)**, on the shores of the Kattegat, Denmark (1955; architects: Jorgen Bo and Vilhelm Wohlert), are interwoven with a mid-nineteenth-century house and park. Into this complex are inserted works with the considered intention, as the catalogue states, of alternating impressions of art and nature. The **sculpture by Alexander Calder (690)** seems to organize sky, sea and wind, much as does **Henry Moore's reclining figure (691)** the ground and surrounding growth. In the **view of a courtyard (692)** the landscape is seen to pass into and through the buildings. Within, an **abstract by Josef Albers (693)** is in association with the trunk of a great beech tree.

690 691

692 693

694

695

696, 697

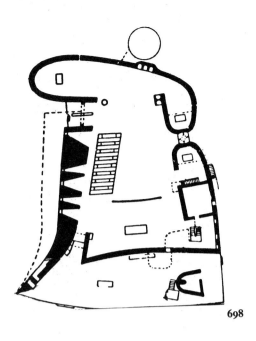

THE LIBERALIZATION OF THE SPIRIT through architecture and the arts has been sought at all times in history. Each civilization may have chosen an individual route, but the final objective seems to have remained the same: subconsciously to seek out and express a correspondence between man himself and the universe. In the **chapel at Ronchamps (694–697)**, completed 1955, Le Corbusier towards the end of his life was grappling, in his own words, with 'mathematics, the creator of the ineffable mysteries of space', now recognized to be a complex of movement and time. Although conditioned by mathematics, **the plan (698)** is no longer that of Platonic geometry. The **panorama (694)** shows the chapel traditionally crowning one of the outcrops of the Vosges mountains; the site is particular but the idea is universal.

On the other side of the Eastern Hemisphere, the **model of a children's playground (699)** near Tokyo by Isamu Noguchi, a Japanese-American sculptor practising in the USA, is similarly and more simply seeking the universal through the particular. Although the design appears to be particularized to the site and evocative of Japanese prehistory, the declared intention is that it will be 'a children's world acceptable to children everywhere'.

698

699

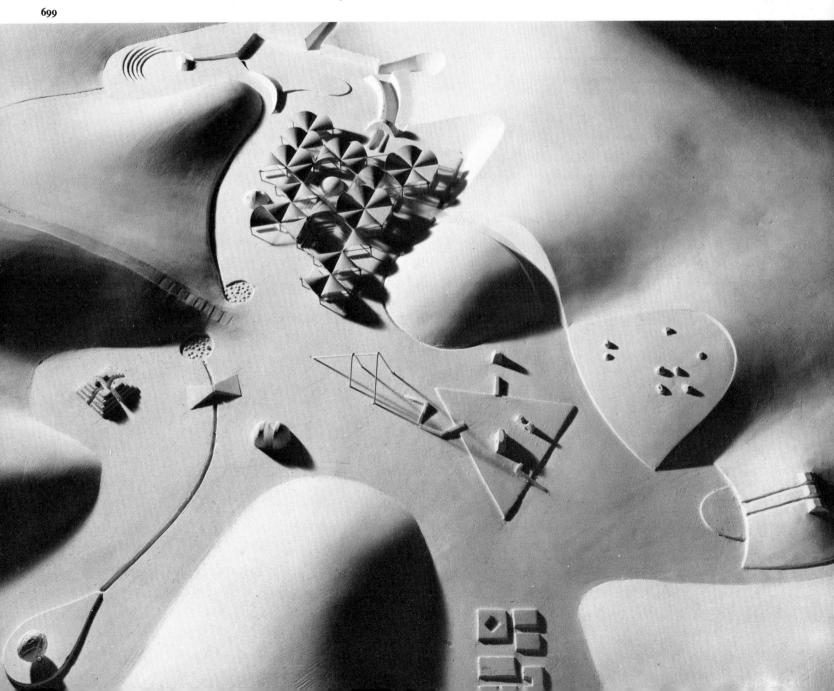

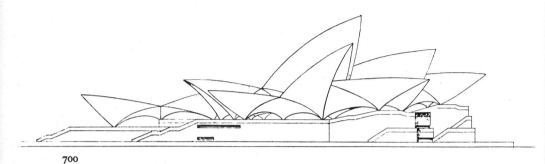

700

THE OPERA HOUSE, SYDNEY, AUSTRALIA, seen from the air (**702**). The design, by the Danish architect Jorn Utzon, was the result of a competition in 1957; Utzon resigned during progress of works. The structural engineers were Ove Arup and Partners. The complex is in the tradition of the great cathedrals, whose brilliant structure expressed poetry rather than function and whose completion was an act of faith. The original drawings of the **plan and section** (**700**, **701**) are typical of the architect, portraying the spirit rather than the actuality of the composition and revealing the underlying man-woman-child symbolism of the beautiful shells. No other building in the modern world can compare with it for the vision it evokes of an idea that transcends logic, reason and common sense.

701

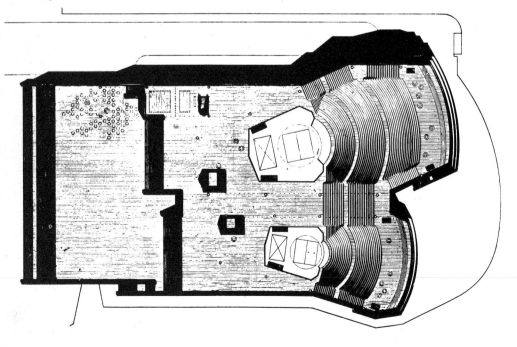

Epilogue: Towards the Landscape of Humanism

THE PHILOSOPHY of landscape design began as belief in myth, merged into humanism based on the establishment of fact, and is now grappling with the realization that facts are no more than assumptions. Humanism is passing into another, unknown, phase. It is possible, for instance, that the present disruption of the environment can be traced beyond the manifest reasons to one basic cause: the subconscious disorientation now in man's mind concerning time and space and his relation to both.

Artists in the nineteenth century had already sensed not only that all things were in flux (as had the Greeks), but that time and space were not two entities, but one. Now that it has been scientifically proved, the concept is so overwhelming and the break with history so abrupt, that this may be the main reason why today, significantly, time plays little part in the arts. It is the present that matters. The imagination, for example, no longer cares to bridge the gap, peculiar to landscape, between the seedling and the tree: landscape must be instant. Architecture is created for a short life and the discord between old and new is without historical precedent. Such absence of a sense of time is contrary to all previous philosophy, metaphysical or humanistic. It is as though action supersedes contemplation. In extreme contrast, Egypt, ancient India and pre-Columbian America were almost wholly preoccupied with abstract time. China considered buildings to be self-reproducing, like plants; but the new landscapes were to be everlasting. Western civilization has consistently balanced time with space; the Italian philosopher-architect Alberti and the English astronomer-architect Wren held equally that all architecture should be built for eternity.

While man's sense of time has diminished, his sense of space seems to have expanded beyond control. He has a command of it, both in microcosm and macrocosm, that would have amazed the ancients; but in filling it he is tending to become personally dissociated from it; it is too big and he is too small. During the last few hundred years, the mathematical laws of the universe, extracted from outer space by scientists and engineers, have slowly come to dominate the biological laws of the biosphere. Second only to the particular significance of nuclear power described in paragraph 149 (p. 321) lies that of pure mathematics. Civilized life for the human race, as emphasized by J. Bronowski in *The Ascent of Man* (Chapter 12: 'Generation upon Generation'), is dependent upon a diversification planned with incredible ingenuity by nature. But mathematics is based on repetition; repetition implies mass production; and this inevitably could lead to the static, efficient and deadly civilization of the bee. Pressure to stamp out individuality is everywhere and is most manifest in state housing or hive; it is no wonder that, under such conditions, the subconscious human instinct for self-expression finds vent in violence and illogical vandalism.

Now that we know and can assess the forces battering our planet, can they first be resisted by the defensive mechanism of instinct and then controlled and put to work by the intellect? Balanced and self-renewing ecosystems had already been evolved by past civilizations (notably the eastern), but their scope was limited and their evolution by trial and error slow and laborious. The possibility now before man is the creation, with the services of the computer, of an ecosystem that is immediate, comprehensive and based on unlimited recurring energies known to exist in the universe. This we can achieve on current theoretical knowledge, but it is not enough. Can we also, as did the simpler past civilizations, turn scientific data into abstract thought and art, thus to sustain and identify ourselves as humans and not as animals in this extraordinary continuum?

The concept of a middle distance, or link between smallness-bigness and immediacy-infinity, is peculiar to the human species. It is primarily concerned with *idea*: that there is a largeness beyond human comprehension and that this can be approached by an intermediary or stepping-stone. All religions are intermediaries, and so is art. In landscape design, the first projection of individual personality has been the complex of home, garden and forest tree; this is the stable foreground from which spring the eternally changing middle distances. In history, the middle distance was almost always metaphysical and abstract, such as the ascending progression of man–sphinx–pyramid–eternity. Although the scene has changed from the metaphysical to the material, the same progression in scale can be experienced today through the enigmatic sculptures and monster structures of Atlanta (**600**). As the man-made world grows increasingly superhuman, so the concept of a meaningful middle distance must be extended and deepened.

What abstract form will this middle distance take? Man's new relation to environment is revolutionary and the landscape designer, unlike the artist, is conditioned by many factors that debar immediate experiment. We must therefore turn to the artists for a vision of the future, gaining confidence in the knowledge that the abstract art that lurks behind all art lives a life of its own, independent of time and space. The interpretation of art into landscape is personal to every designer, but a combined study of the aerial view of Urbino (**659**), the aerial survey of the Philadelphia region (**618**) and the painting by Jackson Pollock (**623**) may suggest the grandeur of a fresh humanistic landscape that will have grown out of history and now lies within our grasp.

For the first time in history, the shape of the world that is unfolding expresses collective materialism rather than prescribed religion. In the advanced countries, the individual is evolving his own personal beliefs within his own home. The greatest threat to his existence may not be commercialism, or war, or pollution, or noise, or consumption of capital resources, or even the threat of extinction from without, but rather the blindness that follows sheer lack of appreciation and the consequent destruction of those values in history that together are symbolic of a single great idea.

Acknowledgments

Select Bibliography

Index

Acknowledgments

ONE OF THE PLEASURES of writing such a wide-ranging book is that it brings the authors into contact with many and varied helpers. To all these we give our grateful thanks and our regrets that space does not allow us to mention them by name. We must, however, record the generous help of Professor Norman Newton of Harvard University, whose scholarly work *Design on the Land* preceded our own and paved the way for a clear understanding of the American scene. With him also we must mention Dean Hubert Owens of the University of Georgia and Mr Sidney Shurcliff, President and Past President respectively of the International Federation of Landscape Architects. In England, Sir Ove Arup and Sir John Pilcher were invaluable in their advice over Denmark, China and Japan.

Sources of Illustrations

Evening Landscape with Horseman and Shepherds by Albert Cuyp (344) is reproduced by gracious permission of Her Majesty the Queen.

Acknowledgment is also made to: A.C.L., Brussels, 238; Aerofilms, 2, 8, 9, 11, 22, 28, 31, 246, 433, 451, 454, 455, 482, 557, 558, 590; American Museum of Natural History, 10; Amsterdam Parks Department, 551–53; Angli Factory, Herning, 680; Architectural Press, 479, 533–35, 621; Richard Arioli, 46–49, 409; Art Institute of Chicago, 418, 448; Austrian National Tourist Office, 335; Aziende Autonoma Turista, Assisi, 222; Bill Barnes, 600; Royal Library of Belgium, 235; Mr George Benson, 421; Bibliothèque Nationale, Paris, 111, 380, 384; Boston Museum of Fine Arts, 93, 95; Derek Bridgwater, 474; M. Brigaud/Photothèque Electricité de France, 669; British-Chinese Friendship Society, 118; British Council, 627; British Museum, 15, 18, 21, 36, 60, 94, 226, 281, 294, 295, 381, 473; British Tourist Authority, 481; Mr Marcus Brumwell, 550; Andreas Bruun, 637–40; Photo Bulloz, 320; Dr G. Bushnell, 149; Caisse Nationale des Monuments Historiques, Paris, 4; Giancarlo de Carlo, 658, 659; J. Allan Cash, 107, 112, 117, 145, 146, 506, 586, 591; Central Electricity Generating Board, 673, 674; Victor Chambi, 154; Thomas Church, 611, 612; Clarke & Rapuano, 588, 589; Country Life, 404, 422, 428, 429, 477, 493; Mrs Albert H. Dedman, 623; Department of the Environment, 341; Rüdiger Dichtel, 685; Direction Générale du Tourisme, Paris, 6, 7, 296, 309, 311, 321; John Donat, 39, 606; Robert Durandaud, 224; Garrett Eckbo, 613, 614; Electricité de France, 668; Ente Provinziale per Turismo, Caserta, 367; Ente Provinziale per il Turismo, Novara, 284; Finnish Tourist Association, 3, 631; Diana Ford, 603; Forestry Commission, 671; Ewing Galloway, 84; the Gaudí Professor, Barcelona University, 515, 516; German Archaeological Institute, Rome, 203; Sir Frederick Gibberd, 629, 675; Government of India Tourist Office, 87; Greek Tourist Office, 213; Irma Groth-Kimball, 151; Guildhall Library, London, 340; Lawrence Halprin, 605; Harvard University, 251, 567; Sheila Haywood, 66; HMSO, 452, 453; Lucien Hervé, 526, 527; Hirmer Archiv, 157, 162; Historisches Museum der Stadt Wien, 441; Mr George Howard, 401; India Office Library and Records, 64, 65, 68, 70, 73, 85, 86, 88; Institute of Archaeology, London, 16; Institut Géographique National, Paris, 434; Iraq Museum, Baghdad, 12; Shojiro Ishibashi, 140; Japan Information Centre, 119–25, 127, 135; Victor Kennett, 395; Dan Kiley, 601, 602; Kungl. Akademien för de fria Konsterna, Stockholm, 390, 414; Kunsthistorisches Museum, Vienna, 346; Ian Mackenzie-Kerr, 632; Mansell Collection, 202, 258, 264, 267, 268, 292; Bildarchiv Marburg, 181, 334, 440; Janet March-Penney, 156, 597–99; Eugene Martini Associates, 622; Dr Roberto Burle Marx, 576–80, 593–96; Mas, Barcelona, 512; Milton Keynes Development Corporation, 656; Ministry of Defence/Air, 14; Mary Mitchell, 100; National Gallery, London, 290, 342, 412, 446, 449; National Gallery of Scotland, 450; Dion

Neutra, 574–75; Novosti Press Agency, 223, 362; City of Oxford, 243; Gordon Patterson, 538, 634; Heinz Pauly, 351; Colin Penn, 103, 104, 113, 385, 386; Alain Percival, 305; Pfalzisches Museum, Heidelberg, 337; Josephine Powell, 83; Radio Times Hulton Picture Library, 158, 165, 167; Rijksmuseum, Amsterdam, 343; Dr J. K. St Joseph, 216, 219; Sasaki, Dawson, Demay Associates, 607–10, 615–17; Schinkel Museum, National Galerie, Berlin, 435; J. C. Shepherd, 510; Smithsonian Institution, Washington, 96; Soprintendenza alle Gallerie, Florence, 247, 248; SPADEM, 236; Stockholm Parks Department, 548; Swiss Government Tourist Office, 524; Tayler & Green, 628; Tennessee Valley Authority, 581, 582, 583; Lady Anne Tree, 91, 214; Eileen Tweedy, 116; US Coast and Geodetic Service, 564; United States Information Service, 1, 377, 498, 559, 560, 585–87; Biblioteca Apostolica Vaticana, 257; Victoria & Albert Museum, 78; University of Virginia, 495, 496; Warwickshire County Council, 396; Mr and Mrs John Hay Whitney, 447; Daniel Wildenstein, 29; Roger Wood, 161.

All photographs not otherwise credited are by Susan Jellicoe.

The maps were prepared by June Harrison.

Drawings and plans have been reproduced from the following books: J. C. A. Alphand, *Les Promenades de Paris* (442, 443, 445, 476, 480); Boston Park Commissioners' *Annual Report 1879* (502) and *Notes on the Plan of Franklin Park* (503); Botta and Flandin, *Monuments de Ninive* (20); J. Boyceau, *Traité du Jardinage* (298); A. Boyd, *Chinese Architecture and Town Planning* (98 a and b); Brooklyn Park Commissioners' *Annual Report 1867* (500); R. Castell, *Villas of the Ancients Illustrated* (199); J.-A. du Cerceau, *Les plus excellents bâtiments de France* (294, 295, 306); Chicago South Park Commissioners' *Annual Report 1872* (505); M. Collignon, *Pergame: Restauration et*

description (205); Le Corbusier, *Towards a New Architecture* (528) and *Complete Architectural Works* (643, 644, 645, 648–50, 698) copyright by SPADEM, Paris; F. Crisp, *Medieval Gardens* (217); Sylvia Crowe et al., *The Gardens of Mughul India* (40, 76); Ernouf and Alphand, *L'Art des Jardins* (297); *The Gardeners' Chronicle* (468); G. Gromort, *Jardins d'Italie* (285); G. Holmdahl, *Gunnar Asplund, Architect* (518); E. Howard, *Tomorrow* (532); G. Kubler, *The Art and Architecture of Ancient America* (149, 152); L. Kuck, *The World of the Japanese Garden* (97 a and b, 143); A. Layard, *Nineveh and its Remains* (19); *New Danish Architecture* (536, 700, 701); N. Rossellini, *I Monumenti dell'Egitto e della Nubia* (163, 164); B. Rowlands, *The Art and Architecture of India* (81, 82); J. C. Shepherd and G. A. Jellicoe, *Italian Gardens of the Renaissance* (259, 270, 274, 282, 286, 288, 293) and *Gardens and Design* (231, 307); O. Sirén, *Gardens of China* (99); C. Th. Sørensen, *Europas Havekunst* (283); L. Thurah, *Den Dansk Vitruv* (365); Vergnaud, *L'Art de Créer les Jardins* (410); W. H. Ward, *The Architecture of the Renaissance in France* (313). The map of Egypt (160) is by A. Moore; the engraving of Durham (237) by Roper and Cole; the engraving of Rome (281) by J. B. Falda; the engraving of Hampton Court (339) by Kip and Knyff; the engraving of the Belvedere Palaces (349) by Salomon Kleiner; the view of Karlsruhe (350) by H. Schwarz; the plan of Leningrad (357) by R. and J. Ottens; the map of Lisbon (370) by A. Tardieu; the drawing of the Chinese Village, Tsarskoe Selo (394), by Quarenghi; the view of the Leasowes (397) by R. Dodsley; the plan of Castle Howard (398) by R. King; the view of the Crystal Palace (478) by Ackerman; the plan of Radburn (568) by Clarence Stein; and the Boston City Plaza (604) by Kallmann and McKinnell. The plan of Oxford (243) is from the RCHM volumes on the City of Oxford. The plans of Painshill (420) and Holland Park (473) are from the London Ordnance Survey, 1st edition.

Drawings not otherwise acknowledged are by Geoffrey Jellicoe, based on the following sources: *American Town Planning Review*, 1916 (504); Amsterdam Parks Department (552, 553); Jorgen Bo and Vilhelm Wohlert (688, 689); Bournville Village Trust (491); A. Boyd, *Chinese Architecture and Town Planning* (102, 105, 106, 108, 109, 110, 114, 115); Le Corbusier, *Complete Architectural Works* (641, 642); Ernouf and Alphand, *L'Art du Jardin* (352, 372); *The Gardener's Chronicle* (469); Sir Frederick Gibberd (676, 677); *Havekunst* 1944/45 (549); Hegemann and Peets, *The American Vitruvius* (299, 371); F. R. Hiorns, *Town-building in History* (208); J. Hoag, *Western Islamic Architecture* (51); G. Holmdahl, *Gunnar Asplund, Architect* (517); Københavns Almindelige Boligselskab (652); G. Kubler, *The Art and Architecture of Ancient America* (145, 153); G. Le Strange, *Baghdad during the Abbasid Caliphate* (30); Olmsted Associates (504); G. Patterson, *The Gardens of Mughul India* (67); Louis de Soissons (530, 531); Clarence Stein (566); C. M. Villiers-Stuart, *Spanish Gardens* (45); Tennessee Valley Authority (582); *Victoria County History of Yorkshire* (218); L. Weaver, *Houses and Gardens by E. Lutyens* (507); M. Yokoyama (129, 132); I Ho Yuan, *A Brief Treatment of . . . the Imperial Summer Palace* (382, 383).

The extract from *The Art and Architecture of Ancient India* on p. 61 is reprinted by permission of Penguin Books Ltd.

Select Bibliography

The subject overlaps into so many areas of study that there can be no comprehensive bibliography. The most constant reference book has been the *Encyclopaedia Britannica* (14th edition). Other works on general history include H. S. Lucas, *A Short History of Civilization* (New York, London and Toronto, 1953), Arnold Toynbee, *A Study of History*, abridged by D. C. Somervell (London, 1946), H. G. Wells, *The Outline of History* (London, 1920), H. A. L. Fisher, *A History of Europe* (London, 1936), and G. M. Trevelyan, *English Social History* (London, 1946); on philosophy Bertrand Russell, *A History of Western Philosophy* (London, 1946); and on architecture Banister Fletcher, *A History of Architecture in the Comparative Method* (17th edition, revised and added to by Professor Cordingly, London, 1963). More recently K. Clark, *Civilisation* (London, 1969), B. Ward and R. Dubos, *Only One Earth* (Harmondsworth, 1972), and J. Bronowski, *The Ascent of Man* (London, 1973), have provided further insight into what is in fact a continuum.

Reliable guides, such as Baedeker and the Blue Guides, were used to supplement notes that, in the majority of examples, were taken directly on the site. Finally, prints and paintings of all periods, although not always factually accurate, have been an added source of understanding of the spirit of historic landscapes.

General World Landscape

Bacon, E., *Design of Cities*, London, 1967.

Clark, K., *Landscape into Art*, London, 1949.

Geddes, P., *Cities in Evolution* (3rd edition), London, 1968.

Giedion, S., *Space, Time and Architecture*, Cambridge, Mass., 1941.

Gothein, M.-L., *A History of Garden Art*, London, 1928.

Gutkind, E. A., *Revolution of Environment*, London, 1946.

Hauser, A., *The Social History of Art*, London, 1951.

Hegemann, W., and E. Peets, *The American Vitruvius*, New York, 1922.

Hiorns, F. R., *Town-building in History*, London, 1956.

Hyams, E., *Soil and Civilization*, London, 1952.

Mumford, L., *The Culture of Cities*, London, 1938.

Newton, N., *Design on the Land: the Development of Landscape*, Cambridge, Mass., 1971.

Sorensen, C. Th., *Europas Havekunst*, Copenhagen, 1959.

Whittick, A., *Encyclopaedia of Urban Planning*, New York, 1974.

1. Origins

Frazer, J., *The Golden Bough*, London, 1922.

Hawkes, J., and Woolley, L., *Prehistory: The Beginnings of Civilization* (Vol. I of *History of Mankind – cultural and scientific development*), London, 1963.

Piggott, S., ed., *The Dawn of Civilization*, London, 1961.

Sandars, N. K., *Prehistoric Art in Europe*, Harmondsworth, 1968.

Ucbo, J. P., Tringham, R., and Dimbleby, G. W., *Man, Settlement and Urbanism*, London, 1972.

Windel, F., *The Lascaux Cave Paintings*, London, 1949.

2. Western Asia to the Muslim Conquest

Cole, S., *The Neolithic Revolution*, London, 1963.

Frankfort, H., *The Art and Architecture of the Ancient Orient*, Harmondsworth, 1954.

Godard, A., *The Art of Iran*, London, 1965.

Koldewey, R., *The Excavations at Babylon*, trans. Johns, A. S., London, 1914.

Saggs, H. W. F., *The Greatness that was Babylon*, London, 1962.

Woolley, L., *The Beginnings of Civilization*, London, 1963; *Ur of the Chaldees*, Harmondsworth, 1929.

3. Islam: Western Asia

Creswell, K. A. C., *A Short Account of Early Muslim Architecture*, Harmondsworth, 1958.

Godard, André, *The Art of Iran*, London, 1965.

Hitti, Philip, *The Near East in History*, New York, 1961.

Le Strange, Guy, *Baghdad during the Abbasid Caliphate*, Oxford, 1900.

Talbot Rice, T., *The Seljuk Turks*, London, 1961.

Ünsal, Behçet, *Turkish Islamic Architecture*, London, 1959.

Upham Pope, Arthur, *A Survey of Persian Art from Persian times to the present day*, London and New York, 1938.

Wheeler, M., ed., *Splendours of the East*, London, 1965.

4. The Western Expansion of Islam: Spain

Clissold, Stephen, *Spain*, London, 1969.

Hoag, John D., *Western Islamic Architecture*, New York, 1963.

Prieto-Moreno, F., *Los Jardines de Granada*, Madrid, 1952.

Villiers Stuart, C. M., *Spanish Gardens*, London, 1929.

5. The Eastern Expansion of Islam: Mughul India

Bernier, François, *Collection of Travels through Turkey into Persia and the East Indies . . . being the travels of Monsieur Tavernier Bernier and other great men*, London, 1684.

Crowe, S. *et al.*, *The Gardens of Mughul India*, London, 1972.

Prawdin, M., *The Builders of the Mogul Empire*, London, 1963.

Smith, V. A., *The Oxford History of India*, Oxford, 1958

Villiers Stuart, C. M., *Gardens of the Great Mughals*, London, 1913.

6. Ancient India

Basham, A. L., *The Wonder that was India* (3rd edition), London, 1967.

Rowlands, Benjamin, *The Art and Architecture of India: Buddhist, Hindu, Jain*, Harmondsworth, 1953.

Rushbrook Williams, L. F., ed., *Murray's Handbook for travellers in India, Pakistan, Burma and Ceylon* (20th edition), London, 1965.

7. China

Boyd, Andrew, *Chinese Architecture and Town Planning, 1500 B.C.–A.D. 1911*, London, 1962.

Cohn, W., *Chinese Painting*, London, 1948.

Graham, D., *Chinese Gardens*, London, 1938.

Lin Yutang, *Imperial Peking: seven centuries of China*, London, 1961.

Polo, Marco, *The Travels of Marco Polo*, London (Everyman ed.), 1908).

Reischauer, E. O., and Fairbank, J. K., *A History of East Asian Civilization*, Vol. I, London, 1958.

Silcock, Arnold, *An Introduction to Chinese Art and History*, London, 1936.

Sirén, Osvald, *Gardens of China*, New York, 1949.

Sullivan, Michael, *The Three Perfections: Walter Neurath Memorial Lecture 1974*, London, 1974.

Waley, Arthur, *Chinese Poems* (translations), London, 1946.

8. Japan

Conder, J., *Landscape Gardening in Japan*, Yokohama, 1893.

Futagawa, Yukio, *The Roots of Japanese Architecture*, Tokyo, 1962.

Ito, Teiji, and Takiji Iwajima, *The Japanese Garden: An Approach to Nature*, New Haven and London, 1972.

Kuck, Loraine, *The World of the Japanese Garden*, New York, 1968.

9. Pre-Columbian America

Burland, C., *Peru under the Incas*, London, 1969.

Bushnell, G.H.S., *Peru* (2nd edition), London, 1963.

Butland, G.J., *Latin America: a regional geography* (2nd edition), London, 1966.

Coe, M.D., *Mexico*, London, 1966.

Kubler, G., *The Art and Architecture of Ancient America*, Harmondsworth, 1962.

Prescott, H.M., *The Conquest of Mexico*, 1843; *The Conquest of Peru*, 1847.

10. Egypt

Cerny, J., *Ancient Egyptian Religion*, London, 1952.

Giedion, S., *The Eternal Present: the beginnings of Architecture*, London, 1964.

Maspero, G.C.R., *Life in Ancient Egypt*, trans. Morton, A., London, 1892.

Stevenson Smith, W., *The Art and Architecture of Ancient Egypt*, Harmondsworth, 1958.

Woenig, F., *Die Pflanzen im alten Aegypten*, Leipzig, 1897.

11. Greece

Bowra, M., *The Greek Experience*, London, 1957.

Herodotus, *The History of Herodotus*, trans. Rawlinson, G. (2 vols.), London and New York, 1948.

Homer, *The Odyssey*, trans. Rieu, E. V., London, 1952.

Hürlimann, M., and Warner, Rex, *Eternal Greece*, London, 1953.

Pausanias, *Description of Greece*, Loeb Classical Library, Cambridge, Mass. and London, 1918–35.

Rodenwaldt, G., and Hege, W., *The Acropolis*, trans. Hartnoll, P., Oxford, c. 1930; *Olympia*, London, 1936.

Wycherley, R. E., *How the Greeks built Cities*, London, 1949.

12. The Roman Empire

Boëthius, A., and Ward Perkins, J. B., *Etruscan and Roman Architecture*, Harmondsworth, 1970.

Grant, M., *The World of Rome*, London, 1960.

Highet, G., *Poets in a Landscape*, Harmondsworth, 1959.

Masson, G., *Italian Gardens*, London, 1961.

Pliny, *Letters*, trans. Melmoth, W., revised Hutchinson, W.M.L., London, 1810.

Stobart, J.C., *The Grandeur that was Rome*, London, 1912.

Virgil, *The Georgics of Virgil*, trans. Day-Lewis, C., London, 1940.

13. The Middle Ages in Europe

Amherst, A., *A History of Gardening in England*, London, 1896.

Coulton, G. G., *Medieval Panorama*, Cambridge, 1938.

Crisp, F., *Mediaeval Gardens* (2 vols.), London, 1924.

Hamilton, G.H., *The Art and Architecture of Russia*, Harmondsworth, 1954.

Henry, F., *Irish Art in the early Christian Period to A.D. 800*, revised edition of 1965; *Irish Art during the Viking Invasions A.D. 800–1020*, 1967; London.

Ivanov, V.N., *Rostov Velikii and Uglich*, Moscow, 1964.

Krautheimer, R., *Early Christian and Byzantine Architecture*, Harmondsworth, 1965.

Mumford, L., *The City in History*, London, 1961.

Parkinson, J., *Paradisi in Sole Paradisus Terrestris*, London, 1629.

14, 15. Italy: Renaissance, Mannerism and Baroque

Alberti, L.B., *Ten Books on Architecture*, trans. Leoni, London, 1955.

Berenson, B., *Italian Painters of the Renaissance*, London, 1930.

Burckhardt, J., *The Renaissance in Italy*, 6th edition, London and New York, 1909.

Gromort, G., *Jardins d'Italie*, Paris, 1931.

Masson, G., *Italian Gardens*; *Italian Villas and Palaces*; London, 1961, 1959.

Percier and Fontaine, *Choix des plus célebres Maisons de Plaisance de Rome*, Paris, 1809.

Richter, J.P., *The Literary Works of Leonardo da Vinci* (2 vols.), 2nd edition, London, 1939.

Scott, G., *The Architecture of Humanism*, London, 1914.

Shepherd, J.C., and Jellicoe, G.A., *Italian Gardens of the Renaissance*, London, 1925.

Symonds, J.A., *The Renaissance in Italy*, London, 1875–86.

Vasari, G., *Lives of the Painters, Sculptors and Architects*, 1550.

Wittkower, R., *Architectural Principles in the Age of Humanism*, London, 1949.

Wölfflin, H., *The Art of the Italian Renaissance*, New York, 1903.

16. France: sixteenth and seventeenth centuries

Androuet du Cerceau, J., *Les plus excellents bâtiments de France*, Paris, 1576.

d'Argenville, A.J. Dézallier, *Theory and Practice of Gardening*, trans. James, J., London, 1712.

Blomfield, R., *A History of French Architecture* (2 vols.), London, 1921.

Blunt, A., *Art and Architecture in France, 1500–1700*, Harmondsworth, 1953.

Boyceau, J., *Traité du Jardinage selons les Raisons de la Nature et de l'Art*, Paris, 1638.

Rigaud, Jean, *Recueil choisi des plus belles Vues de palais, Chateaux, maisons . . . de Paris, et de ses environs*, Paris, 1752.

Ward, W.H., *The Architecture of the Renaissance in France* (2 vols.), London, 1911.

17. Spain, Germany, England, the Netherlands: sixteenth and seventeenth centuries

Caus, Salomon de, *Hortus Palatinus*, Frankfurt, 1620.

Evelyn, John, *Diaries*, ed. Bray, W., London, 1818.

Hadfield, M., *Gardening in Britain*, London, 1960.

Kip and Knyff, *Nouveau Théâtre de la Grande Bretagne*, London, 1708; and numerous prints of English gardens.

Motley, J.L., *The Rise of the Dutch Republic*, London, 1855.

Rosenberg, J., Slive, S., and ter Kuile, E.H., *Dutch Art and Architecture, 1600–1800*, Harmondsworth, 1966.

Villiers Stuart, C.M., *Spanish Gardens*, London, 1929.

Wootton, Henry, *Reliquiae Woottonianae*, 1651.

18. Eighteenth Century: Western Classicism

Egorov, I. A., *The Architectural Planning of St. Petersburg*, Athens, Ohio, 1969.

Hamilton, G.H., *The Art and Architecture of Russia*, Harmondsworth, 1954.

Hempel, E., *Baroque Art and Architecture in Central Europe*, Harmondsworth, 1965.

Jellicoe, G.A., *Baroque Gardens of Austria*, London, 1932; 'Baroque Gardens of Franconia, Germany', *Architectural Review*, London, December 1932.

Kalnein, W.G., and Levey, Michael, *Art and Architecture of the 18th century in France*, Harmondsworth, 1972.

Langley, Batty, *New Principles of Gardening*, London, 1778.

Sale, E. T., *Historic Gardens of Virginia*, Richmond, Va., 1923.

19. Eighteenth Century: The Chinese School

Chambers, William, *A Dissertation on Oriental Gardening*, London, 1772.

Honour, H., *Chinoiserie*, London, 1961.

Lin Yutang, *Imperial Peking*, London, 1961.

Sirén, O., *China in the Gardens of Europe*, New York, 1950.

Temple, William, *Upon the Gardens of Epicurus and of Gardening in the year 1680*, London, 1680.

20. Eighteenth Century: The English School

Clark, H.F., *The English Landscape Garden*, London, 1948.

Hussey, C., *The Picturesque*, new impression, London, 1967; *English Gardens and Landscapes, 1700–1750*, London, 1967.

Jourdain, M., *The Works of William Kent*, London, 1948.

Knight, R, Payne, *The Landscape, a didactic Poem*, London, 1794.

Malins, E., *English Landscaping and Literature, 1660–1840*, London, 1966.

Mason, G., *Essay on Design in Gardening*, London, 1768.

Pevsner, N., *Studies in Art, Architecture and Design*, Vol. I, London, 1968.

Pope, A., *Essay on Criticism*, London, 1711; *Epistle to the Earl of Burlington*, London, 1731.

Price, U., *Essays on the Picturesque as compared with the Sublime and the Beautiful*, London, 1794.

Stroud, D., *Capability Brown*, London, 1950; *Humphry Repton*, London, 1962.

Switzer, S., *The Nobleman, Gentleman and Gardener's Recreation*, London, 1715.

Walpole, H., 'On Modern Gardening', *Anecdotes of Painting*, London, 1786.

Woodbridge, K., *Landscape and Antiquity: aspects of English culture at Stourhead, 1718–1838*, Oxford, 1970.

21. The Nineteenth Century: The European Mainland

Alphand, J.C.A., *Les Promenades de Paris*, Paris, 1867–73.

Briggs, Asa, *The Nineteenth Century*, London, 1970.

Pückler-Muskau, Prince H. L. H. von, *Hints on Landscape Gardening* (translation), Boston, 1917.

Sitte, Camille, *The Art of Building Cities*, trans. Stewart, C. T., New York, 1945.

22. The Nineteenth Century: The British Isles

Chadwick, G., *The Works of Sir Joseph Paxton, 1803–1865*, London, 1961.

Cole, G.D.H., *Life of Robert Owen*, London, 1930.

Jekyll, G., *Colour in the Flower Garden*, London, 1908.

Loudon, J.C., *The Landscape Gardening and Landscape Art of the late Humphry Repton*, London, 1840; *The Suburban Gardener and Villa Companion*, London, 1836.

Robinson, William, *The Wild Garden*, London, 1870; *The English Flower Garden*, London, 1883.

Trevelyan, G.M., *English Social History*, London, 1946.

23. Nineteenth Century: U.S.A.

Downing, A.J., *A Treatise on the Theory and Practice of Landscape Gardening adapted to North America*, New York, 1841.

Eliot, C.W., *Landscape Architect*, Boston, 1902.

Fein, A., *Frederick Law Olmsted and the American Environmental Tradition*, New York, 1972.

Olmsted, F.L., *Forty Years of Landscape Architecture: Central Park*, ed. Olmsted Jr., F. L., and Kimball, T., Cambridge, Mass. and London, 1973.

24. 1900–45: Europe

Abercrombie, P., and Forshaw, J.H., *County of London Plan*, London, 1943.

Abercrombie, P., *Greater London Plan*, London, 1944.

Ashbee, C.R., *Where the Great City Stands*, London, 1917.

Butler, A.S.G., *The Architecture of Sir Edwin Lutyens*, London, 1950.

Chadwick, G.F., *The Park and the Town: public Landscape in the 19th and 20th Centuries*, London, 1966.

Descharnes, R., and Prevost, C., *Gaudí: the Visionary*, London, 1971.

Glikson, A., *Regional Planning and Development*, Leiden, 1955.

Holmdahl, G., *et al.*, *Gunnar Asplund, Architect*, Stockholm, 1950.

Howard, E., *Garden Cities of Tomorrow*, London, 1902.

Le Corbusier, *Towards a new Architecture*, London, 1927.

Martin, J.L., Nicholson, Ben, and Gabo, N., eds., *Circle*, London, 1937/71.

Tansley, A.G., *The British Isles and their Vegetation*, Cambridge, 1939.

Tunnard, C., *Gardens in the Modern Landscape*, London, 1938.

Unwin, R., *Town Planning in Practice*, London, 1909.

25. 1900–45: The Americas

Bardi, P.M., *The Tropical Gardens of Burle Marx*, London, 1964.

Boesiger, W., *Richard Neutra*, Zürich, 1951.

Lilienthal, D.E., *T V A Democracy on the March*, Harmondsworth, 1944.

Stein, C., *Towards New Towns for America*, Chicago, 1951.

Tilden, F., *The National Parks: what they mean to you and me*, New York, 1951.

Wright, F.L., *Modern Architecture*, Princeton, 1931.

26. 1945 to the present: The Western Hemisphere

Beacham, H., *The Architecture of Mexico Yesterday and Today*, New York, 1969.

Church, T., *Gardens are for People*, New York, 1955.

Eckbo, G., *Landscape for Living*, New York, 1950; *The Art of Home Landscaping*, New York, 1964.

Evenson, N., *Two Brazilian Capitals*, New Haven and London, 1973.

Ise, J., *Our National Park Policy: a critical history*, Baltimore, 1961.

Kepes, G., *The New Landscape in Art and Science*, Chicago, 1956.

McCallum, I., *Architecture U.S.A.*, London, 1959.

McHarg, I., *Design with Nature*, New York, 1969.

Marks, R.W., *The Dymaxion World of Buckminster Fuller*, Carbondale, 1960.

Mindlin, H., *Modern Architecture in Brazil*, London, 1956.

Moholy-Nagy, F., *The New Vision*, New York [undated].

Noguchi, I., *A Sculptor's World*, Tokyo and London, 1967.

Rudolph, P., *Architectural Drawings*, London, 1974.

Simonds, J.O., *Landscape Architecture*, New York and London, 1961.

Tennessee Valley Authority, *Annual Report, 1973*.

Tunnard, C., *Man-made America*, New Haven and London, 1963.

Journal: *Landscape Architecture* (Journal of the American Society of Landscape Architects), Louisville, Kentucky.

27. 1900 to the present day: The Eastern Hemisphere

Allen, Lady, and Jellicoe, S., *The New Small Garden*, London, 1956.

Arvill, R., *Man and Environment*, Harmondsworth, 1967.

Buchanan, C., *Traffic in Towns*, London, 1963.

Colvin, B., *Land and Landscape* (2nd edition), London, 1970.

Crowe, S., and Miller, Z., *Shaping Tomorrow's Landscape*, Amsterdam, 1964.

Deilmann, H., Kirschenmann, J., and Pfeiffer, H., *The Dwelling*, Stuttgart, 1973.

Faber, T., *New Danish Architecture*, London, 1968.

Fairbrother, N., *New Lives, New Landscapes*, London, 1970.

Gibberd, F., *Town Design*, London, 1959.

Hackett, B., *Man, Society and Environment*, London, 1950.

Hatje, G., *et al.*, *New German Architecture*, London, 1956.

Kidder Smith, G.E., *Italy Builds*, London, 1955; *Sweden Builds*, London, 1957.

Le Corbusier, *The Complete Architectural Works*, Zürich and London, 1964–66.

Merlin, P., *New Towns*, London, 1971.

Shepheard, P., *Modern Gardens*, London, 1953.

Journals: *Landscape Design* (Institute of Landscape Architects), London; *Havekunst* (Society of Scandinavian Landscape Architects), Copenhagen; *Garten & Landschaft*, Munich; *Espaces Verts*, Paris.

Index of people and places